Pillsbury

Christmas

2007

Pillsbury Christmas 2007

published by

Taste of Home Books
Reiman Media Group, Inc.
5400 S. 60th St., Greendale WI 53129
www.reimanpub.com

This edition published by arrangement
with Wiley Publishing, Inc.

credits

GENERAL MILLS, INC.
PUBLISHER, COOKBOOKS: Maggie Gilbert/Lynn Vettel
EDITOR: Lois Tlusty
RECIPE DEVELOPMENT AND TESTING: Pillsbury Test Kitchens
PHOTOGRAPHY: General Mills Photo Studios

REIMAN MEDIA GROUP, INC.
President and Chief Executive Officer: Mary G. Berner
President, Food & Entertaining: Suzanne M. Grimes
Editor in Chief: Catherine Cassidy
Vice President, Executive Editor/Books: Heidi Reuter Lloyd
Creative Director: Ardyth Cope
Senior Editor/Books: Mark Hagen
Art Director: Gretchen Trautman
Layout Designers: Nancy Novak, Catherine Fletcher and
    Julie Stone
Proofreaders: Linne Bruskewitz and Jean Steiner
Indexer: Jean Steiner

For additional holiday recipes and other delicious dishes, visit

Pillsbury.com.

International Standard Book Number (10): 0-89821-595-1
International Standard Book Number (13): 978-0-89821-595-3
Library of Congress Number: 2007927224
Printed in U.S.A.

Front Cover Photograph:
Chocolate-Cherry Cheesecake, p. 261.

Title Page Photograph:
Glazed Crown Roast with Cranberry-
Cornbread Stuffing, p. 103.

Back Cover Photographs:
Camembert Crowned with Cranberry-Port
Sauce, p. 9; Provençal Roast Chicken, p. 100;
Candy Cane Peppermint Brownie, p. 305;
Pineapple-Cherry Quick Bread, p. 42; Sage 'n
Maple Cornbread Stuffed Pork Chops, p. 104.

contents

Season's Greetings!

With more than 300 tasty recipes

and hundreds of tips, *Pillsbury Christmas 2007* turns holiday

gatherings into treasured memories.

p. 290

p. 100

p. 32

p. 19

p. 267

p. 109

Welcome to the most wonderful time of the year! It's time to make cherished memories with your family…time to enjoy the company of good friends…time to celebrate Christmas!

Smiling faces, glad tidings and bright spirits warm the wintry winds that blow outside. The laughter of children captures the excitement of the holidays. And, of course, comforting aromas waft from the kitchen, ushering in the merriest of seasons.

After all, Christmas just wouldn't be the same without platters of homemade cookies, golden loaves of bread, savory appetizers and all of those special dinner entrees we anticipate throughout the year. That's why we're happy to present Pillsbury Christmas 2007. Here you'll find 330 beloved recipes, each a perfect addition to Yuletide meals.

In fact, because Christmas is so dear to our hearts, we decided to create an entire set of cookbooks, dedicated to bringing the magic of the holidays to your home year after year. We truly hope this first volume helps you prepare all of the phenomenal flavors that accompany the season.

Take a look inside and you'll find crowd-pleasing favorites ideal for large festivities as well as cozy meals for two. From casual winter get-togethers to elegant holiday dinners, Pillsbury Christmas 2007 is sure to make this your most delicious holiday yet.

In addition to chapters such as "Merry Appetizers & Beverages" (p. 6) and "Joyful Entertaining" (p. 116), you'll discover sections devoted entirely to main courses (p. 90), side dishes (p. 64) and simply impressive desserts (p. 256).

Need a present for a friend who has everything? Looking for a unique hostess gift for a holiday open house? The chapter "Gifts from the Kitchen" (p. 164) offers dozens of mouthwatering ideas. You could also consider any of the gorgeous baked goods in "Festive Breads & More" (p. 38) or some of the sweets in "Christmas Cookies & Bars" (p. 186). And if you're looking to bring little ones in on the fun, you won't want to miss "Playful Childhood Treats" (p. 234). See the whimsical Santa Claus Cookies on page 248 to see just what we mean.

We've also included *cook's notes* with many of the recipes. These tidbits suggest ways to trim prep time, substitute ingredients and more. Similarly, *kitchen tips* offer sensible advice on tasks from streamlining cleanup to selecting the best produce. We even share *special touches* that dress up buffet tables and make menus particularly unforgettable.

Most important, you can take comfort in knowing that every single recipe was tested in the Pillsbury Kitchen so that it's easy to prepare, reliable and tastes great. And for additional insurance, we've included many of the Pillsbury Bake-Off® Contest winners…so you know you're preparing the best of the very best!

For more than 100 years, family cooks have turned to Pillsbury to make mealtime special…and that's certainly true when holiday celebrations begin. With this beautiful collection at your fingertips, it's never been easier to find amazing hors d'oeuvres everyone clamors for, hearty soups that warm the soul and memorable entrees destined to become family traditions.

We hope that Pillsbury Christmas 2007 will rekindle all of those heartwarming memories of Christmas past…and spark plenty of new ones, too. *Merry Christmas!*

p. 197

Merry Appetizers & Beverages

Deck the halls this season with an assortment of savory finger food and tongue-tingling beverages that friends and family are sure to remember all year long.

p. 9

p. 31

p. 10

p. 22

p. 12

cheddar-stuffed mushrooms p. 18

pork tenderloin crostini

PREP TIME: 50 Minutes ✳ READY IN: 2 Hours 20 Minutes ✳ SERVINGS: 32 Appetizers

3	green onions		1	teaspoon garlic salt
1	(0.9 oz.) package béarnaise sauce mix		1/4	teaspoon coarsely ground black pepper
3/4	cup milk		32	thin slices baguette-style French bread
1/4	cup butter		4	teaspoons crushed pink peppercorns
1	lb. (2 small) pork tenderloins			or finely chopped red bell pepper

1   Chop onions, separating white portion from green. Place white portion in small saucepan; reserve green portion. Add sauce mix and milk to saucepan; beat with wire whisk to combine. Add butter; cook over medium heat until mixture comes to a boil, stirring constantly. Reduce heat to low; simmer 1 minute. Cover; refrigerate at least 2 hours or until thickened and cool.

2   Meanwhile, heat oven to 400°F. Place pork tenderloins in shallow roasting pan; rub surfaces with garlic salt and pepper. Bake for 25 to 30 minutes or until no longer pink in center and thermometer registers 160°F. Cool 20 minutes or until cool enough to handle and slice.

3   Reduce oven temperature to 375°F. Place bread slices in ungreased 15x10x1-inch baking pan. Bake for 7 to 9 minutes or until crisp. Cool 10 minutes or until completely cooled.

4   When ready to serve, stir reserved green portion of onions into sauce. Cut pork into 32 slices. Place 1 slice pork on each toasted bread slice, folding slice if necessary. Top each with 1 teaspoon sauce; reserve remainder for another use. Top each appetizer with 1/8 teaspoon crushed pink peppercorns.

NUTRITIONAL INFORMATION PER SERVING: Calories 80 • Total Fat 3g • Saturated Fat 1g • Cholesterol 15mg • Sodium 140mg • Total Carbohydrate 8g • Dietary Fiber 0g • Sugars 0g • Protein 5g. DIETARY EXCHANGES: 1/2 Starch • 1/2 Other Carbohydrate • 1/2 Medium-Fat Meat.

camembert crowned with cranberry-port sauce

PREP TIME: 20 Minutes ✳ READY IN: 1 Hour 40 Minutes ✳ SERVINGS: 12

2 tablespoons water	1/4 cup port wine
1/2 teaspoon unflavored gelatin	1 cinnamon stick
1/2 cup chopped fresh or frozen cranberries	1 teaspoon grated orange peel
1/4 cup sugar	1 (8 oz.) round Camembert cheese

1 In glass measuring cup, combine water and gelatin; let stand 5 minutes. In small saucepan, combine cranberries, sugar, wine, gelatin mixture and cinnamon stick. Bring to a boil. Reduce heat to low; simmer 2 to 3 minutes or until cranberries are tender. Remove from heat. Stir in orange peel. Cool 10 minutes.

2 Remove cinnamon stick; pour into small serving bowl. Cover; refrigerate mixture at least 1 hour or overnight.

3 To serve, heat oven to 350°F. Place cheese on ungreased cookie sheet. Bake for 15 to 20 minutes or until thoroughly heated but not melted. Place cheese on serving plate. Spoon cranberry mixture around and on top of warm cheese. Serve with crisp crackers.

NUTRITIONAL INFORMATION PER SERVING: Calories 80 • Total Fat 5g • Saturated Fat 3g • Cholesterol 15mg • Sodium 160mg • Total Carbohydrate 5g • Dietary Fiber 0g • Sugars 5g • Protein 4g. DIETARY EXCHANGES: 1/2 High-Fat Meat • 1/2 Fat.

cook's notes

This Camembert needs a hearty match; present it on a pretty serving platter surrounded by petite toasts, lavosh, toasted baguette slices or whole wheat crackers.

fruit with piña colada dip

READY IN : 25 Minutes ✳ SERVINGS: 15

DIP

- 2 (6 oz.) containers French vanilla fat-free yogurt
- 1 teaspoon rum extract or dark rum
- 3 tablespoons flaked coconut, toasted
- 2 tablespoons finely chopped pineapple

FRUIT

- 15 fresh strawberries, halved
- 30 (1-inch) chunks fresh pineapple
- 30 chunks kiwi fruit (about 5 medium)

1 In small bowl, combine yogurt, rum extract and 2 tablespoons of the coconut; blend well. Stir in pineapple. Serve immediately, or cover and refrigerate until serving time.

2 To serve, arrange fruit on serving platter. Sprinkle dip with remaining tablespoon toasted coconut. If desired, garnish with pineapple leaves. Store dip in refrigerator.

NUTRITIONAL INFORMATION PER SERVING: Calories 60 • Total Fat 1g • Saturated Fat 0 • Cholesterol 0mg • Sodium 15mg • Total Carbohydrate 12g • Dietary Fiber 1g • Sugars 9g • Protein 1g. DIETARY EXCHANGE: 1 Fruit.

---

southwest zesty margarita shrimp

PREP TIME: 30 Minutes ✳ READY IN: 4 Hours 30 Minutes ✳ SERVINGS: 30 Appetizers

- 1/4 cup finely chopped green onions
- 1/4 cup oil
- 1/4 cup tequila
- 1 teaspoon grated lime peel
- 2 tablespoons fresh lime juice
- 2 tablespoons honey
- 2 tablespoons chopped fresh cilantro
- 1/2 teaspoon salt
- 1 lb. (about 30) large tiger (striped) shrimp, shelled, tails left on and deveined

1 In medium bowl, combine all ingredients except shrimp; mix well. Add shrimp; stir to coat. Cover; refrigerate at least 4 hours or up to 8 hours to marinate.

2 Spray broiler pan with nonstick cooking spray. Drain shrimp, discarding marinade. Place shrimp on sprayed broiler pan. Broil 4 inches from heat for 5 to 7 minutes or until shrimp turn pink, turning once.

NUTRITIONAL INFORMATION PER SERVING: Calories 15 • Total Fat 1g • Saturated Fat 0 • Cholesterol 15mg • Sodium 25mg • Total Carbohydrate 0g • Dietary Fiber 0g • Sugars 0g • Protein 2g. DIETARY EXCHANGE: Free.

---

garlic-horseradish roast beef crisps

READY IN: 15 Minutes ✳ SERVINGS: 24 Appetizers

- 1/4 cup light sour cream
- 1/2 teaspoon prepared horseradish
- 1/4 teaspoon Dijon mustard, if desired
- 24 garlic Melba rounds or other low-fat garlic crackers
- 4 slices (about 1/4 lb.) cooked roast beef (from deli), each cut into 6 strips
- 1 tablespoon chopped fresh parsley

1 In small bowl, combine sour cream, horseradish and mustard; blend well. Place 1 roast beef strip on each Melba round. Top each with about 1/2 teaspoon sour cream mixture. Sprinkle each with parsley. Arrange on serving platter.

NUTRITIONAL INFORMATION PER SERVING: Calories 20 • Total Fat 0g • Saturated Fat 0g • Cholesterol 5mg • Sodium 25mg • Total Carbohydrate 3g • Dietary Fiber 0g • Sugars 0g • Protein 2g. DIETARY EXCHANGE: Free.

fruit with piña colada dip
southwest zesty margarita shrimp

gorgonzola-artichoke dip

READY IN: 40 Minutes ✳ SERVINGS: 16

5 slices precooked bacon	1/2 cup Gorgonzola cheese, crumbled (2 oz.)
1 (14 oz.) can artichoke hearts, well drained, chopped	1/2 cup shredded fresh Parmesan cheese (2 oz.)
1 (8 oz.) package cream cheese, softened	2 teaspoons lemon juice

1 Heat oven to 350°F. Spray 8-inch quiche dish or 8 or 9-inch glass pie pan with nonstick cooking spray. Chop 3 slices of the bacon; place in medium bowl. Reserve remaining bacon for garnish. To bacon in bowl, add remaining ingredients; mix well. Spread mixture in sprayed dish.

2 Bake for 10 minutes. Stir dip; bake an additional 10 to 15 minutes or until the dip is bubbly around edges.

3 Chop reserved bacon; sprinkle on top of dip. Serve warm dip with petite toasts, assorted crackers or baguette slices.

NUTRITIONAL INFORMATION PER SERVING: Calories 105 • Total Fat 8g • Saturated Fat 5 • Cholesterol 20mg • Sodium 250mg • Total Carbohydrate 3g • Dietary Fiber 1g • Sugars 1g • Protein 5g. DIETARY EXCHANGES: 1/2 High-Fat Meat • 1 Fat.

cucumber-dill stuffed cherry tomatoes

PREP TIME: 45 Minutes ✳ READY IN: 2 Hours 45 Minutes ✳ SERVINGS: 24

24 cherry tomatoes
1 (3 oz.) package cream cheese, softened
2 tablespoons mayonnaise or salad dressing

1/4 cup finely chopped, seeded cucumber
1 tablespoon finely chopped green onions
2 teaspoons chopped fresh dill or 1/4 teaspoon dried dill weed

1 Remove stems from tomatoes. To level bottoms of tomatoes, cut thin slice from bottom of each. Starting at stem end and using small spoon or melon baller, carefully hollow out each tomato, leaving 1/8-inch shell. Invert tomato shells onto paper towels to drain.

2 In small bowl, combine cream cheese and mayonnaise; blend well. Stir in cucumber, onions and dill; mix well.

3 Fill tomato shells with cream cheese mixture; place on serving platter or tray. Cover loosely; refrigerate at least 2 hours or up to 24 hours before serving. Store in refrigerator.

NUTRITIONAL INFORMATION PER SERVING: Calories 20 • Total Fat 2g • Saturated Fat 1g • Cholesterol 5mg • Sodium 20mg • Total Carbohydrate 1g • Dietary Fiber 0g • Sugars 1g • Protein 0g. DIETARY EXCHANGE: Free.

cook's notes

Use a miniature melon baller to hollow out the tomatoes. To easily fill the tomatoes, place the cream cheese mixture in a plastic squeeze bottle. Snip off three-quarters of the bottle's tip with a kitchen scissors. Squeeze the cream cheese mixture into the tomato shells.

ham and veggie crescent wreath

ham and veggie crescent wreath

PREP TIME: 20 Minutes ✳ READY IN: 1 Hour 10 Minutes ✳ SERVINGS: 20

2 (8 oz.) cans refrigerated crescent dinner rolls	1/4 cup finely chopped green bell pepper
1 (8 oz.) container pineapple cream cheese spread	1/2 cup chopped fresh broccoli florets
1/3 cup chopped cooked ham	1 tablespoon chopped red onion, rinsed, patted dry
1/4 cup finely chopped yellow bell pepper	6 grape tomatoes or small cherry tomatoes, quartered

1 Heat oven to 375°F. Invert 10-oz. custard cup on center of ungreased large cookie sheet. Remove dough from 1 can, keeping dough in 1 piece; do not unroll. (Keep remaining can of dough in refrigerator.) With palms of hands, roll dough in one direction to form 12-inch log. Cut log into 20 slices. Arrange 16 slices, slightly overlapping and in clockwise direction, around custard cup on cookie sheet.

2 Repeat with second can of dough, cutting log into 20 slices. Arrange remaining 4 slices and slices from second can (total of 24 slices) slightly overlapping each other and in counterclockwise direction, close to but not overlapping first ring. Remove custard cup from center of wreath shape.

3 Bake for 15 to 18 minutes or until light golden brown. Gently loosen wreath from cookie sheet; carefully slide onto wire rack. Cool 30 minutes or until completely cooled.

4 Place cooled wreath on serving tray or platter. Spread cream cheese spread over wreath. Sprinkle with ham, peppers, broccoli, onion and tomatoes. Serve immediately or cover and refrigerate up to 4 hours before serving.

NUTRITIONAL INFORMATION PER SERVING: Calories 120 • Total Fat 7g • Saturated Fat 3g • Cholesterol 15mg • Sodium 340mg • Total Carbohydrate 12g • Dietary Fiber 1g • Sugars 4g • Protein 3g. DIETARY EXCHANGES: 1/2 Starch • 1/2 Fruit • 1 Other Carbohydrate • 1 Fat.

asian crab mini quiches

PREP TIME: 20 Minutes ✳ READY IN: 50 Minutes ✳ SERVINGS: 24 Appetizers

1 (15 oz.) box refrigerated pie crusts, softened as directed on package	1 teaspoon grated lime peel
2 eggs	1 teaspoon grated gingerroot
1/2 cup half-and-half	1/2 teaspoon salt
2 tablespoons chopped green onions	1 (6 oz.) can refrigerated pasteurized crabmeat
1 red jalapeño chile, seeded, minced (about 2 tablespoons)	1/4 cup shredded fresh Parmesan cheese

1 Heat oven to 375°F. Remove pie crusts from pouches. Unroll crusts. With 2-1/2-inch round cutter, cut crusts into 24 rounds. Press each round into ungreased miniature muffin cup.

2 Beat eggs in medium bowl. Add half-and-half, onions, chile, lime peel, gingerroot and salt; stir with wire whisk to blend. Stir in crabmeat and cheese. Spoon about 1 tablespoon mixture into each crust-lined cup.

3 Bake for 25 to 30 minutes or until filling is set and crust is golden brown around edges. Serve warm or cool. Store in refrigerator.

NUTRITIONAL INFORMATION PER SERVING: Calories 115 • Total Fat 7g • Saturated Fat 2g • Cholesterol 25mg • Sodium 210mg • Total Carbohydrate 9g • Dietary Fiber 0g • Sugars 0g • Protein 4g. DIETARY EXCHANGES: 1/2 Starch • 1/2 Other Carbohydrate • 1-1/2 Fat.

cook's notes

Assemble and bake the crescent wreath up to 8 hours ahead. Cool it completely, cover it loosely with plastic wrap and store it at room temperature. Up to 4 hours before serving, uncover the wreath and top it with the cream cheese, ham and vegetables.

cook's notes

To prepare Asian Shrimp Mini Quiches, use cooked deveined shrimp in place of the crabmeat. Be sure to peel and chop the shrimp before adding it to the quiche filling.

pinwheel pepperoni trees

PREP TIME: 40 Minutes ✳ READY IN: 1 Hour ✳ SERVINGS: 24

2 (8 oz.) cans refrigerated reduced-fat crescent dinner rolls

1 teaspoon dried oregano leaves or Italian seasoning

2 (2-inch-square) pieces yellow bell pepper

1 (8 oz.) can pizza sauce

1/2 cup chopped pepperoni

1 cup finely shredded mozzarella cheese (4 oz.)

1/4 cup chopped Italian plum tomato (about 1 small)

2 tablespoons chopped green onions

1 Heat oven to 375°F. Spray large cookie sheet with nonstick cooking spray. Separate dough into 8 rectangles; firmly press perforations to seal. Sprinkle about 1/8 teaspoon oregano over each rectangle. Starting with 1 short side, carefully roll up each rectangle. Cut each roll into 6 crosswise slices, making a total of 48 slices.

2 Form 2 trees on sprayed cookie sheet using 24 slices each. For first tree, place 1 slice for top on 1 side of cookie sheet. Arrange 2 slices below top, sides almost touching. Continue arranging rows of 3 slices, 4 slices, and continuing until last row is 6 slices across. Center 3 slices below tree for trunk.

3 Repeat for second tree, assembling in opposite direction on cookie sheet to fit next to first tree. Bake for 14 to 18 minutes or until light golden brown. Meanwhile, with small cookie cutter or sharp knife, cut two 1 to 1-1/2-inch star shapes from bell pepper. Set aside.

4 Remove partially baked trees from oven. Spread 2 tablespoons of the pizza sauce evenly over each tree to within 1/2 inch of edges, leaving trunk uncovered. Sprinkle 1/4 cup chopped pepperoni evenly over sauce on each tree. Sprinkle each with 1/2 cup cheese. Place bell pepper stars on tops of trees.

5 Return to oven; bake an additional 3 to 5 minutes or until cheese is melted. Meanwhile, heat remaining 3/4 cup pizza sauce in small saucepan until hot.

6 Remove trees from oven. Sprinkle each tree with 2 tablespoons tomato and 1 tablespoon onions. Cool trees on cookie sheet for 2 to 3 minutes. Carefully slide trees onto serving platters, trays or cutting boards. Serve warm with warm pizza sauce for dipping.

NUTRITIONAL INFORMATION PER SERVING: Calories 95 • Total Fat 5g • Saturated Fat 2g • Cholesterol 5mg • Sodium 270mg • Total Carbohydrate 9g • Dietary Fiber 2g • Sugars 2g • Protein 3g. DIETARY EXCHANGES: 1/2 Starch • 1 Fat.

mexican vegetable roll-ups

PREP IN: 20 Minutes ✳ READY IN: 1 Hour 20 Minutes ✳ SERVINGS: 24 Appetizers

1 (3 oz.) package cream cheese, softened

1/3 cup sour cream

1 tablespoon taco seasoning mix

1/2 cup fresh corn kernels frozen whole kernel corn, thawed, drained

1/2 cup drained black beans (from 15 oz. can), rinsed

1/4 cup finely chopped fresh cilantro

1 Italian plum tomato, seeded, finely chopped (about 1/4 cup)

2 tablespoons chunky-style salsa

3 (10-inch) garden spinach and vegetable, tomato, or plain flour tortillas

1 In small bowl, combine cream cheese, sour cream and taco seasoning mix; beat until well blended. Stir in corn, beans, cilantro, tomato and salsa.

2 Spread cream cheese mixture over each tortilla to edges. Roll up each; cut off tapered ends. Wrap each tortilla roll in plastic wrap. Refrigerate at least 1 hour or up to 8 hours before serving. To serve, cut each roll into 1-inch slices.

NUTRITIONAL INFORMATION PER SERVING: Calories 65 • Total Fat 3g • Saturated Fat 1g • Cholesterol 5mg • Sodium 90mg • Total Carbohydrate 7g • Dietary Fiber 0g • Sugars 1g • Protein 2g. DIETARY EXCHANGES: 1/2 Starch • 1/2 Fat.

pinwheel pepperoni trees

cheddar-stuffed mushrooms

PREP TIME: 30 Minutes ❋ READY IN: 45 Minutes ❋ SERVINGS: 36 Appetizers

2 (8 oz.) packages fresh whole mushrooms, cleaned

3/4 cup 10-minute herb stuffing mix

1/2 cup shredded extra-sharp Cheddar cheese (2 oz.)

1/4 cup butter, melted

2 tablespoons finely chopped onion

1 Heat oven to 350°F. Remove stems from mushrooms; reserve caps. Finely chop half of the stems; discard remaining stems.

2 In small bowl, combine chopped mushroom stems, stuffing mix, cheese, butter and onion; mix well. Spoon about 1 teaspoon mushroom mixture into each mushroom cap. Place on ungreased cookie sheet. Bake for 10 to 12 minutes or until thoroughly heated. Serve warm.

NUTRITIONAL INFORMATION PER SERVING: Calories 30 • Total Fat 2g • Saturated Fat 1g • Cholesterol 5mg • Sodium 40mg • Total Carbohydrate 2g • Dietary Fiber 0g • Sugars 0g • Protein 1g. DIETARY EXCHANGE: 1/2 Fat.

shrimp crescent bites

READY IN: 45 Minutes ✳ SERVINGS: 24 Appetizers

1 (8 oz.) can refrigerated crescent dinner rolls	1/4 cup apricot preserves
1-1/2 teaspoons curry powder	24 shelled deveined cooked medium shrimp
1/3 cup flaked coconut	24 sprigs fresh cilantro

1 Heat oven to 375°F. Unroll dough into 1 long rectangle; gently press perforations to seal. Place curry powder in small strainer. Shake strainer to sprinkle dough with curry powder; sprinkle evenly with coconut.

2 Starting with one long side, roll up dough, jelly-roll fashion. With serrated knife, cut roll into 24 slices; place, cut side down, on ungreased cookie sheet.

3 Bake for 13 to 15 minutes or until golden brown. Immediately remove from cookie sheet; place on wire rack. Cool 10 minutes or until completely cooled.

4 To serve, top each appetizer with 1/2 teaspoon apricot preserves and 1 shrimp. Garnish each appetizer with cilantro sprig.

NUTRITIONAL INFORMATION PER SERVING: Calories 55 • Total Fat 2g • Saturated Fat 1g • Cholesterol 10mg • Sodium 130mg • Total Carbohydrate 7g • Dietary Fiber 0g • Sugars 3g • Protein 2g. DIETARY EXCHANGES: 1/2 Starch • 1/2 Other Carbohydrate • 1/2 Fat.

kitchen tip

Use a small, fine-mesh strainer to sprinkle curry powder over the unrolled crescent dough. Crescent dough is easy to cut with a long serrated knife such as a bread knife.

creole meatballs

creole meatballs

READY IN: 50 Minutes ✳ SERVINGS: 48

MEATBALLS
- 1   egg
- 1-1/2   lb. lean ground beef
- 1/2   cup Italian-style dry bread crumbs
- 1/4   cup chopped onion
- 1/4   cup chopped green bell pepper
- 3/4   teaspoon salt
- 1/2   teaspoon celery salt
- 1/8   teaspoon ground red pepper (cayenne)
- 1   (15 oz.) can tomato sauce

SAUCE
- 2   tablespoons oil
- 2   tablespoons all-purpose flour
- 2   tablespoons currant jelly
- 1   teaspoon Worcestershire sauce
- 1/2   teaspoon dried Italian seasoning
- 1/4   teaspoon garlic salt
- 1/8   teaspoon ground red pepper (cayenne)

1 Heat oven to 400°F. Beat egg in large bowl. Add ground beef, bread crumbs, onion, bell pepper, salt, celery salt, 1/8 teaspoon ground red pepper and 2 tablespoons of the tomato sauce; mix well. Shape mixture into 48 (1-1/4-inch) meatballs, using about 1 tablespoon mixture for each. Place in ungreased 15x10x1-inch baking pan. Bake for 15 to 20 minutes or until thoroughly cooked and no longer pink in center.

2 Meanwhile, heat oil in medium saucepan over medium-high heat until hot. With wire whisk, stir in flour; cook and stir until mixture turns a deep, rich brown color. Stir in remaining tomato sauce and all remaining sauce ingredients. Bring to a boil. Cook an additional minute, stirring constantly. Add cooked meatballs to sauce; stir gently to coat. Serve with cocktail toothpicks.

NUTRITIONAL INFORMATION PER SERVING: Calories 45 • Total Fat 3g • Saturated Fat 1g • Cholesterol 10mg • Sodium 130mg • Total Carbohydrate 2g • Dietary Fiber 0g • Sugars 1g • Protein 3g. DIETARY EXCHANGE: 1/2 High-Fat Meat.

cook's notes

To prepare the Creole Meatballs ahead of time, simply transfer the cooked meatballs and sauce to a baking dish and cool. Cover the dish and refrigerate it for up to a day. To serve, heat the dish in a 350°F oven for 10 minutes or until heated through.

spinach and feta quesadillas

READY IN: 25 Minutes ✳ SERVINGS: 32 Appetizers

- 1   (8 oz.) container fat-free cream cheese
- 1/4   teaspoon garlic powder
- 1/4   teaspoon pepper
- 8   (8-inch) flour tortillas
- 1   (9 oz.) package frozen spinach, cooked, squeezed to drain
- 1   medium red bell pepper, finely chopped (1 cup)
- 1   cup crumbled feta cheese (4 oz.)

1 In small bowl, combine cream cheese, garlic powder and pepper; blend well. Spread 2 tablespoons cream cheese mixture on each tortilla. Sprinkle about 2 tablespoons each of spinach, bell pepper and cheese on half of each tortilla; fold tortillas in half.

2 Heat large nonstick skillet over medium heat until hot. Place 2 folded tortillas in skillet; cook 1 to 2 minutes on each side or until golden brown.

3 Remove quesadillas from skillet; place on platter. Cover with foil to keep warm. Repeat with remaining folded tortillas. Cut each quesadilla into 4 wedges. Serve warm.

NUTRITIONAL INFORMATION PER SERVING: Calories 55 • Total Fat 2g • Saturated Fat 1g • Cholesterol 5mg • Sodium 130mg • Total Carbohydrate 7g • Dietary Fiber 1g • Sugars 1g • Protein 3g. DIETARY EXCHANGES: 1/2 Starch • 1/2 Other Carbohydrate • 1/2 Fat.

kitchen tip

For crisp spinach quesadillas, arrange the drained greens on a double-thickness of paper towels. Roll the spinach up in the towels. Squeeze and twist to remove the moisture.

fresh vegetable pizza

PREP TIME: 45 Minutes ✳ READY IN: 1 Hour 35 Minutes ✳ SERVINGS: 48

2 (8 oz.) cans refrigerated reduced-fat crescent dinner rolls	2 cups fresh mushrooms, chopped
1 (8 oz.) container light sour cream	1 cup chopped seeded tomatoes
1 to 2 tablespoons prepared horseradish	1 cup finely chopped broccoli florets
1/4 teaspoon garlic salt	1/2 cup chopped green bell pepper
1/8 teaspoon pepper	1/4 cup chopped green onions

1 Heat oven to 375°F. Spray 15x10x1-inch baking pan with nonstick cooking spray. Separate dough into 4 long rectangles. Place rectangles crosswise in sprayed pan; press over bottom and 1 inch up sides to form crust. Seal perforations.

2 Bake crust for 14 to 19 minutes or until golden brown. Cool 30 minutes or until completely cooled.

3 In small bowl, combine sour cream, horseradish, garlic salt and pepper; mix until smooth. Spread evenly over cooled crust. Sprinkle with all remaining ingredients. Cut into small squares to serve. Store in refrigerator.

NUTRITIONAL INFORMATION PER SERVING: Calories 40 • Total Fat 2g • Saturated Fat 1g • Cholesterol 2mg • Sodium 90mg • Total Carbohydrate 5g • Dietary Fiber 1g • Sugars 2g • Protein 1g. DIETARY EXCHANGE: 1/2 Fat.

strawberry champagne punch

READY IN : 30 Minutes ✳ SERVINGS: 24

1 cup water	1 (750 ml) bottle rosé wine, chilled
1 (3 oz.) package strawberry flavor gelatin	1 (750 ml) bottle champagne, chilled
3/4 cup frozen lemonade concentrate, thawed (half 12 oz. can)	2 cups fresh strawberries with stems, frozen (1 pint)
2 cups cold water	

1 Bring water to a boil in small saucepan. Add the gelatin; stir until gelatin is dissolved. Cool 15 minutes.

2 In a large punch bowl, combine the lemonade concentrate, cold water and the gelatin mixture; mix well. Just before serving, stir in the wine, champagne and frozen strawberries.

NUTRITIONAL INFORMATION PER SERVING: Calories 80 • Total Fat 0g • Saturated Fat 0g • Cholesterol 0mg • Sodium 10mg • Total Carbohydrate 10g • Dietary Fiber 0g • Sugars 9g • Protein 0g. DIETARY EXCHANGES: 1 Carbohydrate • 1/2 Fat.

fresh vegetable pizza

teriyaki seafood-stuffed mushrooms
spiced cranberry chutney crackers

teriyaki seafood-stuffed mushrooms

PREP TIME: 45 Minutes ✳ READY IN: 1 Hour 15 Minutes ✳ SERVINGS: 48 Appetizers

48	(1-1/2 to 2-inch) fresh whole mushrooms, washed, stems removed
2	garlic cloves, minced
2-1/4	cups water
1	(15 oz.) bottle teriyaki sauce
1/3	cup chopped imitation crabmeat (surimi)
1/3	cup chopped water chestnuts
1	tablespoon chopped fresh chives

1 Remove stems from mushrooms; discard or reserve for a future use. In Dutch oven, combine mushroom caps, garlic, water and teriyaki sauce. Bring to a boil over medium-high heat.

2 Reduce heat to low; cover and simmer 15 to 20 minutes or until mushrooms are thoroughly cooked, stirring occasionally.

3 Drain mushrooms; place on paper towels to dry. Cool about 15 minutes or until completely cooled. Meanwhile, in medium bowl, combine imitation crabmeat and water chestnuts; mix well.

4 Fill each mushroom cap with about 1/2 teaspoon crabmeat mixture. Sprinkle each with chives. Serve immediately, or cover and refrigerate until serving time.

NUTRITIONAL INFORMATION PER SERVING: Calories 10 • Total Fat 0g • Saturated Fat 0g • Cholesterol 0mg • Sodium 440mg • Total Carbohydrate 3g • Dietary Fiber 0g • Sugars 1g • Protein 1g. DIETARY EXCHANGE: Free.

cook's notes

For Teriyaki Vegetable-Stuffed Mushrooms, omit the surimi and use a few different colors of bell peppers. To keep their colors fresh, finely chop the peppers and combine them with the water chestnuts just before serving.

spiced cranberry chutney crackers

PREP TIME: 30 Minutes ✳ READY IN: 4 Hours 50 Minutes ✳ SERVINGS: 35 Appetizers

1	teaspoon oil
1/4	cup finely chopped onion
1	cup whole berry cranberry sauce (from 16 oz. can)
2	tablespoons cider vinegar
1	teaspoon pumpkin pie spice
1	teaspoon dried thyme leaves
1/4	teaspoon freshly ground black pepper
	Dash hot pepper sauce
3/4	cup (about 6 ounces) fat-free or light cream cheese spread (from 8 oz. container)
35	water crackers

1 Heat oil in small saucepan over medium-low heat until hot. Add onion; cook 3 to 4 minutes or until softened, stirring frequently.

2 Add cranberry sauce, vinegar, pumpkin pie spice, thyme, pepper and hot pepper sauce; mix well. Bring to a boil over medium heat. Cook 10 to 12 minutes or until thickened and reduced slightly, stirring frequently. Cool 20 minutes. Cover; refrigerate at least 4 hours or overnight.

3 Just before serving, spread about 1 teaspoon cream cheese spread on each cracker. Top each with about 1-1/2 teaspoons cranberry mixture. If desired, garnish each with fresh thyme.

NUTRITIONAL INFORMATION PER SERVING: Calories 30 • Total Fat 0g • Saturated Fat 0g • Cholesterol 0mg • Sodium 50mg • Total Carbohydrate 6g • Dietary Fiber 0g • Sugars 3g • Protein 1g. DIETARY EXCHANGES: 1/2 Starch • 1/2 Other Carbohydrate.

cook's notes

For a fast fix, spread the cream cheese on a serving plate. Spoon the chutney over it and serve with crackers.

cajun crab cheesecake

PREP TIME: 20 Minutes ✳ READY IN: 5 Hours 50 Minutes ✳ SERVINGS: 16

CRUST
- 1-3/4 cups unseasoned dry bread crumbs
- 2 teaspoons dried salt-free Cajun seasoning
- 1/2 cup butter, melted

FILLING
- 2 (8 oz.) packages cream cheese, softened
- 1/2 cup shredded fresh Parmesan cheese (2 oz.)
- 1 tablespoon dried salt-free Cajun seasoning
- 2 teaspoons prepared horseradish
- 1/4 cup dry sherry
- 2 eggs
- 2 (6 oz.) cans crabmeat, well drained
- 1/4 to 1/2 teaspoon hot pepper sauce
- 1 tablespoon diced red bell pepper

1 Heat oven to 325°F. In medium bowl, combine all crust ingredients; mix well. Press in bottom and 1 inch up sides of ungreased 9-inch springform pan.

2 In large bowl, combine cream cheese, Parmesan cheese, 1 tablespoon Cajun seasoning and horseradish; beat with electric mixer at medium speed until smooth. Add sherry; beat well. Beat mixture at high speed for 2 minutes. Add eggs, 1 at a time, beating well after each addition. Stir in crabmeat and hot pepper sauce just until combined. Pour into crust-lined pan.

3 Bake for 50 to 60 minutes or until filling is set. Cool in pan on wire rack for 30 minutes. Cover; refrigerate at least 4 hours and up to 24 hours before serving.

4 Just before serving, remove sides of pan; place cheesecake on serving platter. Garnish with bell pepper. Serve immediately, or let stand at room temperature for about 30 minutes before serving. If desired, serve with assorted crackers.

NUTRITIONAL INFORMATION PER SERVING: Calories 240 • Total Fat 18g • Saturated Fat 11g • Cholesterol 95mg • Sodium 360mg • Total Carbohydrate 10g • Dietary Fiber 0g • Sugars 2g • Protein 10g. DIETARY EXCHANGES: 1/2 Starch • 1 Lean Meat • 3 Fat.

chipotle chicken drummettes

PREP TIME: 10 Minutes ✳ READY IN: 1 Hour 10 Minutes ✳ SERVINGS: 20 Appetizers

2 (16 oz.) packages chicken wing drummettes (about 20 drummettes)	2 tablespoons chopped chipotle chiles in adobo sauce
3/4 cup chili sauce	1 teaspoon grated lime peel
3 tablespoons brown sugar	2 garlic cloves, minced

1 Heat oven to 375°F. Line 13x9-inch pan with foil. Arrange drummettes in single layer in the foil-lined pan.

2 In small microwave-safe bowl, combine all remaining ingredients; mix well. Microwave on High for 1 minute or until sugar is dissolved, stirring once halfway through cooking. Pour sauce over drummettes to cover.

3 Bake for 30 minutes. Turn drummettes over; bake an additional 20 to 30 minutes or until drummettes are glazed, fork-tender and no longer pink next to bone.

NUTRITIONAL INFORMATION PER SERVING: Calories 65 • Total Fat 3g • Saturated Fat 1g • Cholesterol 15mg • Sodium 150mg • Total Carbohydrate 5g • Dietary Fiber 0g • Sugars 5g • Protein 5g. DIETARY EXCHANGES: 1/2 Lean Meat • 1/2 Fat.

kitchen tip

Chipotle chiles are dried, smoked jalapeño chiles. They are available dry in bulk or canned in adobo sauce. Adobo sauce is a traditional Mexican paste made from ground chiles, herbs and vinegar. It's not over-ly hot, but it has a rich, spicy flavor.

cheese-filled potato bites
potato and bacon mini pizzas

cheese-filled potato bites

PREP TIME: 40 Minutes ✳ READY IN: 55 Minutes ✳ SERVINGS: 24 Appetizers

POTATOES

- 1 cup water
- 2 tablespoons butter
- 1/2 teaspoon salt
- 1-1/3 cups plain mashed potato mix (dry)
- 1 egg
- 1/4 cup chopped fresh chives

FILLING

- 24 (1/2-inch) cubes pasteurized prepared cheese product (about 2-3/4 oz.)

COATING

- 1 egg
- 1 tablespoon water
- 1 cup plain mashed potato mix (dry)
  Butter-flavor nonstick cooking spray

1. In medium saucepan, bring 1 cup water, butter and salt to a boil. Add 1-1/3 cups mashed potato mix, 1 egg and chives; mix well. Let stand 30 seconds. Stir. Cool 10 minutes.

2. Meanwhile, heat oven to 400°F. Spoon mashed potatoes into 24 mounds, about 1 tablespoon each, onto ungreased cookie sheet. Flatten into disks. Place 1 cheese cube in center of each potato disk. With pancake turner, remove each disk from cookie sheet; pinch potatoes around cheese cube to form ball.

3. In small bowl, beat 1 egg and 1 tablespoon water until well blended. Place 1 cup mashed potato mix in another shallow dish or bowl. Roll balls in potato mix, then in egg mixture and again in potato mix. Place on ungreased cookie sheet.

4. Just before baking, spray coated potato balls with nonstick cooking spray. Bake for 10 to 12 minutes or until potato coating just begins to brown. Serve immediately.

NUTRITIONAL INFORMATION PER SERVING: Calories 50 • Total Fat 3g • Saturated Fat 1g • Cholesterol 25mg • Sodium 110mg • Total Carbohydrate 4g • Dietary Fiber 0g • Sugars 0g • Protein 2g. DIETARY EXCHANGE: 1 Fat.

cook's notes

To prepare the balls ahead of time, arrange them on an ungreased cookie sheet. Cover them with plastic wrap, and refrigerate them for several hours. To serve, uncover and spray the balls with the butter-flavor nonstick cooking spray. Bake them as directed.

potato and bacon mini pizzas

READY IN : 45 Minutes ✳ SERVINGS: 20 Appetizers

- 20 (1/4-inch-thick) slices red boiling potatoes (about 3 medium)
- 8 oz. thick-sliced smoky bacon
- 1 medium onion, sliced

- 1 (12 oz.) can refrigerated flaky biscuits
- 2 tablespoons Dijon mustard
- 1/2 cup sour cream
- 1 tablespoon chopped fresh parsley

1. Heat oven to 400°F. In medium saucepan, cook potato slices in boiling salted water over medium-high heat for 5 minutes. Drain.

2. Fry bacon in large skillet over medium-low heat until crisp. Drain on paper towels. Crumble bacon; set aside. In same skillet with bacon drippings, cook onion 5 to 7 minutes or until softened and separated into rings, stirring frequently.

3. Separate dough into 10 biscuits. Separate each biscuit into 2 layers; place biscuit rounds on ungreased large cookie sheet. Flatten each slightly. Spread each lightly with mustard. Top each dough round with potato slice and onion.

4. Bake for 9 to 15 minutes or until crusts are crisp and golden brown. Top each mini pizza with sour cream and crumbled bacon. Sprinkle with parsley.

NUTRITIONAL INFORMATION PER SERVING: Calories 100 • Total Fat 5g • Saturated Fat 2g • Cholesterol 5mg • Sodium 330mg • Total Carbohydrate 12g • Dietary Fiber 1g • Sugars 3g • Protein 3g. DIETARY EXCHANGES: 1 Starch • 1 Other Carbohydrate • 1/2 Fat.

kitchen tip

Use red boiling potatoes, not bakers, when you need a potato that holds its shape. Boiling potatoes contain less starch, and thus hold their shape well after cooking.

pork riblets with honey-pepper glaze

PREP TIME: 1 Hour ✳ READY IN: 2 Hours 20 Minutes ✳ SERVINGS: 16 Appetizers

RIBLETS

- 1 (2 lb.) rack pork back ribs, cut in half lengthwise across bones
- 3 teaspoons chili powder
- 1 teaspoon celery salt
- 1/2 teaspoon dry mustard

GLAZE

- 1/3 cup honey
- 1 tablespoon lemon juice
- 1/2 teaspoon coarse ground black pepper

1 Line 15x10x1-inch baking pan with foil; spray foil with nonstick cooking spray. Place rack of ribs in single layer in sprayed foil-lined pan.

2 In small bowl, combine chili powder, celery salt and mustard; mix well. Sprinkle one side of ribs with half of spice mixture; turn and sprinkle other side with remaining spice mixture. Let stand at room temperature for 15 to 30 minutes.

3 Heat oven to 300°F. Bake ribs for 1 hour. Meanwhile, in small saucepan, combine all glaze ingredients; mix well. Bring to a boil over medium heat, stirring occasionally.

4 Remove ribs from oven; cool about 10 minutes. Increase oven temperature to 350°F. Cut ribs into individual riblets; return to baking pan in single layer. Brush one side of riblets with glaze.

5 Return to oven; bake for 15 minutes. Turn riblets; brush other side with glaze. Bake an additional 15 minutes. Discard any remaining glaze. Serve warm.

NUTRITIONAL INFORMATION PER SERVING: Calories 110 • Total Fat 8g • Saturated Fat 3g • Cholesterol 35mg • Sodium 125mg • Total Carbohydrate 2g • Dietary Fiber 0g • Sugars 1g • Protein 8g. DIETARY EXCHANGE: 1 High-Fat Meat.

raspberry-brie tarts

READY IN: 30 Minutes ✻ SERVINGS: 30 Appetizers

2 (2.1 oz.) packages frozen mini fillo pastry shells
(30 shells)

1 (8 oz.) round Brie cheese

3 tablespoons raspberry spreadable fruit

1 Heat oven to 350°F. Place pastry shells on ungreased large cookie sheet. Cut cheese into 1/2-inch cubes. Place 3 cheese cubes into each fillo shell. Bake for 10 to 12 minutes or until cheese is melted and bubbly.

2 Remove partially baked shells from oven. Spoon 1/4 teaspoon spreadable fruit over cheese in each shell.

3 Return to oven; bake an additional 2 to 3 minutes or until spreadable fruit is melted. Serve the tarts warm.

NUTRITIONAL INFORMATION PER SERVING: Calories 40 • Total Fat 2g • Saturated Fat 1g • Cholesterol 10mg • Sodium 60mg • Total Carbohydrate 4g • Dietary Fiber 0g • Sugars 1g • Protein 2g. DIETARY EXCHANGE: 1/2 Fat.

special touch

For a surprising bit of flavor and texture, place a walnut half underneath the Brie cheese. Before serving the Raspberry-Brie Tarts, garnish each with a mint leaf.

blue cheese ball with walnuts

READY IN: 15 Minutes ✳ SERVINGS: 8

1 (8 oz.) package cream cheese, softened	2 tablespoons chopped green onions
1 (4 oz.) package blue cheese, room temperature	2/3 cup chopped walnuts

1 In medium bowl, beat cream cheese until soft and creamy. Add blue cheese and onions; beat until well blended.

2 Shape mixture into ball; roll in walnuts. Refrigerate until serving time. Serve with assorted crackers.

NUTRITIONAL INFORMATION PER SERVING: Calories 220 • Total Fat 20g • Saturated Fat 9g • Cholesterol 40mg • Sodium 280mg • Total Carbohydrate 3g • Dietary Fiber 1g • Sugars 1g • Protein 7g. DIETARY EXCHANGES: 1 High-Fat Meat • 2-1/2 Fat.

crabmeat deviled eggs

READY IN: 40 Minutes ✳ SERVINGS: 16 Appetizers

8 eggs	1/2 teaspoon dry mustard
1 (6 oz.) can crab, drained, flaked	1/4 teaspoon ground red pepper (cayenne)
1/4 cup mayonnaise	16 sprigs parsley

1 Place eggs in medium saucepan; cover with cold water. Bring to a boil. Reduce heat to low; simmer about 15 minutes. Immediately drain; run cold water over eggs to stop cooking.

2 Peel eggs; cut in half lengthwise. Scoop yolks from 4 eggs into medium bowl. Remove remaining yolks; reserve for another use.

3 Add crabmeat, mayonnaise, dry mustard and ground red pepper to yolks in bowl; mix and mash with fork until well blended. Mound yolk mixture into center of each cooked egg white. Garnish each with parsley sprig. Cover; refrigerate until serving time.

NUTRITIONAL INFORMATION PER SERVING: Calories 70 • Total Fat 5g • Saturated Fat 1g • Cholesterol 115mg • Sodium 80mg • Total Carbohydrate 0g • Dietary Fiber 0g • Sugars 0g • Protein 5g. DIETARY EXCHANGES: 1/2 Medium-Fat Meat • 1/2 Fat.

special touch

For extra flair, cut the eggs in half with a crinkle-edged cutter. You can find such cutters at most kitchen specialty shops.

cranberry wassail

READY IN: 20 Minutes ✳ SERVINGS: 12

6 each whole cloves and allspice	1/2 teaspoon nutmeg
1 (48 oz.) bottle cranberry juice cocktail	1 (750 ml) bottle dry red wine
1/2 cup firmly packed brown sugar	Cinnamon sticks, if desired

1 Tie whole spices in 2 layers of cheesecloth or place in a tea ball. In a large saucepan or Dutch oven, combine cranberry juice cocktail, brown sugar and nutmeg; mix well.

2 Add spices; cook over medium heat until sugar dissolves, stirring occasionally. Reduce heat; cover and simmer for 10 minutes. Add wine; cook until thoroughly heated. Remove spices. If desired, garnish with cinnamon sticks.

NUTRITIONAL INFORMATION PER SERVING: Calories 150 • Total Fat 0g • Saturated Fat 0g • Cholesterol 0mg • Sodium 10mg • Total Carbohydrate 28g • Dietary Fiber 0g • Sugars 27g • Protein 0g. DIETARY EXCHANGES: 2 Carbohydrate • 1/2 Fat.

crabmeat deviled eggs
blue cheese ball with walnuts

feta cheese package

PREP TIME: 25 Minutes ✳ READY IN: 5 Hours 40 Minutes ✳ SERVINGS: 24

1   medium garlic bulb

1   tablespoon olive oil

2   cups feta cheese, crumbled (8 oz.)

1   (8 oz.) package cream cheese, softened

2   tablespoons finely chopped roasted red bell pepper (from a jar)

2   whole roasted red bell peppers (from a jar)

1 Heat oven to 350°F. Cut about 1/8-inch top off of garlic bulb and discard. Place garlic bulb on sheet of foil. Drizzle with oil; wrap in foil. Bake for 30 to 45 minutes or until garlic is soft. Cool 5 minutes. Unwrap; cool 30 minutes or until cool enough to handle.

2 With small spoon, scoop out soft garlic pulp into food processor bowl with metal blade. Discard skins. Add feta and cream cheese; process about 5 minutes or until light and fluffy. Gently stir in chopped roasted pepper.

3 On sheet of plastic wrap, shape cheese mixture into 4-inch square, 1-1/2 inches thick. Wrap in plastic wrap; refrigerate at least 4 hours or overnight.

4 To serve, unwrap cheese; place on serving plate. Smooth top and sides with small metal spatula. Cut eight 4-inch strips from whole roasted peppers. Wrap cheese square from center down sides with 4 strips of roasted pepper to resemble ribbon. Use 2 strips for loops of bow; use remaining 2 strips for ties that hang over edge of cheese package. Serve with assorted crackers or toasted baguette slices.

NUTRITIONAL INFORMATION PER SERVING: Calories 70 • Total Fat 6g • Saturated Fat 4g • Cholesterol 20mg • Sodium 140mg • Total Carbohydrate 2g • Dietary Fiber 0g • Sugars 1g • Protein 2g. DIETARY EXCHANGES: 1/2 Medium-Fat Meat • 1/2 Fat.

cranberry-barbecue riblets

PREP TIME: 15 Minutes ✳ READY IN: 1 Hour 25 Minutes ✳ SERVINGS: 12

1 (2 lb.) rack pork back ribs, cut in half lengthwise across bones	1/4 cup chopped fresh chives
1 cup barbecue sauce	1/4 teaspoon dry mustard
1/2 cup frozen cranberry-orange fruit for chicken (from 12 oz. container), thawed	1/4 teaspoon dried marjoram leaves

1 Heat oven to 375°F. Line 15x10x1-inch baking pan with foil. Spray foil with nonstick cooking spray. Cut ribs into individual riblets. Place riblets, meaty side down, in sprayed foil-lined pan; cover with foil. Bake for 30 minutes.

2 Meanwhile, in small bowl, combine all remaining ingredients; mix well. Remove riblets from oven. Uncover; drain off liquid in pan. Turn riblets meaty side up; spoon sauce mixture over riblets.

3 Return to oven; bake uncovered an additional 30 to 40 minutes or until riblets are tender and no longer pink next to bone, turning once or twice.

NUTRITIONAL INFORMATION PER SERVING: Calories 195 • Total Fat 11g • Saturated Fat 4g • Cholesterol 45mg • Sodium 250mg • Total Carbohydrate 13g • Dietary Fiber 0g • Sugars 11g • Protein 11g. DIETARY EXCHANGES: 1 Other Carbohydrate • 1-1/2 High-Fat Meat.

green chile cheesecake

green chile cheesecake

PREP TIME: 40 Minutes ✳ READY IN: 5 Hours 45 Minutes ✳ SERVINGS: 20

CRUST

1	cup unseasoned dry bread crumbs
1/2	cup shredded fresh Parmesan cheese (2 oz.)
1-1/2	teaspoons chili powder
1/4	cup butter, melted

FILLING

1	tablespoon oil
1/2	cup chopped red onion
2	tablespoons lime juice
3	garlic cloves, minced
1	cup frozen whole kernel corn, thawed

2	(4.5 oz.) cans chopped green chiles
2	teaspoons cumin
1-1/2	teaspoons salt
1/4	teaspoon hot pepper sauce
3	(8 oz.) packages cream cheese, softened
1/2	cup sour cream
3	eggs
1	cup shredded Monterey Jack cheese (4 oz.)
7	grape or small cherry tomatoes, halved
2	(12 oz.) packages cornbread crackers

1 Heat oven to 325°F. In medium bowl, combine bread crumbs, Parmesan cheese and chili powder; mix well. Stir in melted butter. Pat in bottom and 1 inch up sides of ungreased 9-inch springform pan. Set aside.

2 Heat oil in medium skillet over medium heat until hot. Add onion; stir to coat. Add lime juice; cook 4 to 5 minutes or until onion has softened, stirring frequently.

3 Add garlic; cook and stir 30 to 60 seconds or until fragrant. Remove from heat. Add corn, chiles, cumin, salt and hot pepper sauce; mix well. Set aside.

4 Beat cream cheese in large bowl on Medium speed until fluffy. Beat in sour cream. Reduce speed to Low; beat in eggs one at a time, scraping down sides of bowl after each addition. Stir in Monterey Jack cheese. Stir in chile mixture. Pour into crust-lined pan.

5 Bake for 55 to 65 minutes or just until center of cheesecake is set. Cool cheesecake in pan on wire rack for 1 hour. Cover; refrigerate at least 3 hours before serving.

6 Just before serving, run knife around edge of cheesecake to loosen; remove sides of pan. Arrange halved tomatoes around edge of cheesecake. Serve with crackers.

HIGH ALTITUDE (3500-6500 FT): Bake at 350°F for 55 to 60 minutes.

NUTRITIONAL INFORMATION PER SERVING: Calories 305 • Total Fat 25g • Saturated Fat 12g • Cholesterol 95mg • Sodium 700mg • Total Carbohydrate 10g • Dietary Fiber 1g • Sugars 6g • Protein 11g. DIETARY EXCHANGES: 1/2 Starch • 1/2 Other Carbohydrate • 1 High-Fat Meat • 3-1/2 Fat.

curried gouda spread

PREP TIME: 20 Minutes ✳ READY IN: 4 Hours 20 Minutes ✳ SERVINGS: 20

1	(7 oz.) Gouda cheese with red wax coating
1	(3 oz.) package cream cheese, softened
1	tablespoon honey

2	teaspoons lemon juice
1/4	teaspoon curry powder

1 With sharp knife, remove about 3-inch diameter slice from top of Gouda cheese. Carefully hollow out, leaving wax coating intact to form shell.

2 In food processor bowl with metal blade, combine Gouda cheese, cream cheese, honey, lemon juice and curry powder; process until smooth and well blended. Spoon cheese mixture into shell, mounding in center. Cover; refrigerate at least 3 hours or overnight to blend flavors.

3 For easier spreading, let cheese stand at room temperature for 1 hour before serving. To serve, place cheese on serving tray; surround with wedges of fresh peaches, pears, apple or pineapple, grapes and/or assorted crackers. Spread cheese on fruit or crackers.

NUTRITIONAL INFORMATION PER SERVING: Calories 50 • Total Fat 4g • Saturated Fat 3g • Cholesterol 15mg • Sodium 95mg • Total Carbohydrate 1g • Dietary Fiber 0g • Sugars 1g • Protein 3g. DIETARY EXCHANGE: 1/2 High-Fat Meat.

Festive Breads & More

Welcoming aromas of freshly baked favorites fill homes with good cheer. Usher in the holidays with this cozy collection of golden loaves, scones, muffins and more.

p. 57

p. 48

p. 45

p. 50

p. 49

apricot-orange cream scones p. 53

danish almond crescent ring

PREP TIME: 20 Minutes ✳ READY IN: 45 Minutes ✳ SERVINGS: 8

1/4	cup sugar	
3	tablespoons butter or margarine, softened	
3-1/2	oz. almond paste, broken into pieces	
1	(8 oz.) can refrigerated crescent dinner rolls	

1	egg, beaten
2	teaspoons sugar
2	to 4 tablespoons sliced almonds

1 Heat oven to 375°F. Lightly grease cookie sheet. In small bowl, mix sugar, butter and almond paste with fork until well mixed. Set aside.

2 Unroll dough into 2 long rectangles. Overlap long sides 1/2 inch to form 1 large rectangle; firmly press perforations and edges to seal. Press or roll to form 16x9-inch rectangle. Cut rectangle lengthwise into 3 equal strips.

3 Spoon 3 tablespoons almond paste mixture evenly down center of each strip. Gently press filling to form 1-inch-wide strip. Fold sides of dough over filling; firmly pinch edges to seal.

4 On cookie sheet, loosely braid the 3 filled strips. Shape braid into ring; pinch ends of strips together to seal. Brush with beaten egg. Sprinkle with 2 teaspoons sugar and the almonds.

5 Bake crescent ring 15 to 22 minutes or until golden brown. Cool 5 minutes. Remove from cookie sheet. Serve warm.

NUTRITIONAL INFORMATION PER SERVING: Calories 250 • Total Fat 13g • Saturated Fat 3.5g • Trans Fat 1.5g • Cholesterol 40mg • Sodium 380mg • Total Carbohydrate 28g • Dietary Fiber 1g • Sugars 17g • Protein 4g. DIETARY EXCHANGES: 1 Starch • 1 Other Carbohydrate • 2-1/2 Fat.

potato chive rolls

SERVINGS: 24

4-1/2 to 5 cups all-purpose flour
1 cup mashed potato flakes
1 tablespoon sugar
3 to 4 teaspoons chopped fresh or freeze-dried chives

2 teaspoons salt
2 packages active dry yeast
2 cups milk
1/2 cup dairy sour cream
2 eggs

1 In large bowl, combine 1-1/2 cups flour, potato flakes, sugar, chives, salt and yeast; blend well. In small saucepan, heat milk and sour cream until very warm (120°F to 130°F). Add warm liquid and eggs to flour mixture. Blend at Low speed until moistened; beat 3 minutes at Medium speed. By hand, stir in remaining 3 to 3-1/2 cups flour to form a stiff dough. Cover loosely with plastic wrap and cloth towel. Let rise in warm place (80°F to 85°F) until light and doubled in size, 45 to 55 minutes.

2 Generously grease 13x9-inch pan. On floured surface, knead dough gently until no longer sticky. Divide into 24 pieces; shape into balls. Place in greased pan. Cover; let rise in warm place until light and doubled in size, 30 to 35 minutes.

3 Heat oven to 375°F. Uncover dough. Bake 25 to 35 minutes or until golden brown. Immediately remove from pan; cool on wire rack. If desired, lightly dust tops of rolls with flour.

NUTRITIONAL INFORMATION PER SERVING: Calories 130 • Fat 2g • Sodium 200mg • Total Carbohydrate 24g • Protein 4g.

SUSAN COX
Unionville, Pennsylvania
Bake-Off® Contest 27, 1976
Prize Winner

cook's notes

A little sour cream gives these tender, no-knead rolls a hint of sourdough flavor. Best of all, using mashed potato flakes elminates the need to cook and mash potatoes. Try the rolls with any entree.

muffin mix buffet bread

SERVINGS: 16

1 (8-1/2 oz.) package corn muffin mix
2 packages active dry yeast
3/4 cup warm water
4 cups all-purpose flour

1 (10-3/4 oz.) can condensed Cheddar cheese soup
1/2 cup butter or margarine, melted

1 Grease two 8- or 9-inch square pans. Set aside 2 tablespoons of the dry muffin mix. In large bowl, dissolve yeast in warm water (105°F to 115°F). Add remaining dry muffin mix, 2 cups of the flour, soup and 1/4 cup of the melted butter; mix just until dry ingredients are moistened. Gradually stir in remaining 2 cups flour to form a stiff dough. Knead on floured surface until smooth, about 1 minute. Cover; let rest 15 minutes.

2 Heat oven to 375°F. Divide dough in half; press into greased pans. Cut each into 8 strips. Drizzle remaining 1/4 cup melted butter over loaves; sprinkle with reserved muffin mix. Cover; let rise in warm place 12 to 15 minutes or until light.

3 Bake for 18 to 25 minutes or until golden brown. Immediately remove from pans. Break apart or cut with knife. Serve warm.

NUTRITIONAL INFORMATION PER SERVING: Calories 250 • Fat 9g • Sodium 370mg • Total Carbohydrate 36g • Protein 5g.

MAXINE BULLOCK
Topeka, Kansas
Bake-Off® Contest 18, 1967

pineapple-cherry quick bread

PREP TIME: 30 Minutes ❋ READY IN: 2 Hours 25 Minutes ❋ SERVINGS: 24 Slices (2 Loaves)

4 cups all-purpose flour	4 eggs
1-1/2 cups sugar	1 (8 oz.) can crushed pineapple in unsweetened juice, undrained
1 teaspoon baking soda	1 (10 oz.) jar maraschino cherries, quartered, well drained
1 teaspoon salt	2 teaspoons powdered sugar
3/4 cup oil	
1 tablespoon vanilla	

1 Heat oven to 325°F. Grease and flour bottoms only of two 8x4-inch loaf pans. In large bowl, combine flour, sugar, baking soda and salt; mix well. Add oil, vanilla, eggs and pineapple with liquid; mix with electric mixer at Low speed until combined. Fold in cherries. Spoon into greased and floured pans.

2 Bake for 45 to 55 minutes or until toothpick inserted in center comes out clean. Cool in pans for 10 minutes. Remove from pans; place on wire racks. Cool 1 hour or until completely cooled. Sprinkle cooled loaves with powdered sugar.

HIGH ALTITUDE (3500-6500 FT): Bake 8x4-inch pans at 350°F for 60 to 65 minutes. Bake mini loaf pans at 350°F for 40 to 50 minutes.

NUTRITIONAL INFORMATION PER SERVING: Calories 220 • Total Fat 8g • Saturated Fat 1g • Cholesterol 35mg • Sodium 170mg • Total Carbohydrate 34g • Dietary Fiber 0g • Sugars 18g • Protein 3g. DIETARY EXCHANGES: 1 Starch • 1 Other Carbohydrate • 1-1/2 Fat.

crescent cranberry wreaths

READY IN: 30 Minutes ❋ SERVINGS: 6

1/3 cup finely chopped sweetened dried cranberries	1 oz. white chocolate baking bar, chopped
2 tablespoons cherry or strawberry preserves	1/2 teaspoon oil
1 (8 oz.) can refrigerated crescent dinner rolls	

1 Heat oven to 375°F. Lightly spray cookie sheet with nonstick cooking spray. In small bowl, combine cranberries and preserves; mix well.

2 Unroll dough into 2 rectangles. Press each to form 8x6-inch rectangle, pressing perforations to seal. Spread cranberry mixture over 1 rectangle to edges. Place second rectangle on top; press lightly. With sharp knife or pizza cutter, cut lengthwise into six 8-inch-long strips. Twist each strip 3 times and shape into ring on sprayed cookie sheet; pinch ends to seal.

3 Bake for 9 to 12 minutes or until golden brown. Cool on cookie sheet for 2 minutes. Meanwhile, in small microwavable bowl, combine baking bar and oil. Microwave on High for 30 seconds; stir until melted and smooth. If necessary, microwave an additional 10 to 20 seconds. Drizzle over warm wreaths. Serve warm.

NUTRITIONAL INFORMATION PER SERVING: Calories 200 • Total Fat 7g • Saturated Fat 2g • Cholesterol 0mg • Sodium 460mg • Total Carbohydrate 31g • Dietary Fiber 1g • Sugars 16g • Protein 3g. DIETARY EXCHANGES: 1 Starch • 1 Other Carbohydrate • 1-1/2 Fat.

pineapple-cherry quick bread

Lois Mattson
Duluth, Minnesota
Bake-Off® Contest 16, 1964

cook's notes

*Similar to the focaccia bread
found in restaurants and bak-
eries, this easy version makes
mealtime special. It's a memorable addition to holiday
menus, particularly those that
include red sauces.*

cheese-crusted flat bread

SERVINGS: 16 Wedges (2 Loaves)

BREAD
2-1/2	to 3 cups all-purpose flour
1	tablespoon sugar
1	teaspoon salt
1	package active dry yeast
3/4	cup milk
1/4	cup water
2	tablespoons butter or margarine

TOPPING
1/4	cup butter or margarine, melted
2	tablespoons chopped onion
1/2	teaspoon dried oregano leaves
1/2	teaspoon paprika
1/4	teaspoon garlic salt
1/4	teaspoon celery seed
1	cup shredded Cheddar cheese (4 oz.)

1 In large bowl, combine 2 cups flour, sugar, salt and yeast; mix well. In small saucepan, combine milk, water and 2 tablespoons butter. Heat until very warm (120°F to 130°F). Add warm liquid to flour mixture; mix well. Stir in remaining 1/2 to 1 cup flour to form a stiff dough.

2 On lightly floured surface, knead dough until smooth, about 5 minutes. Place dough in greased bowl. Cover loosely with greased plastic wrap and cloth towel. Let rise in warm place (80°F to 85°F) until light and doubled in size, 45 to 60 minutes.

3 Grease two 9-inch round cake or pie pans. Divide dough in half; press each half in greased pan. In small bowl, combine 1/4 cup butter, onion, oregano, paprika, garlic salt and celery seed; mix well. Spread mixture over dough. Prick tops generously with fork. Sprinkle evenly with cheese. Cover; let rise in warm place until light and doubled in size, 30 to 45 minutes. Heat oven to 375°F. Uncover dough. Bake 20 to 25 minutes or until golden brown. Serve warm.

NUTRITIONAL INFORMATION PER SERVING: Calories 160 • Fat 7g • Sodium 260mg • Total Carbohydrate 20g • Protein 5g.

onion-garlic loaf

PREP TIME: 20 Minutes ✳ READY IN: 50 Minutes ✳ SERVINGS: 5

1 tablespoon butter	1 (11 oz.) can refrigerated French loaf
1/2 cup thinly sliced green onions, including tops	1/4 cup grated Parmesan cheese
1 garlic clove, minced	

1 Heat oven to 350°F. Spray cookie sheet with nonstick cooking spray. Melt butter in small skillet over medium heat. Add onions and garlic; cook and stir 2 to 3 minutes or until tender.

2 Carefully unroll dough. Spread onion mixture evenly over dough. Reserve 1 teaspoon of the cheese for topping; sprinkle remaining cheese over onion mixture. Roll up dough; place seam side down on sprayed cookie sheet.

3 With sharp or serrated knife, make 4 or 5 diagonal slashes on top of loaf. Sprinkle with reserved 1 teaspoon cheese.

4 Bake for 26 to 30 minutes or until deep golden brown. Immediately remove from cookie sheet; cool 10 minutes. Cut diagonally into slices with serrated knife. Serve warm.

NUTRITIONAL INFORMATION PER SERVING: Calories 195 • Total Fat 6g • Saturated Fat 3g • Cholesterol 10mg • Sodium 480mg • Total Carbohydrate 28g • Dietary Fiber 1g • Sugars 3g • Protein 7g. DIETARY EXCHANGES: 2 Starch • 1 Fat • 2 Carbohydrate Choices.

special touch

Want to add a little spice to Onion-Garlic Loaf? Try sprinkling fresh basil or dried oregano over the filling before rolling up the loaf.

christmas tree coffee cake

READY IN: 25 Minutes ✳ SERVINGS: 8

BREAD	**DECORATIONS AND GLAZE**
1 (8 oz.) can refrigerated crescent dinner rolls	1/4 cup powdered sugar
2 teaspoons sugar	1 to 2 teaspoons orange juice
1 teaspoon grated orange peel	4 red candied cherries, halved
	4 green candied cherries, halved

1 Heat oven to 375°F. Unroll dough into 2 long rectangles; firmly press perforations to seal. Cut each rectangle lengthwise into 4 strips.

2 Twist each dough strip several times. On ungreased cookie sheet, form tree shape by starting at top of tree. Zigzag twisted strips of dough back and forth across cookie sheet, touching previous strip and making tree wider towards bottom, adding strips as each is finished. End with curl of dough at center of bottom to form trunk. Tree will be about 8 inches from tip to trunk.

3 In small bowl, combine sugar and orange peel; mix well. Sprinkle over dough. Bake for 12 to 16 minutes or until golden brown. Immediately remove from cookie sheet; place on serving tray.

4 In small bowl, combine powdered sugar and enough orange juice for desired drizzling consistency; beat until smooth. Drizzle glaze over bread. Garnish with cherries. Serve warm.

NUTRITIONAL INFORMATION PER SERVING: Calories 150 • Total Fat 6g • Saturated Fat 1g • Cholesterol 0mg • Sodium 230mg • Total Carbohydrate 21g • Dietary Fiber 0g • Sugars 10g • Protein 2g. DIETARY EXCHANGES: 1/2 Starch • 1 Fruit • 1-1/2 Other Carbohydrate • 1 Fat.

special touch

Whether serving Christmas Tree Coffee Cake for brunch, afternoon tea or even dessert, try presenting it on a silver tray with rosemary sprigs and whole candied cherries.

overnight caramel-apple rolls

PREP TIME: 35 Minutes ✳ READY IN: 10 Hours 30 Minutes ✳ SERVINGS: 12

ROLLS

3	to 3-1/2 cups all-purpose flour
1/4	cup sugar
1	teaspoon salt
1	package active dry yeast
1/2	cup applesauce
1/2	cup milk
1/4	cup butter
1	egg

TOPPING

1/2	cup firmly packed brown sugar
1/2	cup applesauce
3	tablespoons butter, melted

FILLING

2	tablespoons butter, softened
1/3	cup sugar
1	teaspoon cinnamon

1. In large bowl, combine 1 cup of the flour, 1/4 cup sugar, the salt and yeast; mix well. In small saucepan, heat 1/2 cup applesauce, the milk and 1/4 cup butter over medium heat until very warm (120°F to 130°F), stirring constantly.

2. Add warm mixture and egg to flour mixture; beat with electric mixer at low speed until moistened. Beat 2 minutes at medium speed. By hand, stir in 1-1/2 to 1-3/4 cups flour until dough pulls cleanly away from sides of bowl.

3. On floured surface, knead in an additional 1/2 to 3/4 cup flour until dough is smooth and elastic, about 5 minutes. Place dough in greased bowl; cover loosely with greased plastic wrap and cloth towel. Let rise in warm place (80°F to 85°F) until light and doubled in size, 45 to 60 minutes.

4. Grease 13x9-inch pan. Combine all topping ingredients in pan; mix well. Spread evenly in pan. On lightly floured surface, roll dough to 15x12-inch rectangle. Spread dough with 2 tablespoons butter. In small bowl, combine 1/3 cup sugar and cinnamon; mix well. Sprinkle over butter.

5. Starting with 15-inch side, roll up tightly, pinching edges to seal. Cut roll into 12 slices; place cut side down over topping in pan. Cover; refrigerate at least 8 hours or overnight.

6. When ready to bake, let rolls stand at room temperature for 30 to 60 minutes. Heat oven to 400°F. Uncover rolls; bake 20 to 25 minutes or until golden brown. Cool in pan for 1 minute. Invert rolls onto serving tray; remove pan. Scrape any remaining topping onto rolls. Serve warm.

NUTRITIONAL INFORMATION PER SERVING: Calories 300 • Total Fat 10g • Saturated Fat 6g • Cholesterol 40mg • Sodium 270mg • Total Carbohydrate 48g • Dietary Fiber 1g • Sugars 23g • Protein 4g. DIETARY EXCHANGES: 1 Starch • 2 Fat • 2 Other Carbohydrate • 3 Carbohydrate Choices.

STEPHANIE LUETKEHANS
Chicago, Illinois
Bake-Off® Contest 33, 1988
Prize Winner

lemon raspberry muffins

SERVINGS: 12

2	cups all-purpose flour
1	cup sugar
3	teaspoons baking powder
1/2	teaspoon salt
1	cup half-and-half

1/2	cup oil
1	teaspoon lemon extract
2	eggs
1	cup fresh or frozen raspberries without syrup (do not thaw)

1. Heat oven to 425°F. Line 12 muffin cups with paper baking cups. In large bowl, combine flour, sugar, baking powder and salt; mix well. In small bowl, combine half-and-half, oil, lemon extract and eggs; blend well. Add to dry ingredients; stir just until ingredients are moistened. Carefully fold in raspberries. Divide batter evenly into paper-lined muffin cups. Bake for 18 to 23 minutes or until golden brown. Cool 5 minutes; remove from pans.

HIGH ALTITUDE (3500-6500 FT): Line 16 muffin cups with paper baking cups. Decrease baking powder to 2 teaspoons. Bake as directed above. Yield: 16 muffins.

NUTRITIONAL INFORMATION PER SERVING: Calories 260 • Fat 12g • Sodium 230mg • Total Carbohydrate 35g • Protein 4g.

overnight caramel-apple rolls

dill-parmesan popovers

PREP TIME: 10 Minutes ✳ READY IN: 1 Hour ✳ SERVINGS: 8

3 eggs, room temperature	2 tablespoons grated Parmesan cheese
1-1/4 cups milk, room temperature	1 teaspoon dried dill weed
1-1/4 cups all-purpose flour	1/2 teaspoon salt

1 Heat oven to 450°F. Generously grease 8 popover cups or 6-oz. custard cups. In small bowl, beat eggs with eggbeater or wire whisk until lemon colored and foamy. Add milk; blend well.

2 Add all remaining ingredients; beat with eggbeater just until batter is smooth and foamy on top. Pour batter evenly into greased cups, filling each about 1/3 full.

3 Bake for 20 minutes. (Do not open.) Reduce oven temperature to 350°F; bake an additional 15 to 30 minutes or until deep golden brown. Remove from oven; insert sharp knife into each popover to allow steam to escape. Remove from cups. Serve warm.

NUTRITIONAL INFORMATION PER SERVING: Calories 120 • Total Fat 3g • Saturated Fat 1g • Cholesterol 85mg • Sodium 220mg • Total Carbohydrate 17g • Dietary Fiber 0g • Sugars 2g • Protein 6g. DIETARY EXCHANGES: 1 Starch • 1/2 Medium-Fat Meat • 1 Carbohydrate Choice.

white chocolate-iced cranberry bread

PREP TIME: 30 Minutes ✳ READY IN: 2 Hours 30 Minutes ✳ SERVINGS: 12

BREAD

2-1/4 cups all-purpose flour	2 teaspoons grated orange peel
3/4 cup sugar	2 eggs
1-1/2 teaspoons baking powder	1/2 cup butter or margarine, melted
1/2 teaspoon baking soda	1/4 cup orange juice
1/2 teaspoon salt	**ICING**
1/2 cup coarsely chopped sweetened dried cranberries	1 oz. white chocolate baking bar, chopped
3/4 cup half-and-half	1 to 2 tablespoons half-and-half
	1/2 cup powdered sugar

1 Heat oven to 350°F. Grease bottom only of 8x4-inch loaf pan. In large bowl, combine flour, sugar, baking powder, baking soda and salt; mix well. Stir in cranberries.

2 In small bowl, combine 3/4 cup half-and-half, orange peel and eggs; beat well. Add half-and-half mixture, melted butter and orange juice to flour mixture; stir just until dry ingredients are moistened. Pour batter into greased pan.

3 Bake for 50 to 60 minutes or until deep golden brown and toothpick inserted in center comes out clean. Cool in pan for 10 minutes. Run knife around edges of pan to loosen. Remove loaf from pan; place on wire rack. Cool 1 hour or until completely cooled.

4 In small microwavable bowl, combine baking bar and 1 tablespoon of the half-and-half. Microwave on High for 30 seconds; stir until melted and smooth. If necessary, microwave an additional 10 to 20 seconds. With wire whisk, beat in powdered sugar until smooth. If necessary, add additional half-and-half, 1/2 teaspoon at a time, until of desired consistency. Spoon and spread icing over cooled loaf, allowing some to run down sides.

HIGH ALTITUDE (3500-6500 FT): Bake at 350°F for 60 to 70 minutes.

NUTRITIONAL INFORMATION PER SERVING: Calories 285 • Total Fat 11g • Saturated Fat 7g • Cholesterol 65mg • Sodium 280mg • Total Carbohydrate 42g • Dietary Fiber 0g • Sugars 24g • Protein 4g. DIETARY EXCHANGES: 1 Starch • 2 Other Carbohydrate • 2 Fat.

pumpkin-cranberry-pecan bread

PREP TIME: 15 Minutes ✻ READY IN: 2 Hours 25 Minutes ✻ SERVINGS: 12

BREAD

- 1 (14 oz.) package pumpkin quick bread and muffin mix
- 1 cup water
- 3 tablespoons oil
- 2 eggs
- 1/2 cup sweetened dried cranberries
- 1/2 cup chopped pecans

TOPPING

- 1/4 cup white vanilla chips
- 1-1/2 teaspoons oil
- 2 tablespoons chopped pecans

1 Heat oven to 375°F. Generously grease bottom only of 8x4- or 9x5-inch loaf pan. In large bowl, combine quick bread mix, water, 3 tablespoons oil and eggs; beat 50 to 75 strokes with spoon until mix is moistened. Stir in cranberries and 1/2 cup pecans. Pour batter into greased pan.

2 Bake for 40 to 55 minutes or until toothpick inserted in center comes out clean. Cool in pan on wire rack for 15 minutes. Loosen sides of loaf with knife or metal spatula; remove from pan. Cool 1 hour or until completely cooled.

3 Melt vanilla chips with 1-1/2 teaspoons oil as directed on package. Cool about 3 minutes or until slightly cooled. Place mixture in resealable food storage plastic bag; seal bag. Cut small hole in bottom corner of bag. Squeeze bag to drizzle topping over cooled loaf. Immediately sprinkle with 2 tablespoons pecans. Let stand until topping sets before wrapping tightly. Store in refrigerator.

HIGH ALTITUDE (3500-6500 FT): Add 1/4 cup flour to dry quick bread mix. Bake at 375°F for 45 to 60 minutes.

NUTRITIONAL INFORMATION PER SERVING: Calories 260 • Total Fat 12g • Saturated Fat 2g • Cholesterol 35mg • Sodium 240mg • Total Carbohydrate 35g • Dietary Fiber 2g • Sugars 21g • Protein 3g. DIETARY EXCHANGES: 1 Starch • 1-1/2 Fruit • 2-1/2 Other Carbohydrate • 2 Fat.

special touch

This festive bread makes a wonderful hostess gift. Wrap the cooled loaf in a colorful cellophane bag tied with a pretty, plaid ribbon. Or, follow the instructions on the box of the bread-muffin mix, and prepare the heartwarming recipe in miniature loaf pans. If your host isn't keen on cranberries, simply replace them with dried cherries or currants. Instead of pecans, feel free to use whatever nuts you prefer.

orange-chocolate bubble bread

PREP TIME: 10 Minutes ✳ READY IN: 1 Hour ✳ SERVINGS: 12

4 tablespoons butter, softened	1/2 cup orange marmalade
2 (13.9 oz.) cans refrigerated orange flavor sweet rolls with icing	1/4 cup miniature semisweet chocolate chips, if desired

1 Heat oven to 375°F. Using 1 tablespoon of the butter, generously grease 12-cup fluted tube pan. Place remaining butter in small microwavable bowl. Microwave on High for 30 seconds or until melted; stir.

2 Separate dough into 16 rolls. Cut each in half crosswise. Place half of the roll pieces, cut edge down, in greased pan. Spoon and spread half of marmalade over rolls, avoiding touching sides of pan. Drizzle with half of melted butter. Layer with remaining roll pieces and marmalade. Sprinkle with chocolate chips. Drizzle with remaining butter.

3 Bake for 22 to 32 minutes or until rolls are golden brown and dough appears done when slightly pulled apart. Cool in pan for 2 minutes. Invert onto serving platter. Cool 15 minutes. Stir icing to soften. Spread over warm bread. Slice or pull apart bread to serve.

HIGH ALTITUDE (3500-6500 FT): Bake at 375°F for 28 to 33 minutes.

NUTRITIONAL INFORMATION PER SERVING: Calories 290 • Total Fat 12g • Saturated Fat 5g • Cholesterol 25mg • Sodium 570mg • Total Carbohydrate 42g • Dietary Fiber 1g • Sugars 16g • Protein 4g. DIETARY EXCHANGES: 1 Starch • 2 Other Carbohydrate • 2 Fat.

SUSAN BRINKLEY
Eminence, Missouri
Bake-Off® Contest 37, 1996

savory cheese and scallion scones

SERVINGS: 8

SCONES

2-3/4 cups all-purpose flour	4 scallions or green onions, chopped
5 teaspoons baking powder	1 cup half-and-half or milk
1/2 teaspoon salt, if desired	1 egg
1 cup crumbled feta cheese (4 oz.)	**GLAZE, IF DESIRED**
4 oz. cream cheese or 1/3-less-fat cream cheese (Neufchatel), cut into 1-inch cubes	1 egg
	2 tablespoons milk

1 Heat oven to 400°F. Grease large cookie sheet. In large bowl, combine flour, baking powder and salt; mix well. With pastry blender or fork, cut in feta cheese and cream cheese until mixture is crumbly. Add scallions; toss gently until combined. In small bowl, combine half-and-half and 1 egg; blend well. Add half-and-half mixture to flour mixture; stir lightly, just until soft dough forms.

2 Turn dough out onto well-floured surface; knead lightly 5 or 6 times. Pat or press dough into 1-inch-thick round. With floured knife, cut into 8 wedges. Place wedges 2 inches apart on greased cookie sheet. In small bowl, combine glaze ingredients; blend well. Brush over tops of wedges.

3 Bake for 25 to 30 minutes or until golden brown. Remove scones from cookie sheet. Cool 5 minutes. Serve warm or cool. Store in refrigerator.

NUTRITIONAL INFORMATION PER SERVING: Calories 310 • Fat 13g • Sodium 670mg • Total Carbohydrate 37g • Protein 10g.

orange-chocolate bubble bread

apricot-orange cream scones

apricot-orange cream scones

READY IN: 30 Minutes ✳ SERVINGS: 8

2 cups all-purpose flour	1/2 cup chopped dried apricots
3 tablespoons sugar	1/2 cup white vanilla chips
3 teaspoons baking powder	1-1/3 cups whipping cream
2 teaspoons grated orange peel	1 cup powdered sugar
1/2 teaspoon salt	2 to 3 tablespoons orange juice

1 Heat oven to 400°F. Lightly grease cookie sheet. In large bowl, combine flour, sugar, baking powder, orange peel and salt; mix well. Add apricots and white vanilla chips; mix well. Add whipping cream all at once; stir just until dry ingredients are moistened.

2 On lightly floured surface, knead dough 6 or 7 times until smooth. Divide dough in half. Pat halves into 6-inch rounds; cut each into 4 wedges. Place 2 inches apart on greased cookie sheet.

3 Bake for 10 to 13 minutes or until light golden brown. Cool 5 minutes. Meanwhile, in small bowl, blend powdered sugar and enough orange juice for desired drizzling consistency. Drizzle icing over warm scones. Serve warm.

HIGH ALTITUDE (3500-6500 FT): Increase flour to 2-1/4 cups; decrease whipping cream to 1 cup and add 1/3 cup water. Cut each 6-inch round of dough into 6 wedges. Bake as directed above. Yield: 12 scones.

NUTRITIONAL INFORMATION PER SERVING: Calories 420 • Total Fat 18g • Saturated Fat 11g • Cholesterol 50mg • Sodium 360mg • Total Carbohydrate 60g • Dietary Fiber 1g • Sugars 35g • Protein 5g. DIETARY EXCHANGES: 2 Starch • 2 Other Carbohydrate • 3-1/2 Fat.

salsa bread olé

SERVINGS: 24

3 eggs	1/4 cup shredded Monterey Jack cheese, if desired (1 oz.)
1/2 cup cornmeal	2 cups all-purpose flour
2/3 cup buttermilk	1 cup mashed potato flakes
1/2 cup butter or margarine, softened	4 teaspoons taco seasoning mix
1 (16 oz.) jar mild salsa, well drained	3 teaspoons baking powder
1/2 cup chopped ripe olives	1 teaspoon baking soda
1/4 cup chopped green onions	1/4 teaspoon salt
1 tablespoon chopped fresh parsley	1/4 teaspoon pepper
1-1/4 cups shredded Cheddar cheese (5 oz.)	

1 Heat oven to 350°F. Grease and flour 10-inch tube or 12-cup Bundt® pan. In large bowl, beat eggs at high speed for 1 minute. Add cornmeal, buttermilk, butter and salsa; beat 1 minute at medium speed or until well blended. With spoon, stir in olives, onions, parsley and cheeses.

2 In medium bowl, combine flour and all remaining ingredients; mix well. Add to salsa mixture; stir until well blended. Spoon batter into greased and floured pan.

3 Bake for 45 to 50 minutes or until toothpick inserted in center comes out clean. Cool 15 minutes. Remove from pan. Cool 20 minutes. Serve warm.

NUTRITIONAL INFORMATION PER SERVING: Calories 140 • Fat 7g • Sodium 360mg • Total Carbohydrate 14g • Protein 4g.

cook's notes

The night before, stir together the first seven ingredients for the scones; cover and let them stand at room temperature. In the morning, preheat the oven, stir the cream into the dry ingredients, then shape and bake the tasty treats.

CINDY ATWOOD
Taunton, Massachusetts
Bake-Off® Contest 37, 1996

dried cherry-cardamom bread

PREP TIME: 25 Minutes ✷ READY IN: 3 Hours 15 Minutes ✷ SERVINGS: 16

3/4 cup sugar	1 cup dried cherries, chopped
1/2 cup butter, softened	1 teaspoon grated lemon peel
1 teaspoon vanilla	1/2 teaspoon baking powder
1 cup buttermilk	1/2 teaspoon baking soda
2 eggs	1/2 teaspoon salt
2 cups all-purpose flour	1/2 teaspoon cardamom

1 Heat oven to 350°F. Spray bottom only of 9x5- or 8x4-inch loaf pan with nonstick cooking spray. In large bowl, combine sugar and butter; beat until light and fluffy. Beat in vanilla. Add buttermilk and eggs; blend well. (Mixture will appear curdled.)

2 In small bowl, combine all remaining ingredients; mix well. Add to buttermilk mixture; stir just until dry ingredients are moistened. Pour batter into sprayed pan.

3 Bake until toothpick inserted in center comes out clean. Bake 9x5-inch pan for 50 to 65 minutes; bake 8x4-inch pan for 55 to 75 minutes. Loosen edges of bread; cool in pan on wire rack for 15 minutes. Remove bread from pan; place on wire rack. Cool 1-1/2 hours or until completely cooled. Wrap tightly and store in refrigerator.

HIGH ALTITUDE (3500-6500 FT): Bake at 375°F. Bake 9x5-inch pan for 50 to 65 minutes; bake 8x4-inch pan for 55 to 75 minutes.

NUTRITIONAL INFORMATION PER SERVING: Calories 190 • Total Fat 7g • Saturated Fat 4g • Cholesterol 45mg • Sodium 200mg • Total Carbohydrate 29g • Dietary Fiber 1g • Sugars 15g • Protein 3g. DIETARY EXCHANGES: 1 Starch • 1 Fruit • 2 Other Carbohydrate • 1 Fat.

upside-down cinnamon-apple coffee cake

PREP TIME: 20 Minutes ✷ READY IN: 1 Hour ✷ SERVINGS: 8

1-1/2 cups chopped peeled apples	2 tablespoons butter or margarine, melted
1 (12.4 oz.) can refrigerated cinnamon rolls with icing	1/3 cup packed brown sugar
1/2 cup pecan halves or pieces	2 tablespoons corn syrup

1 Heat oven to 350°F. Spray 9-inch glass pie plate with cooking spray. Spread 1 cup of the apples in pie plate.

2 Separate dough into 8 rolls. Cut each roll into quarters; place in large bowl. Add remaining 1/2 cup apples and pecans.

3 In small bowl, mix butter, brown sugar and corn syrup until well blended. Add brown sugar mixture to dough mixture; toss gently to combine. Spoon mixture over apples in pan.

4 Bake 28 to 38 minutes or until deep golden brown. Cool 5 minutes. Invert onto serving platter. Remove lid from icing. Microwave icing on High 10 to 15 seconds or until of drizzling consistency. Drizzle over warm coffee cake. Serve warm.

NUTRITIONAL INFORMATION PER SERVING: Calories 290 • Total Fat 13g • Saturated Fat 2g • Cholesterol 0mg • Sodium 390mg • Total Carbohydrate 40g • Dietary Fiber 2g • Sugars 23g • Protein 3g. DIETARY EXCHANGES: 1 Starch • 1-1/2 Fruit • 2-1/2 Other Carbohydrate • 2-1/2 Fat.

dried cherry-cardamom bread

Kitchen tip

To help speed up preparation time, always slice, chop or snip dried fruits with knives or kitchen scissors that have been sprayed with a little nonstick cooking spray.

holiday focaccia

PREP TIME: 30 Minutes ✳ READY IN: 2 Hours 40 Minutes ✳ SERVINGS: 12

FOCACCIA

  3 to 3-3/4 cups all-purpose flour
  3 tablespoons sugar
  1 teaspoon salt
  1 teaspoon grated lemon peel
1/2 teaspoon cardamom
  1 package active dry yeast
  1 cup warm water (120°F to 130°F)

  2 tablespoons oil
1/2 cup chopped candied cherries or mixed fruit
1/3 cup coarsely chopped almonds
1/4 cup dried currants or raisins

TOPPING

  1 tablespoon butter, melted
  2 tablespoons sugar

1 In large bowl, combine 1-1/2 cups flour, 3 tablespoons sugar, salt, lemon peel, cardamom and yeast; mix well. Add water and oil; beat 2 minutes at Medium speed.

2 By hand, stir in cherries, almonds, currants and 1-1/2 cups flour. If necessary, add 1/4 to 3/4 cup additional flour until dough pulls cleanly away from sides of bowl.

3 On lightly floured surface, knead dough 5 to 10 times. Place in sprayed bowl; turn dough to grease top. Cover with sprayed plastic wrap and cloth towel. Let rise in warm place (80°F to 85°F) until doubled in size, 45 to 60 minutes.

4 Spray cookie sheet with nonstick cooking spray. Remove dough from bowl; lightly knead to form round ball. With sprayed hands, stretch and press dough to form 12-inch round. Place on sprayed cookie sheet. Brush with melted butter. Prick dough several times with fork. Cover; let rise in warm place until light and doubled in size, 40 to 50 minutes.

5 Heat oven to 400°F. Uncover dough; sprinkle with 2 tablespoons sugar. Bake for 15 to 20 minutes or until golden brown. Immediately remove from cookie sheet; place on serving tray. Cool 10 minutes. With pizza cutter or serrated knife, cut into wedges. Serve warm.

NUTRITIONAL INFORMATION PER SERVING: Calories 240 • Total Fat 5g • Saturated Fat 1g • Cholesterol 3mg • Sodium 210mg • Total Carbohydrate 44g • Dietary Fiber 2g • Sugars 12g • Protein 5g. DIETARY EXCHANGES: 2 Starch • 1 Fruit • 3 Other Carbohydrate • 1/2 Fat.

double chocolate batter bread

PREP TIME: 30 Minutes ❋ READY IN: 2 Hours 40 Minutes ❋ SERVINGS: 12

3-1/2	cups all-purpose flour	1-1/2	cups buttermilk
1/3	cup unsweetened cocoa	1/4	cup butter
1/3	cup sugar	2	eggs
1/4	teaspoon salt	1	(12 oz.) package semisweet chocolate chips (2 cups)
1/4	teaspoon baking soda		
1	package active dry yeast	2	teaspoons oil

1 Generously grease 12-cup fluted tube cake pan. In large bowl, combine 2-1/2 cups of the flour, cocoa, sugar, salt, baking soda and yeast; mix well. In small saucepan, heat buttermilk and butter until very warm (120°F to 130°F). Add warm liquid and eggs to flour mixture; beat at Low speed until moistened. Beat 3 minutes at High speed.

2 By hand, stir in remaining 1 cup flour and 1-1/2 cups chocolate chips. Spoon dough evenly into greased pan. Cover with plastic wrap and cloth towel; let rise in warm place (80°F to 85°F) until light and doubled in size, 30 to 40 minutes.

3 Heat oven to 350°F. Uncover dough; bake 35 to 45 minutes or until toothpick inserted near center comes out clean. Immediately invert bread onto wire rack; remove pan. Cool 45 minutes or until completely cooled.

4 Place remaining 1/2 cup chocolate chips and oil in resealable food storage freezer plastic bag; seal bag. Knead bag to evenly distribute oil. Microwave on High for 30 to 60 seconds or until melted. Cut small hole in bottom corner of bag. Squeeze bag to drizzle melted chocolate over cooled bread.

NUTRITIONAL INFORMATION PER SERVING: Calories 380 • Total Fat 15g • Saturated Fat 8g • Cholesterol 45mg • Sodium 160mg • Total Carbohydrate 54g • Dietary Fiber 4g • Sugars 24g • Protein 8g, DIETARY EXCHANGES: 2-1/2 Starch • 1 Fruit • 3-1/2 Other Carbohydrate • 2-1/2 Fat.

special touch

Warm slices of this chocolate bread are simply delicious when served with cream cheese. Consider using a whipped cream cheese for easy spreading. Or, for added richness, try a mascarpone cheese spread instead.

sweet nutcracker braid

PREP TIME: 20 Minutes ❋ READY IN: 1 Hour ❋ SERVINGS: 8

BREAD

2/3	cup chopped pecans
1/2	cup finely chopped dates
1/4	cup raisins
1	tablespoon sugar
1/8	teaspoon cinnamon
1	sheet frozen puff pastry, thawed

1/3	cup apricot preserves

GLAZE

3/4	cup powdered sugar
1/4	teaspoon vanilla
1	to 2 tablespoons milk
1/4	cup chopped pecans

1 Heat oven to 375°F. Spray large cookie sheet with nonstick cooking spray. In small bowl, combine 2/3 cup pecans, dates, raisins, sugar and cinnamon; mix well.

2 Unfold puff pastry; place on sprayed cookie sheet. Roll to form 14x10-inch rectangle. Spread preserves in 4-inch-wide strip lengthwise down center of pastry. Sprinkle fruit and nut mixture over preserves.

3 With scissors or sharp knife, make cuts 1 inch apart on long sides of pastry to within 1/2 inch of filling. Fold strips at an angle across filling mixture, overlapping ends and alternating from side to side.

4 Bake for 20 to 25 minutes or until golden brown. Immediately remove from cookie sheet; place on serving platter. Cool 15 minutes.

5 In small bowl, blend powdered sugar, vanilla and enough milk for desired drizzling consistency. Drizzle over cooled braid. Sprinkle with 1/4 cup pecans.

NUTRITIONAL INFORMATION PER SERVING: Calories 410 • Total Fat 22g • Saturated Fat 4g • Cholesterol 0mg • Sodium 85mg • Total Carbohydrate 50g • Dietary Fiber 3g • Sugars 30g • Protein 4g, DIETARY EXCHANGES: 1 Starch • 2-1/2 Fruit • 3-1/2 Other Carbohydrate • 4 Fat.

cook's notes

Make the braid ahead of time. Just bake and cool it; don't glaze it. Wrap the cooled braid tightly in plastic wrap, seal it in a food storage plastic freezer bag and freeze it for up to 4 days. To serve, unwrap and thaw it at room temperature before glazing it.

pumpkin-pecan braid

PREP TIME: 20 Minutes ❋ READY IN: 50 Minutes ❋ SERVINGS: 6

COFFEE CAKE
- 3/4 cup canned pumpkin
- 1/3 cup firmly packed brown sugar
- 1 teaspoon cinnamon
- 1/8 teaspoon ginger
- 1/8 teaspoon nutmeg
- 1 egg, separated
- 1/2 cup chopped pecans
- 1 (8 oz.) can refrigerated crescent dinner rolls

GLAZE
- 1/2 cup powdered sugar
- 2 to 3 teaspoons milk
- 1 tablespoon chopped pecans

1 Heat oven to 350°F. Spray cookie sheet with nonstick cooking spray. In medium bowl, combine pumpkin, brown sugar, cinnamon, ginger, nutmeg and egg yolk; blend well. Stir in 1/2 cup of the pecans.

2 Unroll dough onto sprayed cookie sheet; firmly press edges and perforations to seal. Press to form 13x7-inch rectangle. Spread filling in 3-1/2-inch-wide strip lengthwise down center of dough rectangle to within 1 inch of ends.

3 With scissors or sharp knife, make cuts 1 inch apart on long sides of dough rectangle just to edge of filling. Fold strips at an angle across filling, overlapping ends and alternating from side to side. Beat egg white in small bowl until foamy; brush over dough.

4 Bake for 20 to 30 minutes or until deep golden brown. Immediately remove from cookie sheet; place on serving platter.

5 In small bowl, blend powdered sugar and enough milk for desired drizzling consistency. Drizzle over warm coffee cake. Sprinkle with 1 tablespoon pecans.

NUTRITIONAL INFORMATION PER SERVING: Calories 330 • Total Fat 17g • Saturated Fat 3g • Cholesterol 35mg • Sodium 300mg • Total Carbohydrate 38g • Dietary Fiber 3g • Sugars 23g • Protein 5g. DIETARY EXCHANGES: 2 Starch • 1/2 Fruit • 2-1/2 Other Carbohydrate • 3 Fat.

parmesan-herb muffins

READY IN: 30 Minutes ❋ SERVINGS: 12

- 2 cups all-purpose flour
- 3/4 cup grated Parmesan cheese
- 1 tablespoon sugar
- 1-1/2 teaspoons baking powder
- 1/2 teaspoon baking soda
- 1/2 teaspoon dried sage leaves, crumbled
- 1/2 cup chopped fresh parsley
- 1-1/4 cups buttermilk
- 1/4 cup butter or margarine, melted
- 1 egg, slightly beaten

1 Heat oven to 400°F. Grease bottoms only of 12 medium muffin cups or line with paper baking cups. In large bowl, combine flour, cheese, sugar, baking powder, baking soda, sage and parsley; mix well.

2 Add buttermilk, butter and egg; stir just until dry ingredients are moistened. Divide batter evenly into greased muffin cups, filling each about 1/3 full.

3 Bake for 15 to 20 minutes or until toothpick inserted in center comes out clean. Immediately remove from pan. Serve warm.

NUTRITIONAL INFORMATION PER SERVING: Calories 165 • Total Fat 7g • Saturated Fat 4g • Cholesterol 35mg • Sodium 290mg • Total Carbohydrate 19g • Dietary Fiber 0g • Sugars 3g • Protein 6g. DIETARY EXCHANGES: 1 Starch • 1/2 Lean Meat • 1 Fat • 1 Carbohydrate Choice.

pumpkin-pecan braid

onion lover's twist
whole wheat raisin loaf

NAN ROBB
Huachucha City, Arizona
Bake-Off® Contest 21, 1970
Grand Prize Winner

special touch

Present slices of the large onion

loaf in a pretty basket with a

holiday cloth. It may be served

either warm from the oven or at

room temperature, and it is

particularly tasty with beef and

poultry dishes.

onion lover's twist

SERVINGS: 32

BREAD

3-1/2	to 4-1/2 cups all-purpose flour
1/4	cup sugar
1-1/2	teaspoons salt
1	package active dry yeast
3/4	cup water
1/2	cup milk
1/4	cup margarine or butter
1	egg

FILLING

1/4	cup margarine or butter
1	cup finely chopped onions or 1/4 cup instant minced onion
1	tablespoon grated Parmesan cheese
1	tablespoon sesame or poppy seed
1/2	to 1 teaspoon garlic salt
1	teaspoon paprika

1 In large bowl, combine 2 cups of the flour, sugar, salt and yeast; blend well. In small saucepan, heat water, milk and 1/4 cup margarine until very warm (120°F to 130°F). Add warm liquid and egg to flour mixture. Blend at Low speed until moistened; beat 3 minutes at Medium speed. By hand, stir in remaining 1-1/2 to 2-1/2 cups flour to form a soft dough. Cover loosely with greased plastic wrap and cloth towel. Let rise in warm place (80°F to 95°F) until light and doubled, 45 to 60 minutes.

2 Grease large cookie sheet. Melt 1/4 cup margarine in small saucepan; stir in remaining filling ingredients. Set aside. Stir down dough to remove all air bubbles. On floured surface, toss dough until no longer sticky. Roll dough into 18x12-inch rectangle. Cut rectangle in half crosswise to make two 12x9-inch rectangles; cut each rectangle into three 9x4-inch strips. Spread about 2 tablespoons onion mixture over each strip to 1/2 inch of edges. Bring lengthwise edges of each strip together to enclose filling; pinch edges and ends to seal.

3 On greased cookie sheet, braid 3 rolls together; pinch ends to seal. Repeat with remaining 3 rolls for second loaf. Cover; let rise in warm place until light and doubled in size, 25 to 30 minutes.

4 Heat oven to 350°F. Uncover dough. Bake 27 to 35 minutes or until golden brown and loaves sound hollow when lightly tapped. Immediately remove from cookie sheet; cool on wire racks.

NUTRITIONAL INFORMATION PER SERVING: Calories 130 • Fat 6g • Sodium 230mg • Total Carbohydrate 16g • Protein 3g.

whole wheat raisin loaf

SERVINGS: 32 Slices (2 Loaves)

2 to 3 cups all-purpose flour	3/4 cup water
1/2 cup sugar	1/4 cup oil
3 teaspoons salt	4 cups whole wheat flour
1 teaspoon cinnamon	1 cup rolled oats
1/2 teaspoon nutmeg	1 cup raisins
2 packages active dry yeast	1 tablespoon margarine or butter, melted
2 cups milk	1 teaspoon sugar, if desired

1 In large bowl, combine 1-1/2 cups all-purpose flour, 1/2 cup sugar, salt, cinnamon, nutmeg and yeast; mix well. In medium saucepan, heat milk, water and oil until very warm (120°F to 130°F). Add warm liquid to flour mixture. Blend at Low speed until moistened; beat 3 minutes at Medium speed. By hand, stir in whole wheat flour, rolled oats, raisins and an additional 1/4 to 3/4 cup all-purpose flour until dough pulls cleanly away from sides of bowl.

2 On floured surface, knead in remaining 1/4 to 3/4 cup all-purpose flour until dough is smooth and elastic, about 5 minutes. Place dough in greased bowl; cover loosely with greased plastic wrap and cloth towel. Let rise in warm place (80°F to 85°F) until light and doubled, 20 to 30 minutes.

3 Grease two 9x5- or 8x4-inch loaf pans. Punch down dough several times to remove all air bubbles. Divide dough in half; shape into loaves. Place in greased pans. Cover; let rise in warm place until light and doubled in size, 30 to 45 minutes.

4 Heat oven to 375°F. Uncover dough. Bake 40 to 50 minutes or until deep golden brown and loaves sound hollow when lightly tapped. If loaves become too brown, cover loosely with foil last 10 minutes of baking. Immediately remove from pans; cool on wire racks. Brush tops of loaves with margarine; sprinkle with 1 teaspoon sugar.

NUTRITIONAL INFORMATION PER SERVING: Calories 160 • Fat 3g • Sodium 210mg • Total Carbohydrate 29g • Protein 5g.

LENORA SMITH
Harahan, Louisiana
Bake-Off® Contest 27, 1976
Grand Prize Winner

special touch

For a no-fuss spread, create your own flavored cream cheese. Stir tablespoons of your favorite preserves into a tub of cream cheese to taste. Try apricot or berry preserves with the raisin loaf.

banana-wheat quick bread

SERVINGS: 16

1-1/4 cups all-purpose flour	1/4 cup margarine or butter, softened
1/2 cup whole wheat flour	2 tablespoons orange juice
1 cup sugar	1/4 teaspoon lemon juice, if desired
1 teaspoon baking soda	1 egg
1 teaspoon salt	1/4 to 1/2 cup raisins
1-1/2 cups mashed ripe bananas (3 medium)	

1 Heat oven to 350°F. Grease and flour bottom only of 9x5- or 8x4-inch loaf pan. In large bowl, combine all ingredients except raisins; beat 3 minutes at Medium speed. Fold in raisins. Pour batter into greased and floured pan.

2 Bake 55 to 65 minutes or until toothpick inserted in center comes out clean. Cool 10 minutes; remove from pan. Cool on wire rack. Wrap tightly and store in refrigerator.

HIGH ALTITUDE (3500-6500 FT): Increase all-purpose flour to 1-1/2 cups. Bake as directed above.

NUTRITIONAL INFORMATION PER SERVING: Calories 160 • Fat 3g • Sodium 250mg • Total Carbohydrate 31g • Protein 2g.

BARBARA GOLDSTEIN
New York, New York
Bake-Off® Contest 24, 1973

CLAUDIA HOWE
Hickory Hills, Illinois
Bake-Off® Contest 34, 1990

cook's notes

To make a cream-cheese fruit spread, substitute an 8 oz. package of reduced-fat cream cheese, softened, for the margarine. Increase the pineapple spread to 1/2 cup. Prepare as directed.

tropical oat bran muffins

SERVINGS: 22

MUFFINS

- 2 cups all-purpose flour
- 3/4 cup fortified whole bran cereal with oat bran or fortified whole bran cereal
- 1/2 cup coconut
- 2 teaspoons baking powder
- 1 teaspoon cinnamon
- 1 (3-1/2 oz.) jar macadamia nuts, chopped, if desired
- 1/2 cup margarine or butter, softened
- 1 cup sugar
- 1/4 cup firmly packed brown sugar
- 3 eggs
- 3/4 cup mashed ripe bananas (about 2 medium)
- 2 teaspoons vanilla
- 1 (8 oz.) can crushed pineapple in unsweetened juice, drained

FRUIT SPREAD

- 1/2 cup margarine or butter, softened
- 1/3 cup low-calorie pineapple fruit spread, preserves or jam

1 Heat oven to 350°F. Line with paper baking cups or grease bottoms only of 22 regular-sized muffin cups or 12 jumbo muffin cups. In large bowl, combine flour, cereal, coconut, baking powder, cinnamon and macadamia nuts; mix well.

2 In another large bowl, combine 1/2 cup margarine, sugar and brown sugar; beat until light and fluffy. Add eggs; blend well. Stir in mashed bananas, vanilla and pineapple; blend well. Add to dry ingredients all at once; stir until dry ingredients are just moistened. Fill greased muffin cups 2/3 full.

3 Bake for 20 to 30 minutes or until light golden brown and toothpick inserted in center comes out clean. Cool 2 minutes; remove from pans. In small bowl, combine the fruit spread ingredients at low speed until well blended. Serve with muffins.

HIGH ALTITUDE (3500-6500 FT): Decrease sugar to 3/4 cup. Bake as directed above.

NUTRITIONAL INFORMATION PER SERVING: Calories 240 • Fat 13g • Sodium 160mg • Total Carbohydrate 28g • Protein 3g.

SALLY VOG
Springfield, Oregon
Bake-Off® Contest 34, 1990

cook's notes

You can prepare the muffins with the flavor of jam you think that your friends and family members will enjoy the most.

chocolate chunk pistachio muffins

SERVINGS: 10

- 2 cups all-purpose flour
- 3/4 cup sugar
- 2 teaspoons baking powder
- 1/2 teaspoon cinnamon
- 1/4 teaspoon baking soda
- 1/4 teaspoon salt
- 6 oz. sweet cooking chocolate, coarsely chopped
- 1/2 cup coarsely chopped pistachios
- 1 cup milk
- 1/2 cup margarine or butter, melted
- 1 teaspoon grated lemon peel
- 1 teaspoon vanilla
- 1 egg, slightly beaten
- 1/3 cup seedless raspberry jam

1 Heat oven to 375°F. Line with paper baking cups or grease bottoms only of 10 jumbo muffin cups. In large bowl, combine flour, sugar, baking powder, cinnamon, baking soda and salt; mix well. Reserve 1/3 cup of the largest pieces of chopped chocolate; reserve 2 tablespoons of the pistachios. Stir remaining chopped chocolate and pistachios into dry ingredients. In small bowl, combine milk, margarine, lemon peel, vanilla and egg; blend well. Add to dry ingredients all at once; stir just until dry ingredients are moistened.

2 Fill each paper-lined muffin cup with 2 heaping tablespoons batter. Spoon rounded teaspoon jam into center of batter in each cup. Spoon about 1 heaping tablespoon of the remaining batter over jam in each cup. Top each with reserved chopped chocolate and pistachios.

3 Bake for 20 to 25 minutes or until toothpick inserted in center comes out clean. Cool 5 minutes; remove from pan. Serve warm or cool.

HIGH ALTITUDE (3500-6500 FT): Increase flour to 2-1/4 cups. Bake as directed above.

NUTRITIONAL INFORMATION PER SERVING: Calories 420 • Fat 20g • Sodium 260mg • Total Carbohydrate 54g • Protein 6g.

tropical oat bran muffins
chocolate chunk pistachio muffins

Seasonal Salads & Sides

Christmas menus are absolutely a joy to plan with this assortment of refreshing salads, savory side dishes and mouth-watering soups. Each rounds out meals perfectly.

p. 67

p. 76

p. 88

p. 66

p. 75

spinach salad with cranberry vinaigrette p. 85

baked brandied cranberries

PREP TIME: 5 Minutes ✳ READY IN: 1 Hour 5 Minutes ✳ SERVINGS: 8

1 (12 oz.) bag fresh cranberries	2 teaspoons grated orange peel
1-1/2 cups sugar	3 tablespoons brandy or orange juice

1 Heat oven to 350°F. In ungreased 1-1/2-quart casserole, mix all ingredients. Cover. Bake 20 minutes. Uncover casserole; stir mixture. Bake uncovered 30 to 40 minutes longer or until cranberries pop and mixture is slightly thickened. Serve warm or cold.

NUTRITIONAL INFORMATION PER SERVING: Calories 170 • Total Fat 0g • Saturated Fat 0g • Trans Fat 0g • Cholesterol 0mg • Sodium 0mg • Total Carbohydrate 43g • Dietary Fiber 2g • Sugars 40g • Protein 0g. DIETARY EXCHANGES: 1 Fruit • 2 Other Carbohydrate.

garden salad with herbed vinaigrette

READY IN: 15 Minutes ✳ SERVINGS: 4

SALAD

4	cups torn leaf lettuce
1	cup sliced fresh mushrooms
1/2	cup sliced radishes
1	large tomato, chopped

VINAIGRETTE

2	tablespoons chopped fresh basil
1	tablespoon chopped fresh chives
2	teaspoons sugar
1/2	teaspoon dry mustard
1/4	teaspoon salt
1/4	teaspoon pepper
3	tablespoons tarragon or white wine vinegar
2	tablespoons extra-virgin olive oil

1 In large bowl, combine all salad ingredients. In small bowl or jar with tight-fitting lid, combine all dressing ingredients; blend or shake until sugar is dissolved. Add dressing to salad; toss gently to coat.

NUTRITIONAL INFORMATION PER SERVING: Calories 110 • Total Fat 7g • Saturated Fat 1g • Cholesterol 0mg • Sodium 150mg • Total Carbohydrate 10g • Dietary Fiber 3g • Sugars 5g • Protein 2g. DIETARY EXCHANGES: 1-1/2 Vegetable • 1-1/2 Fat.

cook's notes

Prepare the salad mixture and vinaigrette up to 4 hours in advance. Refrigerate the salad and dressing separately. Toss the two together just before serving time.

Marlys Ward
Mankato, Minnesota
Bake-Off® Contest 34, 1990

mediterranean fennel salad

READY IN: 20 Minutes ✳ SERVINGS: 10

2 (14 oz.) packages frozen whole green beans	1 tablespoon Dijon mustard
2 bulbs fresh fennel	1 teaspoon minced garlic
2 medium red bell peppers, cut into bite-sized strips	1/2 teaspoon salt
3 tablespoons red wine vinegar	1/2 cup extra-virgin olive oil
	1/4 cup pine nuts

1 Cook green beans as directed on package. Drain; rinse with cold water to cool. Trim fennel bulbs; cut in half. Cut each half into 1/4-inch-thick slices. In large bowl, combine fennel, bell peppers and cooked green beans.

2 In small bowl, combine vinegar and mustard; beat with wire whisk until well blended. On cutting board, mash garlic and salt together with fork to make a paste. Beat into vinegar mixture. Slowly beat in oil until well blended.

3 Add dressing to vegetable mixture; toss gently to mix. Arrange on large serving platter. Sprinkle with pine nuts. If desired, garnish with fresh fennel tops.

NUTRITIONAL INFORMATION PER SERVING: Calories 170 • Total Fat 13g • Saturated Fat 2g • Cholesterol 0mg • Sodium 190mg • Total Carbohydrate 11g • Dietary Fiber 4g • Sugars 4g • Protein 2g. DIETARY EXCHANGES: 2 Vegetable • 2-1/2 Fat • 1 Carbohydrate Choice.

spicy corn and black bean salad

SERVINGS: 11

SALAD

2 (11 oz.) cans vacuum-packed whole kernel corn with red and green sweet peppers, drained

1 (15 oz.) can black beans, drained, rinsed

1 (4.5 oz.) jar sliced mushrooms, drained

1/2 cup sliced green onions

1/2 cup peeled, thinly sliced cucumber

2 tablespoons finely chopped fresh jalapeño pepper

DRESSING

1/3 cup oil

1/4 cup rice wine vinegar or white vinegar

1/4 cup orange juice

1 teaspoon finely chopped garlic

1/2 teaspoon salt

1/4 cup chopped fresh cilantro

1 tablespoon grated orange peel

1 to 2 teaspoons cumin seed

Lettuce leaves

1 In large bowl, combine all salad ingredients; blend well. In small bowl using wire whisk, blend oil, vinegar, orange juice, garlic and salt. Pour over salad; toss gently. Cover; refrigerate 1 to 2 hours to blend flavors.

2 Just before serving, drain salad. Stir in cilantro, orange peel and cumin seed. Serve in lettuce-lined bowl or on lettuce-lined plates. Store in refrigerator.

NUTRITIONAL INFORMATION PER SERVING: Calories 110 • Fat 2g • Sodium 200mg • Carbohydrate 18g • Protein 4g.

mediterranean fennel salad

turkey and pasta coleslaw

turkey and pasta coleslaw

SERVINGS: 5

1 (1 lb.) package frozen pasta, broccoli, corn and carrots in a garlic-seasoned sauce

3 cups finely shredded green cabbage

1 cup cubed cooked turkey

1/2 cup shredded carrot

1 green onion, chopped

1/3 cup purchased reduced-calorie coleslaw salad dressing

5 lettuce leaves

5 lime slices

5 fresh parsley sprigs

1 Prepare frozen vegetables and pasta according to package directions until vegetables are crisp-tender. Place in large bowl. Cool 15 minutes in refrigerator.

2 Add cabbage, turkey, carrot and green onion to vegetable and pasta mixture; mix well. Pour dressing over salad; toss gently to combine. Cover; refrigerate at least 1 hour to blend flavors. Serve on lettuce-lined plates; garnish with lime slices and parsley.

NUTRITIONAL INFORMATION PER SERVING: Calories 210 • Fat 8g • Sodium 560mg • Total Carbohydrate 26g • Protein 13g.

NANCY E. SMITH
The Woodlands, Texas
Bake-Off® Contest 35, 1992

santa fe corn and cheese bake

SERVINGS: 8

2 eggs, beaten

1 cup creamed cottage cheese

1/2 cup dairy sour cream

1/3 cup chopped green chiles, drained

3 tablespoons all-purpose flour

3 tablespoons milk

2 to 3 teaspoons sugar

1 teaspoon onion salt

1/4 to 1/2 teaspoon pepper

1 (15.25 oz.) can whole kernel corn, drained

3 tablespoons chopped ripe olives

1/4 cup shredded Cheddar cheese (1 oz.)

1 Heat oven to 350°F. In large bowl, combine eggs and cottage cheese; blend well. Add sour cream and chiles; mix well. In small bowl, combine flour and milk; beat until smooth. Add to cottage cheese mixture. Stir in sugar, onion salt, pepper and corn; blend well. Pour into ungreased 8-inch square (1-1/2-quart) baking dish or 2-quart casserole.

2 Bake for 30 to 40 minutes or until knife inserted near center comes out clean. Sprinkle top with olives and Cheddar cheese. Bake an additional 1 to 2 minutes or until cheese is melted.

NUTRITIONAL INFORMATION PER SERVING: Calories 160 • Fat 8g • Sodium 580mg • Total Carbohydrate 15g • Protein 8g.

ALDA MENONI
Santa Barbara, California
Bake-Off® Contest 33, 1988

cook's notes

You can serve the corn side dish as a meatless main course for casual, holiday get-togethers. It also makes a great contribution to potlucks.

seasoned chicken caesar salad

READY IN: 10 Minutes ✳ SERVINGS: 3

1 (9 oz.) package frozen southwestern-flavored cooked chicken breast strips

4 cups lightly packed torn romaine lettuce

1/3 cup purchased creamy Caesar salad dressing

1/2 cup crumbled basil and tomato feta cheese (2 oz.)

1/4 cup crushed tortilla chips

1 Heat chicken as directed on package using microwave. In large bowl, combine all ingredients except tortilla chips; toss gently. Top with tortilla chips.

NUTRITIONAL INFORMATION PER SERVING: Calories 310 • Total Fat 20g • Saturated Fat 6g • Cholesterol 60mg • Sodium 910mg • Total Carbohydrate 9g • Dietary Fiber 2g • Sugars 3g • Protein 24g. DIETARY EXCHANGES: 1/2 Starch • 1/2 Other Carbohydrate • 1 Vegetable • 3 Very Lean Meat • 3-1/2 Fat.

MILDRED WITTAN
Boca Raton, Florida
Bake-Off® Contest 36, 1994

cook's notes

Entertaining during the holidays doesn't have to be hard. Just serve this hearty chicken soup with a salad and a crusty loaf of bread.

garlic chicken provençal soup

SERVINGS: 4

SOUP

2　tablespoons butter or margarine
1/2　cup chopped onion
1/4　cup butter or margarine
4　boneless, skinless chicken breast halves
2　(16 oz.) cans Italian plum tomatoes or whole tomatoes, undrained, cut into pieces

1　cup dry white wine or water
1　(16 oz.) package frozen pasta, broccoli, corn and carrots in a garlic-seasoned sauce

GARNISHES, IF DESIRED

1/4　cup grated Parmesan cheese
1/4　cup chopped fresh parsley

1　Melt 2 tablespoons butter in Dutch oven over medium-high heat. Add onion; cook and stir 3 to 5 minutes or until softened. Remove from pan; set aside.

2　In same Dutch oven, melt 1/4 cup butter; add chicken and cook 8 to 10 minutes or until golden brown, turning once. Add tomatoes, wine and reserved onion. Bring to a boil. Reduce heat; simmer uncovered 10 to 15 minutes or until chicken is no longer pink. Stir in frozen vegetables with pasta. Bring to a boil. Reduce heat; simmer 3 to 5 minutes or until vegetables are crisp-tender.

3　To serve, place 1 chicken breast half in each of 4 large shallow soup bowls; ladle hot soup over chicken. Garnish with Parmesan cheese and parsley.

NUTRITIONAL INFORMATION PER SERVING: Calories 570 • Fat 29g • Sodium 1120mg • Total Carbohydrate 34g • Protein 36g.

creamy corn with chives

READY IN: 10 Minutes ✳ SERVINGS: 4

2　cups frozen extra sweet whole kernel corn
2　tablespoons chopped fresh chives
1/4　teaspoon salt

1/4　teaspoon garlic-pepper blend
2　tablespoons light sour cream

1　In medium saucepan or microwavable dish, cook corn as directed on package. Drain; return to saucepan. Add all remaining ingredients; toss to coat. Heat just until thoroughly heated.

NUTRITIONAL INFORMATION PER SERVING: Calories 70 • Total Fat 2g • Saturated Fat 1g • Cholesterol 4mg • Sodium 160mg • Total Carbohydrate 11g • Dietary Fiber 2g • Sugars 5g • Protein 2g. DIETARY EXCHANGES: 1/2 Starch • 1/2 Other Carbohydrate • 1/2 Fat.

DOROTHY CROW
Ocean City, Maryland
Bake-Off® Contest 38, 1998
Prize Winner

sherried mushroom bisque

SERVINGS: 6

2　to 4 tablespoons butter or margarine
1/2　cup finely chopped onion
2　(4.5 oz.) jars sliced mushrooms, drained
1/2　cup cream sherry or chicken broth
3　cups chicken broth
1　(4.5 to 5.5 oz.) container garlic and herb soft spreadable cheese

2　cups half-and-half or milk
1　cup mashed potato flakes
1/8　teaspoon salt
1/8　teaspoon pepper
　Chopped fresh chives, if desired
　Garlic croutons, if desired

1　Melt butter in large saucepan over medium-high heat. Add onion; cook and stir 3 to 5 minutes or until tender. Increase heat to high. Add mushrooms and sherry; cook and stir 3 to 5 minutes or until liquid is reduced by half. Stir in broth; bring to a boil. Add cheese, half-and-half, potato flakes, salt and pepper; cook and stir just until cheese is melted and mixture is thoroughly heated, reducing heat if necessary. Do not boil. Garnish each serving with chives or croutons.

NUTRITIONAL INFORMATION PER SERVING: Calories 370 • Fat 27g • Sodium 1010mg • Total Carbohydrate 21g • Protein 10g.

garlic chicken provençal soup

JUDITH METTLIN
Snyder, New York
Bake-Off® Contest 39, 2000
Prize Winner

cook's notes

Island Paradise Salad is a delicious way to brighten up holiday menus. Feel free to replace the mango with a small can of mandarin oranges if you wish.

island paradise salad

SERVINGS: 8

DRESSING

- 1 teaspoon grated lime peel
- 3 tablespoons honey
- 2 tablespoons fresh lime juice
- 1 tablespoon canola or vegetable oil

SALAD

- 2 cups frozen sugar snap peas (from 1 lb. pkg.)
- 3 cups torn romaine lettuce
- 3 cups torn Bibb lettuce
- 1 avocado, peeled, pitted and cut into 1/2-inch cubes
- 1 large ripe mango, peeled, seed removed and cut into 1/2-inch cubes
- 1 small red onion, thinly sliced, separated into rings
- 1/2 cup unsweetened or regular shredded coconut

1 In small bowl, combine all dressing ingredients; mix well. Cook sugar snap peas as directed on package. Drain. Rinse with cold water to cool. Drain well.

2 In large bowl, combine cooked sugar snap peas and all remaining salad ingredients except coconut. Add dressing; toss to coat. Sprinkle with coconut.

NUTRITIONAL INFORMATION PER SERVING: Calories 160 • Fat 9g • Sodium 10mg • Total Carbohydrate 18g • Protein 2g.

honey-walnut-wild rice stuffed butternut squash

PREP TIME: 15 Minutes ✳ READY IN: 1 Hour 10 Minutes ✳ SERVINGS: 4

- 2 medium butternut squash, halved lengthwise, seeds removed
- 1 (15 oz.) can cooked wild rice, drained
- 1/2 cup sweetened dried cranberries
- 1/4 cup chopped walnuts
- 2 tablespoons honey
- 1/2 teaspoon dried marjoram leaves
- 1/2 teaspoon salt
- 2 tablespoons frozen apple juice concentrate, thawed
- 2 teaspoons butter, melted

1 Heat oven to 375°F. Spray 15x10x1-inch baking pan with nonstick cooking spray. Place squash, cut side down, in sprayed pan. Bake for 30 minutes.

2 Meanwhile, in medium bowl, combine wild rice, cranberries, walnuts, 1 tablespoon of the honey, marjoram and 1/4 teaspoon of the salt; mix well. In small bowl, combine remaining tablespoon honey, apple juice concentrate and butter.

3 Remove squash from oven. Turn cut side up. Sprinkle with remaining 1/4 teaspoon salt. Brush with honey-butter mixture. Spoon wild rice mixture into each half. Drizzle with any remaining honey-butter mixture.

4 Return to oven; bake an additional 30 minutes or until squash is tender and filling is thoroughly heated, covering with foil during last 10 minutes of baking.

NUTRITIONAL INFORMATION PER SERVING: Calories 370 • Total Fat 7g • Saturated Fat 2g • Cholesterol 5mg • Sodium 550mg • Total Carbohydrate 71g • Dietary Fiber 10g • Sugars 34g • Protein 6g. DIETARY EXCHANGES: 2 Starch • 2-1/2 Fruit • 4-1/2 Other Carbohydrate • 1-1/2 Fat.

cook's notes

Two cups of cooked wild rice can be used in place of the canned rice in the butternut squash side dish.

CHRIS HURST
Atlanta, Georgia
Bake-Off® Contest 37, 1996
Prize Winner

cook's notes

Never seen a side dish steal the show from the entree? Try this potato pie at your next celebration. The impressive dish is wonderful with nearly any main course. Feel free to exchange the Cheddar for Swiss cheese if you'd like.

savory mashed potato pie

SERVINGS: 8

CRUST

1 refrigerated pie crust (from 15 oz. pkg.)

FILLING

2 cups water

3 tablespoons butter or margarine

1/2 teaspoon salt, if desired

1/2 teaspoon garlic powder

1/8 teaspoon white pepper

2-1/2 cups mashed potato flakes

1/2 cup sour cream

1/4 cup purchased real bacon bits, or 4 slices bacon, cooked, crumbled

1/2 cup thinly sliced green onions

1 cup shredded Cheddar cheese (4 oz.)

2 small tomatoes, thinly sliced

1 tablespoon olive oil or vegetable oil

GARNISH

2 tablespoons thinly sliced green onions

1/2 cup sour cream

1 Heat oven to 450°F. Prepare pie crust according to package directions for one-crust baked shell using 9-inch deep-dish pie pan or 9-inch pie pan. Bake for 9 to 11 minutes or until light golden brown. Cool while preparing mashed potatoes.

2 Meanwhile, in large saucepan, combine water, butter, salt, garlic powder and pepper. Bring to a boil. Remove from heat; stir in potato flakes, 1/2 cup sour cream and bacon bits; mix well.

3 Sprinkle 1/2 cup onions over bottom of cooled baked shell; sprinkle with cheese. Spoon and spread potato mixture evenly over cheese. Arrange tomatoes around edge, overlapping if necessary. Brush potato mixture and tomatoes with oil.

4 Reduce oven temperature to 400°F. Bake pie for 15 to 20 minutes or until thoroughly heated in center. Cool 5 minutes. To serve, sprinkle with 2 tablespoons onions. Cut into wedges; top each serving with 1 tablespoon sour cream.

NUTRITIONAL INFORMATION PER SERVING: Calories 390 • Fat 25g • Sodium 590mg • Total Carbohydrate 33g • Protein 9g.

VICKIE COX
Wilkes-Barre, Pennsylvania
Bake-Off® Contest 35, 1992
Prize Winner

special touch

For extra flair, gently spoon the prepared salad into a large, clear-glass serving bowl lined with crisp lettuce leaves. Guests are sure to notice your attention to detail.

antipasto tortellini salad

SERVINGS: 12

1 (16 oz.) package fresh or frozen uncooked cheese tortellini

1 cup chopped salami (4 oz.)

4 oz. provolone cheese, cut into 2x1/4x1/4-inch strips

1 (11 oz.) can vacuum-packed whole kernel corn, drained

1 (9 oz.) package frozen spinach in a pouch, thawed, squeezed to drain

1 (6 oz.) jar marinated artichoke hearts, drained, chopped

1 (6 oz.) can pitted ripe olives, drained, sliced (1-1/2 cups)

1-1/2 cups purchased creamy Italian salad dressing

1 teaspoon Dijon mustard

1/2 cup grated Parmesan cheese

1 (2 oz.) jar diced pimiento, drained, if desired

1 Cook tortellini to desired doneness as directed on package. Drain; rinse with cold water. In very large bowl, combine tortellini, salami, provolone cheese, corn, spinach, artichoke hearts and 1 cup of the olives.

2 In small bowl, combine salad dressing, mustard and 1/4 cup of the Parmesan cheese; blend well. Pour dressing over salad; toss gently. Top with remaining olives and Parmesan cheese. Cover; refrigerate 1 to 2 hours to blend flavors. Just before serving, garnish with pimiento.

NUTRITIONAL INFORMATION PER SERVING: Calories 350 • Fat 21g • Sodium 910mg • Total Carbohydrate 28g • Protein 13g.

savory mashed potato pie

fiesta chicken salad

fiesta chicken salad

READY IN: 30 Minutes ✳ SERVINGS: 8

1/4 cup margarine or butter, cut into 4 pieces	1/2 teaspoon ground oregano
6 boneless, skinless chicken breast halves	4 green onions, sliced
2 eggs	1 (16 oz.) package mixed salad greens
1-1/4 cups medium chunky-style picante	3 medium tomatoes, chopped
1-1/3 cups unseasoned bread crumbs	1 (8 oz.) bottle red wine vinegar and oil salad dressing
1 teaspoon salt	1 avocado, peeled, sliced
1 teaspoon cumin	1 cup sour cream
1 teaspoon chili powder	

1 Heat oven to 400°F. Place margarine in 15x10x1-inch baking pan. Place pan in oven; heat 3 minutes or until margarine is melted. Tilt pan to coat with margarine.

2 Meanwhile, cut chicken breast halves in half lengthwise. Cut crosswise into 1/2-inch slices. In large bowl, beat eggs; stir in chicken and 1/4 cup of the picante.

3 In shallow bowl, combine bread crumbs, salt, cumin, chili powder and oregano; mix well. Add chicken pieces to bread crumb mixture, a few at a time; turn to coat. Place coated chicken in margarine-coated pan. Bake for 15 to 20 minutes or until chicken is no longer pink.

4 Reserve 1 tablespoon of the green onions for garnish. In large bowl, combine remaining onions, salad greens and tomatoes; toss gently. Pour half of the dressing over salad; toss to coat. Arrange evenly on 8 individual plates.

5 Spoon chicken into center of each salad. Top each with 1 tablespoon sour cream and about 1/2 teaspoon reserved green onions. Garnish each plate with avocado slices. Serve with remaining half of salad dressing, 1/2 cup sour cream and 1 cup picante.

NUTRITIONAL INFORMATION PER SERVING: Calories 530 • Fat 36g • Sodium 740mg • Total Carbohydrate 25g • Protein 27g.

sweet potatoes with apples and onions

READY IN: 40 Minutes ✳ SERVINGS: 8

1-1/2 lb. dark-orange sweet potatoes (4 to 5 medium), peeled, cut in half lengthwise and sliced	1 Granny Smith apple, peeled, sliced
1 tablespoon olive oil	1-1/2 cups apple juice
2 cups sliced red onion (1 large)	1/4 cup firmly packed brown sugar
	1/4 teaspoon salt
	Dash pepper

1 Place sweet potato slices in large saucepan or Dutch oven; add enough cold water to cover. Bring to a boil. Cover loosely; cook over medium heat for 9 to 13 minutes or until tender. Drain.

2 Meanwhile, heat oil in large nonstick skillet over medium-high heat until hot. Add onion; cook 2 minutes. Add all remaining ingredients; mix well. Cook 10 to 15 minutes or until mixture is reduced to a glaze, stirring occasionally.

3 Add cooked sweet potatoes to skillet; stir gently to coat. Remove from heat; let stand 1 minute before serving.

NUTRITIONAL INFORMATION PER SERVING: Calories 160 • Total Fat 2g • Saturated Fat 0g • Cholesterol 0mg • Sodium 85mg • Total Carbohydrate 33g • Dietary Fiber 2g • Sugars 24g • Protein 2g. DIETARY EXCHANGES: 1 Starch • 1/2 Fat • 1 Other Carbohydrate • 2 Carbohydrate Choices.

GRETA EBERHARDT
San Pedro, California
Bake-Off® Contest 37, 1996
Prize Winner

cook's notes

Ready in just half an hour, this main dish salad is perfect for a casual meal after a fun day of holiday shopping with family or friends.

cook's notes

Sweet potatoes can vary from pale yellow to dark orange. The dark-orange variety tends to work best in this particular recipe. Get the kids involved in prepping by having them peel the potatoes—just be sure that the potatoes are cool enough to handle.

MARILOU ROBINSON
Portland, Oregon
Bake-Off® Contest 35, 1992

kitchen tip

To toast pine nuts, spread them

on a cookie sheet and bake at

350°F for 3 to 6 minutes or

until light golden brown, stir-

ring occasionally.

corn and pumpkin soup with jalapeño pesto

SERVINGS: 11

JALAPEÑO PESTO

- 1 cup fresh cilantro
- 1 cup fresh parsley
- 1/2 cup pine nuts, lightly toasted
- 1/2 cup grated Parmesan cheese
- 5 garlic cloves, minced
- 4 jalapeño peppers, cut up
- 1 teaspoon lime juice
- 1/2 teaspoon grated lime peel
- 3/4 cup olive oil

SOUP

- 4 (14-1/2 oz.) cans ready-to-serve chicken broth
- 2 (11 oz.) cans vacuum-packed whole kernel corn, drained
- 1/4 cup finely chopped onion
- 2 tablespoons finely chopped jalapeño pepper
- 1 (16 oz.) can pumpkin
- 1 cup half-and-half
- 1/2 teaspoon salt
- 1/4 teaspoon pepper
- 11 (8 or 6-inch) corn tortillas or 8-inch flour tortillas, warmed

1 In food processor bowl with metal blade or blender container, combine cilantro, parsley, pine nuts, cheese and garlic. Process 10 to 15 seconds to chop mixture. Add 4 cut-up jalapeño peppers, lime juice and lime peel; process 5 to 10 seconds to blend. With machine running, add oil through feed tube or opening in blender lid in slow, steady stream just until well blended. Set aside.

2 In large saucepan, combine broth, corn, onion and 2 tablespoons jalapeño pepper. Bring to a boil. Reduce heat; cover and simmer 20 to 25 minutes or until onion and jalapeño pepper are tender. Stir in pumpkin; blend well. Cover; simmer 5 to 10 minutes or until thoroughly heated. Add half-and-half, salt and pepper; cook and stir until thoroughly heated. Do not boil.

3 To serve, line 11 soup bowls with warmed tortillas; ladle hot soup into tortilla-lined bowls. Spoon scant 2 tablespoons pesto onto each serving.

NUTRITIONAL INFORMATION PER SERVING: Calories 370 • Fat 23g • Sodium 840mg • Total Carbohydrate 32g • Protein 11g.

kitchen tip

Use a swivel-type vegetable

peeler to easily remove only the

thin brown peel from pota-

toes. For even cooking, cut the

peeled potatoes into similar-

size pieces.

perfect mashed potatoes

PREP TIME: 15 Minutes ✳ READY IN: 35 Minutes ✳ SERVINGS: 8

- 4 medium russet or Idaho baking potatoes (about 1-1/2 lb.)
- 3/4 teaspoon salt
- 1 to 2 tablespoons butter or margarine, if desired
- Dash pepper
- 1/4 to 1/3 cup hot milk

1 Wash and peel potatoes; cut into quarters. Place potatoes in 3-quart saucepan; add enough water to cover. Add 1/2 teaspoon of the salt. Heat to boiling. Reduce heat to medium-low; cover loosely and boil gently 15 to 20 minutes or until potatoes break apart easily when pierced with fork.

2 Drain potatoes well; return to saucepan. Shake saucepan gently over low heat 1 to 2 minutes to evaporate any excess moisture.

3 With potato masher, mash potatoes until no lumps remain. Add butter, remaining 1/4 teaspoon salt and the pepper; continue mashing, gradually adding enough milk until potatoes are smooth and creamy. Serve immediately.

NUTRITIONAL INFORMATION PER SERVING: Calories 50 • Total Fat 0g • Saturated Fat 0g • Cholesterol 0mg • Sodium 230mg • Total Carbohydrate 12g • Dietary Fiber 0g • Sugars 0g • Protein 1g. DIETARY EXCHANGE: 1 Starch.

corn and pumpkin soup
with jalapeño pesto

Pillsbury Bake-Off

ROCKY BROWN
Carmichaels, Pennsylvania
Bake-Off® Contest 35, 1992

cook's notes

For a heartier dish, add strips of cooked and cooled chicken to the couscous salad, or stir in cooked, cubed ham.

southwestern couscous salad

SERVINGS: 12

SALAD

1-1/2	cups water
1	cup uncooked couscous
1-1/2	cups frozen corn (from 1 lb. pkg.), cooked, cooled
1	(15 oz.) can black beans, drained, rinsed
1/4	cup chopped seeded tomato
1/4	cup chopped green bell pepper
1/4	cup chopped red bell pepper
2	tablespoons sliced green onions
2	tablespoons chopped fresh cilantro or parsley

DRESSING

1/3	cup olive oil or vegetable oil
1/4	to 1/3 cup lime juice
1/4	teaspoon salt, if desired
1/4	teaspoon garlic powder
1/4	teaspoon cumin
1/8	teaspoon ground red pepper (cayenne)

GARNISH, IF DESIRED

Lettuce leaves
Fresh cilantro
Lime slices

1 Bring water to a boil in small saucepan; remove from heat. Stir in couscous. Cover; let stand 5 minutes. Cool completely.

2 In large bowl, combine cooked couscous and all remaining salad ingredients; toss to combine. In small jar with tight-fitting lid, combine all dressing ingredients; shake well. Pour over salad; toss to coat. Cover; refrigerate 1 hour to blend flavors.

3 Line serving platter with lettuce leaves; spoon salad over lettuce leaves. Garnish with cilantro and lime slices.

NUTRITIONAL INFORMATION PER SERVING: Calories 150 • Fat 6g • Sodium 120mg • Total Carbohydrate 21 g • Protein 4g.

light and zesty vegetable coleslaw

PREP TIME: 15 Minutes ✳ READY IN: 2 Hours 15 Minutes ✳ SERVINGS: 16

1 (16 oz.) package coleslaw blend	1/4 cup orange marmalade
2 cups small fresh broccoli florets	1/4 teaspoon celery seed
1/4 cup sliced green onions	1 (11 oz.) can mandarin orange segments, drained
3/4 cup purchased fat-free Italian salad dressing	

1 In large bowl, combine coleslaw blend, broccoli and onions; stir gently to mix. In small bowl, combine salad dressing, marmalade and celery seed; blend well. Pour over coleslaw mixture; toss to coat.

2 Add mandarin orange segments; toss gently. Cover; refrigerate at least 2 hours or until serving time to blend flavors.

NUTRITIONAL INFORMATION PER SERVING: Calories 40 • Total Fat 0g • Saturated Fat 0g • Cholesterol 0mg • Sodium 170mg • Total Carbohydrate 9g • Dietary Fiber 1g • Sugars 6g • Protein 1g. DIETARY EXCHANGES: 1/2 Fruit • 1/2 Other Carbohydrate.

cook's notes

Consider the coleslaw if shrimp or other seafood is on your yuletide menu.

spinach salad with cranberry vinaigrette

spinach salad with cranberry vinaigrette

READY IN: 25 Minutes ✳ SERVINGS: 8

DRESSING
- 1/2 cup whole berry cranberry sauce
- 1/4 cup vegetable oil
- 2 tablespoons orange juice
- 2 tablespoons honey
- 2 tablespoons balsamic vinegar
- 1/4 teaspoon salt

SALAD
- 1 (10 oz.) bag fresh baby spinach leaves
- 2 avocados, peeled, pitted and sliced
- 1 tablespoon orange juice
- 1/2 cup pomegranate seeds

1 In jar with tight-fitting lid, place cranberry sauce, vegetable oil, orange juice, honey, balsamic vinegar and salt; shake until well blended. Refrigerate.

2 Arrange spinach leaves on individual salad plates. Coat avocado slices with 1 tablespoon orange juice; arrange over spinach. Sprinkle with pomegranate seeds. Drizzle salads with dressing.

NUTRITIONAL INFORMATION PER SERVING: Calories 220 • Total Fat 15g • Saturated Fat 2g • Cholesterol 0mg • Sodium 105mg • Total Carbohydrate 18g • Dietary Fiber 4g • Sugars 12g • Protein 2g. DIETARY EXCHANGES: 1 Fruit • 1 Other Carbohydrate • 1 Vegetable • 3 Fat.

kitchen tip

Cut avocados in half length-wise, cutting around the large seed in the center. Twist the halves to separate. Next, carefully strike the seed with the blade of the knife, and lift out the seed.

winter greens with pomegranate-champagne vinaigrette

READY IN: 20 Minutes ✳ SERVINGS: 12-16

- 2 (10 oz.) packages mixed salad greens
- 1 pomegranate
- 1/4 cup champagne wine vinegar
- 1 tablespoon Dijon mustard
- 3/4 cup vegetable oil
- 1/4 teaspoon salt
-   Dash freshly ground black pepper

1 Place greens in large salad bowl. Peel and seed pomegranate, reserving seeds. In small bowl, combine vinegar and mustard; blend well. With wire whisk, slowly beat in oil until thick. Add salt and pepper. Stir in half of the pomegranate seeds.

2 Just before serving, add dressing to greens; toss to coat. Scatter remaining pomegranate seeds over salad.

NUTRITIONAL INFORMATION PER SERVING: Calories 105 • Total Fat 10g • Saturated Fat 1g • Cholesterol 0mg • Sodium 70mg • Total Carbohydrate 3g • Dietary Fiber 0g • Sugars 2g • Protein 1g. DIETARY EXCHANGES: 2 Fat • 0 Carbohydrate Choice.

cook's notes

White wine vinegar can be used in place of the champagne vinegar if you would like. Remember to dress the salad greens immediately before serving so that the greens do not wilt.

honey-mustard dilled brussels sprouts

READY IN: 15 Minutes ✳ SERVINGS: 4

- 12 oz. fresh Brussels sprouts (about 2-1/4 cups)
- 1 tablespoon butter, melted
- 1 tablespoon honey
- 1 teaspoon Dijon mustard
- 1/8 teaspoon onion powder
- 1/8 teaspoon dried dill weed

1 Trim Brussels sprouts; cut small X in stem end. Place in medium saucepan; add 1/2 cup water. Cover; cook over medium-high heat 8 minutes or until tender. Drain; return to saucepan.

2 Add butter, honey, Dijon mustard, onion powder and dill weed to cooked Brussels sprouts; toss gently to coat.

NUTRITIONAL INFORMATION PER SERVING: Calories 90 • Total Fat 3.5g • Saturated Fat 1.5g • Trans Fat 0g • Cholesterol 10mg • Sodium 65mg • Total Carbohydrate 11g • Dietary Fiber 3g • Sugars 6g • Protein 3g. DIETARY EXCHANGES: 1/2 Other Carbohydrate • 1 Vegetable • 1/2 Fat.

JUDITH METTLIN
Snyder, New York
Bake-Off® Contest 35, 1992

cook's notes

Replace the red and yellow bell peppers with whatever bell peppers you have. You can also mix up the variety of beans.

bean and pepper salad with citrus dressing

SERVINGS: 8

SALAD

1	(15.5 oz.) can great northern beans, drained, rinsed
1	cup red bell pepper strips (2x1/4-inch)
1	cup yellow bell pepper strips (2x1/4-inch)
1/2	cup sliced green onions
1/4	cup crumbled gorgonzola or blue cheese

CITRUS DRESSING

2	to 4 tablespoons olive oil or vegetable oil
2	tablespoons orange juice
1	tablespoon red wine vinegar
1	tablespoon finely chopped fresh basil or 1 teaspoon dried basil leaves
1	teaspoon grated orange peel
1/4	teaspoon salt
	Lettuce leaves

1 In medium bowl, combine all salad ingredients; toss to combine. In small jar with tight-fitting lid, combine all dressing ingredients; shake well. Pour over salad; toss gently to coat. Cover; refrigerate 1 hour to blend flavors. Line 8 individual serving plates with lettuce leaves; spoon salad onto lettuce.

NUTRITIONAL INFORMATION PER SERVING: Calories 120 • Fat 8g • Sodium 210mg • Total Carbohydrate 10g • Protein 4g.

shrimp cocktail salad

READY IN: 15 Minutes ❋ SERVINGS: 4

1/3 cup mayonnaise	1 cup coarsely chopped celery
3 tablespoons seafood cocktail sauce	3 tablespoons coarsely chopped dill pickle
3/4 lb. frozen shelled deveined cooked bay shrimp, thawed	6 cups shredded leaf lettuce

1 In small bowl, combine mayonnaise and cocktail sauce; blend well. In medium bowl, combine shrimp, celery and pickle. Stir in mayonnaise mixture. Serve immediately, or cover and refrigerate until serving time.

2 To serve, arrange the lettuce on a large serving platter or on individual serving plates. Spoon the salad onto lettuce.

NUTRITIONAL INFORMATION PER SERVING: Calories 250 • Total Fat 16g • Saturated Fat 3g • Cholesterol 175mg • Sodium 560mg • Total Carbohydrate 7g • Dietary Fiber 2g • Sugars 4g • Protein 20g. DIETARY EXCHANGES: 1 Vegetable • 2-1/2 Very Lean Meat • 3 Fat.

special touch

Based on a classic appetizer, this salad is a hit any time of day. Serve it with lemon wedges on the side.

three-potato gratin

PREP TIME: 20 Minutes ✳ READY IN: 1 Hour 20 Minutes ✳ SERVINGS: 9

3 medium dark-orange sweet potatoes or yams (1 lb.), peeled	2 cups finely shredded Swiss cheese (8 oz.)
3 medium red-skinned potatoes (1 lb.), unpeeled	1 cup beef broth
3 medium Yukon Gold potatoes (1 lb.), unpeeled	1 teaspoon dried rosemary leaves, crushed
	1/4 teaspoon pepper
	2 garlic cloves, minced

1 Heat oven to 400°F. Spray 12x8-inch (2-quart) glass baking dish and a sheet of foil with nonstick cooking spray. Cut all potatoes into 1/8-inch-thick slices. Layer half of potatoes in sprayed baking dish. Top with half of the Swiss cheese. Cover with remaining potatoes.

2 In medium saucepan, combine broth, rosemary, pepper and garlic. Bring to a boil. Pour boiling broth over potatoes. Loosely cover with sprayed sheet of foil. Bake for 45 minutes.

3 Remove baking dish from oven. Uncover dish; sprinkle with remaining half of cheese. Return to oven; bake uncovered for an additional 15 minutes or until potatoes are tender and cheese is melted.

NUTRITIONAL INFORMATION PER SERVING: Calories 240 • Total Fat 7g • Saturated Fat 5g • Cholesterol 25mg • Sodium 190mg • Total Carbohydrate 34g • Dietary Fiber 3g • Sugars 8g • Protein 10g. DIETARY EXCHANGES: 1 Starch • 1 High-Fat Meat • 1 Other Carbohydrate • 2 Carbohydrate Choices.

baby peas with lemon-pepper and honey

READY IN: 15 Minutes ✳ SERVINGS: 6

1 (1 lb.) package frozen baby sweet peas	1/4 teaspoon lemon-pepper seasoning
2 teaspoons honey	1/4 teaspoon salt
1 teaspoon butter	

1 In medium saucepan or microwavable dish, cook peas as directed on package. Drain; return to saucepan. Add honey, butter, lemon-pepper seasoning and salt; toss to coat.

NUTRITIONAL INFORMATION PER SERVING: Calories 70 • Total Fat 1g • Saturated Fat 0g • Cholesterol 0mg • Sodium 260mg • Total Carbohydrate 12g • Dietary Fiber 4g • Sugars 7g • Protein 4g. DIETARY EXCHANGES: 1 Starch • 1 Other Carbohydrate.

italian cauliflower and broccoli medley

READY IN: 15 Minutes ✳ SERVINGS: 4

2 cups frozen cauliflower florets	1/4 cup purchased light Italian salad dressing
2 cups frozen broccoli florets	2 tablespoons shredded fresh Parmesan cheese

1 Bring 1 inch of water to a boil in medium saucepan. Reduce heat to medium-low. Add cauliflower and broccoli; cover and simmer 5 to 7 minutes or until the vegetables are crisp-tender. Drain.

2 Add salad dressing to vegetables; toss to coat. Sprinkle with cheese. Cover; let stand 1 to 2 minutes or until cheese melts.

NUTRITIONAL INFORMATION PER SERVING: Calories 70 • Total Fat 4g • Saturated Fat 1g • Cholesterol 0mg • Sodium 190mg • Total Carbohydrate 5g • Dietary Fiber 2g • Sugars 2g • Protein 3g. DIETARY EXCHANGES: 1 Vegetable • 1 Fat.

three-potato gratin

Holiday Entreés

Celebrate the season in style with this chapter's exceptional assortment of main courses. Turn the page for tender cuts of beef, juicy poultry and other Christmas staples.

p. 99

p. 100

p. 104

p. 103

p. 104

pepper-crusted prime rib
with zinfandel sauce p. 109

holiday baked ham

PREP TIME: 15 Minutes ✳ START TO FINISH: 3 Hours ✳ SERVINGS: 12 to 16

HAM
- 1 fully cooked bone-in ham (6 to 8 lb.)

BROWN SUGAR-CIDER GLAZE
- 1/2 cup packed brown sugar
- 1/2 cup apple cider
- 1 teaspoon ground cinnamon

CHERRY-APRICOT SAUCE
- 1-1/2 cups frozen sweet cherries (from 12 oz. bag), halved
- 1/2 cup apricot jam
- 2 teaspoons cornstarch

1 Heat oven to 325°F. If using shallow roasting pan without rack, line pan with foil. Trim fat from ham if necessary. Score ham diagonally at 1-inch intervals, cutting about 1/4 inch deep; score in opposite direction to form diamond shapes. Insert ovenproof meat thermometer so bulb reaches center of thickest part of ham, but does not rest in fat or on bone.

2 Place ham, fat side up, in foil-lined pan or on rack in roasting pan; add 1 cup water to pan. If using Brown Sugar-Cider Glaze, in 1-quart saucepan, mix all ingredients; heat to boiling over medium-high heat, stirring frequently. Brush 1/3 of glaze mixture over ham.

3 Bake uncovered 1 hour. Brush another 1/3 of glaze over ham; bake uncovered 1 hour to 1 hour 30 minutes longer, spooning pan drippings frequently over ham and brushing with remaining 1/3 of glaze, until thermometer reads 135°F. Remove from oven.

4 Let ham stand in roasting pan 15 minutes before slicing, spooning pan drippings frequently over ham, until thermometer reads 140°F. If using Cherry-Apricot Sauce, in 1-quart saucepan, mix all ingredients; cook over medium-high heat 3 to 5 minutes, stirring frequently, until mixture boils and sauce has thickened. Serve sauce with ham.

NUTRITIONAL INFORMATION PER SERVING: Calories: 280 • Total Fat 7g • Saturated Fat 2.5g • Cholesterol 65mg • Sodium 1480mg • Total Carbohydrate 29g • Dietary Fiber 0g • Sugars 25g • Protein 26g. DIETARY EXCHANGES: 2 Other Carbohydrate • 3-1/2 Very Lean Meat • 1 Fat.

pesto and pepper-stuffed leg of lamb

PREP TIME: 15 Minutes ✳ READY IN: 1 Hour 30 Minutes ✳ SERVINGS: 12

PESTO

3/4	cup firmly packed fresh parsley
1/4	cup fresh rosemary leaves
1/4	cup fresh mint leaves
3	garlic cloves
2	tablespoons olive oil

LAMB

1	(5 lb.) rolled boneless leg of lamb
1	(7.5 oz.) jar roasted red bell peppers, well drained
2	teaspoons lemon-pepper seasoning

1 Heat oven to 350°F. In food processor bowl with metal blade, combine all pesto ingredients; process until smooth.

2 Unroll lamb, cut side up, onto work surface. Spread pesto over lamb. Place roasted peppers over pesto. Roll up lamb. Tie with kitchen string or secure edges with metal skewers. Rub surface with lemon-pepper seasoning. Place on rack in shallow roasting pan.

3 Bake for 60 to 75 minutes or until meat thermometer inserted in center registers 145°F for medium-rare. Remove string from lamb; cut into slices.

NUTRITIONAL INFORMATION PER SERVING: Calories 300 • Total Fat 15g • Saturated Fat 5g • Cholesterol 130mg • Sodium 100mg • Total Carbohydrate 1g • Dietary Fiber 0g • Sugars 1g • Protein 40g. DIETARY EXCHANGE: 5-1/2 Lean Meat.

cook's notes

You have lots of options for getting a head start on making this dish. You can mix the pesto and refrigerate it overnight, and the roast can be stuffed, tied, covered and refrigerated for up to 3 hours. You can also skip making the pesto altogether and buy it instead.

party chicken cacciatore

party chicken cacciatore

PREP TIME: 30 Minutes ✳ READY IN: 1 Hour 15 Minutes ✳ SERVINGS: 10

3-1/2 to 4 lb. boneless skinless chicken thighs

2 tablespoons olive oil

2 cups chopped onions (about 4 medium)

2 tablespoons minced garlic (about 6 to 7 cloves)

2 (28 oz.) cans crushed tomatoes, undrained

1 cup dry red wine or chicken broth

1 teaspoon sugar

2 teaspoons dried rosemary leaves, crushed

1/2 teaspoon salt

1 bay leaf

1/4 cup chopped fresh parsley

1 Pat chicken dry with paper towels. Heat oil in Dutch oven over medium-high heat until hot. Add chicken; cook in batches until browned. Remove chicken from Dutch oven; set aside.

2 Add onions to same Dutch oven; cook and stir 2 to 3 minutes. Add garlic; cook 1 to 2 minutes. Add tomatoes, wine, sugar, rosemary, salt and bay leaf; stir gently to mix.

3 Add chicken with any juices to tomato mixture. Bring to a boil. Reduce heat to low; simmer 45 minutes or until chicken is fork-tender, its juices run clear and sauce has thickened.

4 Remove bay leaf. Sprinkle chicken mixture with parsley. If desired, garnish with freshly shredded or shaved Parmesan cheese.

NUTRITIONAL INFORMATION PER SERVING: Calories 345 • Total Fat 16g • Saturated Fat 4g • Cholesterol 100mg • Sodium 450mg • Total Carbohydrate 11g • Dietary Fiber 2g • Sugars 6g • Protein 36g. DIETARY EXCHANGES: 1/2 Starch • 1 Vegetable • 4-1/2 Lean Meat • 1/2 Fat.

cook's notes

This recipe can be made early in the day so you can focus on other party preparations. Just cover and refrigerate. When you are about ready to serve, reheat it over medium-low heat, stirring occasionally, until it is thoroughly heated. It should take only about 15 to 20 minutes.

apple-glazed pork chops with sage-apple stuffing

PREP TIME: 20 Minutes ✳ READY IN: 1 Hour 30 Minutes ✳ SERVINGS: 4

4 (1 inch thick) boneless pork loin chops (about 1-1/2 lb.)

1 tablespoon butter or margarine

1/2 cup chopped celery

1/2 cup chopped green onions

1/2 cup chopped apple

1/4 cup raisins

1/4 to 1/2 teaspoon dried sage leaves, crushed

2 cups sage and onion-seasoned stuffing cubes

3 tablespoons apple juice

1/2 teaspoon peppered seasoned salt

1/4 cup apple jelly

1 Heat oven to 350°F. Cut deep horizontal pocket in side of each pork chop. Melt butter in medium nonstick skillet over medium heat. Add celery and 1/4 cup of the onions; cook and stir 2 to 3 minutes or until crisp-tender. Add apple, raisins and sage; mix well. Remove from heat. Stir in stuffing cubes and apple juice.

2 Stuff each pork chop with about 1/2 cup stuffing mixture. Place in ungreased 13x9-inch pan. Sprinkle pork chops with peppered seasoned salt. Arrange any remaining stuffing mixture around chops. Cover with foil.

3 Bake for 45 minutes. Meanwhile, in small saucepan, combine remaining 1/4 cup onions and the jelly; heat over low heat until melted, stirring occasionally.

4 Uncover pork chops; brush with jelly mixture. Bake uncovered an additional 20 to 30 minutes or until pork chops are no longer pink in center, brushing with jelly mixture once or twice.

NUTRITIONAL INFORMATION PER SERVING: Calories 425 • Total Fat 12g • Saturated Fat 5g • Cholesterol 75mg • Sodium 790mg • Total Carbohydrate 52g • Dietary Fiber 3g • Sugars 20g • Protein 27g. DIETARY EXCHANGES: 2 Starch • 1/2 Fruit • 3 Lean Meat • 1 Other Carbohydrate • 3-1/2 Carbohydrate Choices.

cook's notes

This delicious dish is a great choice for casual entertaining, especially when kids are invited to the table. The apple-pork chop combo suits pint-sized palates. Older children can even help out by chop ingredients and stuffing the dressing into the chops.

deviled lobster tails

READY IN: 45 Minutes ❋ SERVINGS: 4

2 teaspoons salt	1/4 cup cocktail sauce
4 frozen lobster tails (about 10 oz. each)	2 teaspoons Worcestershire sauce
4 tablespoons butter, melted	1 teaspoon dry mustard
4 green onions, sliced	1/2 teaspoon salt
2 tablespoons all-purpose flour	1/2 teaspoon hot pepper sauce
1-1/2 cups half-and-half	1/3 cup unseasoned dry bread crumbs

1 In Dutch oven, combine 2 quarts water and 2 teaspoons salt; bring to a boil. Add lobster tails; return to a boil. Cook 8 to 10 minutes or until lobster shells turn red and meat is opaque. Immediately plunge lobster tails into cold water to stop cooking. (Lobster will not be thoroughly cooked, but will continue to cook during baking step.)

2 Meanwhile, heat oven to 450°F. In medium saucepan, combine 2 tablespoons of the melted butter and the onions; cook and stir over medium heat for 2 minutes or until onions are tender. Add flour; cook and stir until mixture is smooth and bubbly. Gradually add half-and-half, stirring constantly. Bring to a boil. Cook 1 minute, stirring constantly. Add cocktail sauce, Worcestershire sauce, dry mustard, 1/2 teaspoon salt and the hot pepper sauce; mix well. Remove from heat.

3 With kitchen scissors, cut and remove membrane from under side of each lobster tail; discard membrane. Remove lobster meat; cut into chunks (reserve shell). Add meat to sauce; mix well.

4 Return mixture to lobster tail shells. Place in ungreased shallow baking dish. To prevent lobster tails from tipping over, place small crumbled pieces of foil between tails.

5 In small bowl, combine remaining 2 tablespoons melted butter and the bread crumbs; mix well. Sprinkle over lobster mixture. Bake for 10 minutes or until thoroughly heated and bread crumbs are browned.

NUTRITIONAL INFORMATION PER SERVING: Calories 430 • Total Fat 23g • Saturated Fat 14g • Cholesterol 170mg • Sodium 1860mg • Total Carbohydrate 21g • Dietary Fiber 1g • Sugars 10g • Protein 35g. DIETARY EXCHANGES: 1 Starch • 4-1/2 Lean Meat • 2 Fat • 1-1/2 Carbohydrate Choices.

EVELYN ROBINSON
Bellevue, Washington
Bake-Off® Contest 11, 1959

crab meat salad pie

SERVINGS: 6

CRUST

1 refrigerated pie crust (from 15 oz. pkg.)

FILLING

3/4 cup dry bread crumbs
1 cup chopped celery
1 tablespoon finely chopped onion

1 tablespoon finely chopped green bell pepper
1 tablespoon lemon juice
1 (6 oz.) can crab meat, drained
3/4 to 1 cup mayonnaise or salad dressing
1/2 cup shredded Cheddar cheese (2 oz.)

1 Heat oven to 450°F. Prepare and bake pie crust according to package directions for one-crust baked shell using 9-inch pie pan. Bake for 9 to 11 minutes or until light golden brown. Cool completely.

2 Reserve 2 tablespoons of the bread crumbs. In large bowl, combine remaining bread crumbs, celery, onion, bell pepper, lemon juice and crab meat; toss lightly. Add enough mayonnaise for desired consistency; mix well. Spoon into cooled baked shell. Sprinkle with reserved 2 tablespoons bread crumbs and cheese. Bake for 8 to 10 minutes or until cheese is melted.

NUTRITIONAL INFORMATION PER SERVING: Calories 390 • Fat 26g • Sodium 600mg • Total Carbohydrate 28g • Protein 10g.

deviled lobster tails

easy pork chops with stuffing

PREP TIME: 15 Minutes ❋ READY IN: 55 Minutes ❋ SERVINGS: 4

4 bone-in pork loin chops (1/2 inch thick)	1-1/2 cups water
1/2 teaspoon seasoned salt	1 (6 oz.) box one-step herb stuffing mix for pork
1/4 teaspoon pepper	
2 teaspoons vegetable oil	2 cups frozen broccoli florets (from 14 oz. bag)

1 Heat oven to 350°F. Sprinkle pork chops with seasoned salt and pepper. In 10-inch nonstick skillet, heat oil over medium-high heat. Add pork chops; cook 4 to 6 minutes or until browned on both sides. Remove chops from skillet.

2 Heat water to boiling in same skillet. Remove from heat. Stir in stuffing until moistened. Spoon into ungreased 12x8-inch (2-quart) glass baking dish.

3 Arrange broccoli and pork chops over stuffing. Cover tightly with foil; bake 30 to 40 minutes or until pork chops are no longer pink in center.

NUTRITIONAL INFORMATION PER SERVING: Calories: 370 • Total Fat 12g • Saturated Fat 3.5g • Trans Fat 0g • Cholesterol 65mg • Sodium 900mg • Total Carbohydrate 36g • Dietary Fiber 3g • Sugars 2g • Protein 30g. DIETARY EXCHANGES: 2 Starch • 1 Vegetable • 3 Lean Meat • 1/2 Fat.

oven-baked marinated beef roast

PREP TIME: 15 Minutes ✳ READY IN: 10 Hours ✳ SERVINGS: 8

3/4 cup chili sauce	1/2 teaspoon garlic-pepper blend
1/4 cup red wine vinegar	1/2 teaspoon ginger
2 tablespoons sugar	1 (2 to 2-1/2 lb.) eye of round beef roast
2 tablespoons soy sauce	

1 In large resealable food storage plastic bag, combine all ingredients except roast; mix well. Add roast; seal bag and turn to coat. Refrigerate at least 8 hours or overnight to marinate.

2 Heat oven to 325°F. Remove beef from marinade; reserve marinade. Place beef in shallow roasting pan. Bake for 1-1/2 to 1-3/4 hours or until of desired doneness, brushing occasionally with marinade.

3 To serve, bring any remaining marinade to a boil in small saucepan. Slice the beef thinly; serve with marinade.

NUTRITIONAL INFORMATION PER SERVING: Calories 200 • Total Fat 5g • Saturated Fat 2g • Cholesterol 65mg • Sodium 670mg • Total Carbohydrate 10g • Dietary Fiber 0g • Sugars 8g • Protein 28g. DIETARY EXCHANGES: 1/2 Fruit • 1/2 Other Carbohydrate • 4 Lean Meat.

special touch

Arrange roasted new potatoes and carrots on each dinner plate with slices of this roast. Pass a tossed salad and some crusty bread.

cook's notes

Garnish the chicken with fresh herbs such as rosemary or thyme. Herbes de Provence is an herb blend that typically includes basil, fennel, marjoram, rosemary, sage, and thyme. It is often used in French cooking.

provençal roast chicken

PREP TIME: 20 Minutes ✳ READY IN: 1 Hour 50 Minutes ✳ SERVINGS: 6

1 whole chicken (3 to 3-1/2 lb.)	1-1/2 lb. small red potatoes (about 10 to 12), cut into fourths
1 lemon	2 medium zucchini, cut into 1-1/2-inch pieces
1 teaspoon olive oil	1/2 cup chopped pitted kalamata olives
1 tablespoon herbes de Provence or dried rosemary leaves, crushed	1 (14.5 oz.) can diced tomatoes with basil, garlic and oregano, drained
1/4 teaspoon freshly ground black pepper	

1 Heat oven to 400°F. Remove and discard giblets from chicken. Rinse chicken inside and out with cold water; drain. Pat dry with paper towels. In shallow roasting pan, place chicken, breast side up. Grate peel from lemon. Cut lemon in half; squeeze and reserve juice from lemon. Reserve lemon halves. In small bowl, mix lemon peel, lemon juice and oil until well blended.

2 Drizzle half of lemon mixture over chicken. Sprinkle and pat herbes de Provence and pepper over the skin of the chicken. Place squeezed lemon halves inside chicken. Using string, tie legs and tail together. Insert ovenproof meat thermometer so tip is in thickest part of inside thigh and does not touch bone.

3 In large bowl, mix potatoes, zucchini, olives, tomatoes and remaining lemon juice mixture. Arrange vegetables around chicken in pan.

4 Bake 1 hour to 1 hour 30 minutes or until thermometer reads 180°F and legs move easily when lifted or twisted, and vegetables are tender. Remove and discard lemon halves. If desired, add salt and pepper to taste.

NUTRITIONAL INFORMATION PER SERVING: Calories 510 • Total Fat 18g • Saturated Fat 4g • Cholesterol 90mg • Sodium 430mg • Total Carbohydrate 53g • Dietary Fiber 7g • Sugars 5g • Protein 34g. DIETARY EXCHANGES: 3 Starch • 3 Other Carbohydrate • 1 Vegetable • 3-1/2 Lean Meat • 1 Fat.

german wiener schnitzel

READY IN: 30 Minutes ✳ SERVINGS: 6

6 veal cutlets (3/8 inch thick)	2 eggs, slightly beaten
2 tablespoons all-purpose flour	1 tablespoon milk
1/2 teaspoon salt	1 to 1-1/2 cups unseasoned dry bread crumbs
1/4 teaspoon pepper	6 tablespoons oil

1 Place 1 veal cutlet between 2 pieces of plastic wrap or waxed paper. Working from center, gently pound cutlet with flat side of mallet or rolling pin until about 1/8 inch thick; remove wrap. Repeat with remaining cutlets.

2 In small bowl, combine the flour, salt and pepper; mix well. In another bowl, combine egg and milk. Blend well. Coast each cutlet with seasoned flour; dip in egg mixture. Coat with crumbs.

3 In large skillet, heat 3 tablespoons of oil over medium-high heat until hot. Cook 3 cutlets at a time for 5 to 7 minutes or until golden brown on both sides. Repeat with remaining 3 tablespoons oil and remaining 3 cutlets.

NUTRITION INFORMATION PER SERVING: Calories 390 • Total Fat 20g • Saturated Fat 4g • Cholesterol 165mg • Sodium 480mg • Total Carbohydrate 22g • Dietary Fiber 1g • Sugars 2g • Protein 31g. Dietary Exchanges: 1-1/2 Other Carbohydrate • 4 Very Lean Meat • 3 Fat.

special touch

To customize this dish to your liking, just add a dash or two of your favorite seasoning or dried herb to the simple flour mixture.

provençal roast chicken

glazed crown roast with
cranberrry-cornbread stuffing

glazed crown roast with cranberry-cornbread stuffing

PREP TIME: 35 Minutes ✳ READY IN: 3 Hours 35 Minutes ✳ SERVINGS: 12

STUFFING

3 (6 oz.) packages one-step cornbread stuffing mix

Butter or margarine

Water

3/4 cup sweetened dried cranberries

3/4 cup chopped dried apples

ROAST

1 (12-bone) pork crown roast (about 7 lb.)

1/4 cup apple jelly

2 tablespoons jellied cranberry sauce

1 Heat oven to 350°F. In large saucepan, prepare stuffing mix as directed on package, using butter and water. Stir in cranberries and apples. Set aside.

2 Place pork roast on rack in shallow roasting pan. Fill cavity with as much of the prepared stuffing as it will hold. Cover stuffing and bones loosely with foil. Spray 1-quart casserole with nonstick cooking spray. Spoon remaining stuffing into sprayed casserole. Cover; refrigerate until 45 minutes before serving time.

3 Bake roast for 2-1/4 to 3 hours, allowing 25 to 30 minutes per pound, or until meat thermometer inserted in center registers 155°F.

4 Meanwhile, in small saucepan, combine apple jelly and cranberry sauce; mix well. Heat over low heat until mixture is melted and smooth.

5 During last 45 minutes of baking time, brush roast with jelly mixture and bake any remaining stuffing.

6 Remove roast from pan. Cover with foil; let stand 15 minutes. Remove string from roast; cut between bones. Serve with stuffing from center of roast and additional baked stuffing.

NUTRITIONAL INFORMATION PER SERVING: Calories 590 • Total Fat 26g • Saturated Fat 12g • Cholesterol 135mg • Sodium 820mg • Total Carbohydrate 48g • Dietary Fiber 2g • Sugars 14g • Protein 41g. DIETARY EXCHANGES: 2 Starch • 1 Fruit • 5 Lean Meat • 2 Fat • 3 Carbohydrate Choices.

roasted orange-fennel halibut with dijon sauce

READY IN: 35 Minutes ✳ SERVINGS: 4

SAUCE

1/2 cup fat-free or light mayonnaise

2 tablespoons finely chopped fresh parsley

1 tablespoon Dijon mustard

1 teaspoon grated orange peel

2 tablespoons orange juice

2 tablespoons finely chopped fresh parsley

2 teaspoons grated orange peel

1/2 teaspoon fennel seed, crushed

1/2 teaspoon garlic salt

HALIBUT

1 (1-1/2 lb.) halibut fillet, cut into 4 pieces

1 Heat oven to 425°F. Spray shallow baking pan with nonstick cooking spray. In small bowl, combine all sauce ingredients; mix well. Cover; refrigerate until serving time.

2 Place halibut in sprayed pan. Brush with orange juice. Sprinkle with 2 tablespoons parsley, 2 teaspoons orange peel, the fennel and garlic salt; rub in with fingers. Bake for 15 to 20 minutes or until fish flakes easily with fork. Serve fish with sauce.

NUTRITIONAL INFORMATION PER SERVING: Calories 170 • Total Fat 2g • Saturated Fat 1g • Cholesterol 90mg • Sodium 600mg • Total Carbohydrate 5g • Dietary Fiber 0g • Sugars 3g • Protein 32g. DIETARY EXCHANGES: 4-1/2 Very Lean Meat • 0 Carbohydrate Choice.

cook's notes

Save yourself some time in the kitchen by serving this elegant holiday dish with Caesar salad from a bag and purchased dinner rolls.

sage 'n maple cornbread stuffed pork chops

Prep Time: 20 Minutes ✳ READY IN: 1 Hour 15 Minutes ✳ SERVINGS: 4

- 2 tablespoons butter or margarine
- 1 cup frozen bell pepper and onion stir fry (from 1 lb. bag), large pieces cut up
- 3/4 cup water
- 1 teaspoon dried sage leaves
- 3/4 teaspoon seasoned salt

- 2 cups cornbread stuffing mix (from 6 oz. package)
- 3 tablespoons real maple syrup or maple-flavored syrup
- 4 bone-in pork loin chops, about 1-1/2 inches thick (2-1/2 to 3 lb.)

1 Heat oven to 350°F. Spray 13x9-inch (3-quart) glass baking dish with cooking spray. In 10-inch skillet, melt butter over medium-high heat. Add bell pepper and onion stir-fry; cook 3 to 5 minutes, stirring occasionally, just until tender.

2 Stir in water, 1/2 teaspoon of the sage and 1/4 teaspoon of the seasoned salt. Heat to boiling. Stir in stuffing mix and 1 tablespoon of the syrup until moistened. Remove from heat.

3 Cut pocket in each pork chop, cutting into side towards bone. Spoon about 1/2 cup cornbread mixture into each chop, pressing in firmly. Sprinkle both sides of stuffed pork chops with remaining 1/2 teaspoon sage and 1/2 teaspoon seasoned salt; place in baking dish. Drizzle remaining 2 tablespoons syrup over chops. Spoon any remaining stuffing around chops.

4 Cover tightly with foil; bake 45 minutes. Uncover dish; bake 10 minutes longer or until meat thermometer inserted in pork next to bone reads 160°F. If desired, serve with pan drippings.

HIGH ALTITUDE (3500-6500 FT): Heat oven to 375°F. Increase water to 1 cup.

NUTRITIONAL INFORMATION PER SERVING: Calories 550 • Total Fat 23g • Saturated Fat 9g • Cholesterol 145mg • Sodium 910mg • Total Carbohydrate 39g • Dietary Fiber 2g • Sugars 11g • Protein 48g. DIETARY EXCHANGES: 1-1/2 Starch • 6 Lean Meat • 1 Fat • 1 Other Carbohydrate • 2-1/2 Carbohydrate Choice.

chicken picadillo pie

SERVINGS: 8

NINA REYES
Miami, Florida
Bake-Off® Contest 32, 1986

CRUST
- 1 (15 oz.) package refrigerated pie crusts

FILLING
- 3 tablespoons margarine or butter
- 1 tablespoon cornstarch
- 1/8 teaspoon ginger
- Dash pepper
- 1 tablespoon prepared mustard
- 1 tablespoon soy sauce, if desired
- 1 tablespoon Worcestershire sauce
- 1 cup orange juice
- 2 tablespoons margarine or butter

- 2 large whole chicken breasts, skinned, boned, cut into bite-sized pieces
- 1 cup finely chopped onions
- 1/4 cup finely chopped green bell pepper
- 2 garlic cloves, minced
- 1/2 cup coconut
- 1/4 cup slivered almonds
- 1/4 cup raisins
- 1/4 to 1/2 cup chopped pimiento-stuffed green olives
- 2 tablespoons capers, if desired

1 Prepare pie crust according to package directions for two-crust pie using 9-inch pie pan. Heat oven to 400°F. Melt 1 tablespoon margarine in small saucepan. Blend in cornstarch, ginger, pepper, mustard, soy sauce and Worcestershire sauce. Gradually add orange juice. Bring to a boil; cook until mixture thickens, stirring constantly. Set aside.

2 Melt 2 tablespoons margarine in large skillet. Cook chicken, onions, bell pepper and garlic over medium heat until chicken is completely cooked. Stir in coconut, almonds, raisins, olives, capers and the orange sauce. Continue to cook until thoroughly heated, stirring occasionally. Spoon into pie crust-lined pan. Top with second crust and flute; cut slits in several places.

3 Bake for 30 to 40 minutes or until golden brown. Cover edge of crust with strips of foil after 15 to 20 minutes of baking to prevent excessive browning. Let stand 5 minutes before serving.

NUTRITIONAL INFORMATION PER SERVING: Calories 470 • Fat 26g • Sodium 680mg • Total Carbohydrate 37g • Protein 21g.

sage 'n maple cornbread
stuffed pork chops

MARY LOU COOK
Fallbrook, California
Bake-Off® Contest 36, 1994

rosemary chicken and brie en croute

SERVINGS: 4

1   (8 oz.) can refrigerated crescent dinner rolls
2   tablespoons finely chopped green onions
6   oz. Brie cheese, rind removed, cubed
1-1/2   cups chopped cooked chicken breast
1   egg, beaten

1   teaspoon crushed dried rosemary leaves
1   tablespoon grated Parmesan cheese

GARNISH, IF DESIRED
1   medium tomato, cut into 8 wedges
4   green onions

1   Heat oven to 350°F. Separate dough into 4 rectangles; firmly press perforations to seal. Spoon 1/4 of chopped green onions onto center of each rectangle; top with 1/4 of cheese cubes. Top each with 1/4 of chicken, pressing into cheese. Fold short ends over chicken, overlapping slightly. Fold open ends over about 1/2 inch to form rectangle. Press all edges to seal. Place seam side down on ungreased 15x10x1-inch baking pan or cookie sheet. Cut three 1-inch slashes on top of each roll to form steam vents. Brush with egg; sprinkle with rosemary and Parmesan cheese.

2   Bake for 21 to 26 minutes or until golden brown. Garnish each sandwich with 2 tomato wedges and 1 green onion. Let stand 5 minutes before serving.

NUTRITIONAL INFORMATION PER SERVING: Calories 450 • Fat 25g • Sodium 790mg • Total Carbohydrate 25g • Protein 30g.

baked ham with zesty cranberry sauce

PREP TIME: 20 Minutes ❋ READY IN: 2 Hours 5 Minutes ❋ SERVINGS: 12

1 fully cooked rump half, bone-in ham (6 lb.)	2 teaspoons sugar
1 (16 oz.) can jellied cranberry sauce	2 teaspoons grated lemon peel
1/3 cup apple juice	2 teaspoons grated orange peel
1/4 cup port wine or apple juice	1/4 teaspoon white pepper
2 tablespoons lemon juice	1/4 teaspoon ground ginger
1 tablespoon Dijon mustard	

1 Heat oven to 325°F. Place ham on rack in shallow roasting pan. Add 1/4 to 1/2 inch water to pan. Cover pan.

2 Bake 45 minutes. Uncover pan; bake 45 minutes to 1 hour 15 minutes longer or until meat thermometer inserted in center, but not touching bone, registers 140°F.

3 To make sauce, in small saucepan, mix all remaining ingredients with wire whisk until well blended. Cook over medium heat 10 minutes or until cranberry sauce is melted and mixture is thoroughly heated, stirring frequently. Cut ham into slices. Serve with sauce.

NUTRITIONAL INFORMATION PER SERVING: Calories 220 • Total Fat 6g • Saturated Fat 2g • Trans Fat 0g • Cholesterol 60mg • Sodium 1350mg • Total Carbohydrate 19g • Dietary Fiber 0g • Sugars 17g • Protein 23g. DIETARY EXCHANGES: 1 Fruit • 3 Very Lean Meat • 1 Fat.

cook's notes

Cut down on the time you spend in the kitchen on Christmas Day by making this flavorful sauce the night before. When you're ready to use it, just heat before serving. The sauce also makes a thoughtful hostess gift. Pour it into a decorative jar, and store in the refrigerator until you're ready to give it to your host.

pepper-crusted prime rib
with zinfandel sauce

pepper-crusted prime rib with zinfandel sauce

PREP TIME: 25 Minutes ✳ READY IN: 2 Hours 10 Minutes ✳ SERVINGS: 12

ROAST

- 1 (6 lb.) boneless prime or choice beef rib roast
- 3 garlic cloves, sliced
- 1 tablespoon mixed peppercorns, coarsely ground
- 1 tablespoon mustard seed
- 1 tablespoon Worcestershire sauce
- 1 tablespoon Dijon mustard

SAUCE

- 2 tablespoons finely chopped shallots
- 1 cup red Zinfandel wine
- 1 (14 oz.) can beef broth
- 1/4 cup all-purpose flour
- 2 tablespoons brandy or beef broth
- 1 tablespoon chopped fresh parsley

1 Heat oven to 450°F. Make shallow slits in surface of beef roast. Insert slices of garlic. In small bowl, combine ground peppercorns, mustard seed, Worcestershire sauce and Dijon mustard; mix well. Spread over surface of roast. Place roast on rack in shallow metal roasting pan.

2 Bake for 15 minutes. Reduce oven temperature to 350°F; bake an additional 1-1/4 to 1-1/2 hours or until meat thermometer inserted in center registers 140°F for medium-rare.

3 Remove roast from pan; cover roast with foil to keep warm. Remove and discard all but 2 tablespoons drippings from pan. Add shallots; cook and stir over medium heat for 2 to 3 minutes or until shallots are tender. Add wine; cook over medium-high heat until mixture boils, scraping brown bits from bottom of pan.

4 In small bowl, combine broth and flour; blend well. Stir into wine mixture. Cook until mixture comes to a boil, stirring frequently. Boil 3 minutes or until slightly thickened. Stir in brandy. Cut roast into slices. Serve with sauce. Sprinkle individual servings with parsley.

NUTRITIONAL INFORMATION PER SERVING: Calories 470 • Total Fat 26g • Saturated Fat 10g • Cholesterol 140mg • Sodium 310mg • Total Carbohydrate 3g • Dietary Fiber 0g • Sugars 0g • Protein 47g. DIETARY EXCHANGE: 6-1/2 Medium-Fat Meat.

cook's notes

Red Zinfandel, a fruity wine, is a good match for this robust beef dish. Another fruity red wine, such as Cabernet Sauvignon or Pinot Noir, can be used in place of the red Zinfandel.

creamy spinach and tortellini

SERVINGS: 4

- 1 lb. fresh or frozen cheese tortellini
- 2 tablespoons olive oil or vegetable oil
- 1/2 cup chopped onion
- 3 garlic cloves, minced
- 1 (9 oz.) package frozen spinach in a pouch, thawed
- 1 cup cubed, seeded tomato

- 1/4 cup chopped fresh basil or 1-1/2 teaspoons dried basil leaves
- 1/2 teaspoon salt
- 1/2 teaspoon pepper
- 1 cup whipping cream
- 1/4 cup grated Parmesan or Romano cheese

1 Cook frozen cheese tortellini to desired doneness as directed on package. Drain the tortellini; keep it warm.

2 Meanwhile, heat oil in large skillet over medium heat until hot. Add onion and garlic; cook until tender and lightly browned, about 4 minutes. Add spinach, tomato, basil, salt and pepper; cook 5 minutes, stirring occasionally. Stir in whipping cream and Parmesan cheese; cook until mixture just comes to a boil. Reduce heat to low; stir in cooked tortellini. Cook an additional 4 to 5 minutes or until thoroughly heated. Serve with additional Parmesan cheese, if desired.

NUTRITIONAL INFORMATION PER SERVING: Calories 670 • Fat 37g • Sodium 1080mg • Total Carbohydrate 62g • Protein 25g.

JEANINE ALFANO
Montauk, New York
Bake-Off® Contest 34, 1990
Prize Winner

kitchen tip

Sweet potatoes are an excellent source of vitamin A and a good source of vitamin C.

orange-glazed roast chicken breasts with sweet potatoes

PREP TIME: 15 Minutes ✻ READY IN: 1 Hour ✻ SERVINGS: 4

BASTING SAUCE

1/4	cup orange marmalade
2	tablespoons orange juice
1	tablespoon balsamic vinegar
1	teaspoon dried thyme leaves
1/4	teaspoon salt
1/8	teaspoon pepper

CHICKEN AND VEGETABLES

4	bone-in skinless chicken breasts
2	medium dark-orange sweet potatoes, peeled, cut into 1-inch cubes
1	medium onion, cut into 8 wedges
1	teaspoon olive oil
1/3	cup sweetened dried cranberries
1/4	cup orange juice

1 Heat oven to 375°F. In small saucepan, cook all basting sauce ingredients over low heat 3 to 4 minutes or until marmalade is melted, stirring occasionally.

2 In 15x10x1-inch pan, place chicken breasts. Brush with half of basting sauce. In medium bowl, toss potatoes and onion with oil; place around chicken. Bake 25 minutes.

3 Meanwhile, in small bowl, soak cranberries in 1/4 cup orange juice. Brush chicken again with remaining basting sauce. Stir gently to coat vegetables with pan juices. With slotted spoon, sprinkle cranberries over vegetables; drizzle with juice. Bake 20 minutes longer or until juice of chicken is clear when thickest part is cut to bone (170°F), and vegetables are tender.

NUTRITIONAL INFORMATION PER SERVING: Calories 340 • Total Fat 5g • Saturated Fat 1g • Cholesterol 75mg • Sodium 220mg • Total Carbohydrate 46g • Dietary Fiber 3g • Sugars 26g • Protein 28g. DIETARY EXCHANGES: 2 Starch • 1 Fruit • 3 Other Carbohydrate • 3 Very Lean Meat • 1/2 Fat.

festive oyster stew

READY IN: 30 Minutes ✻ SERVINGS: 8

2	(8 oz.) cans whole oysters, drained, liquid reserved
1/4	cup butter or margarine
1	medium red bell pepper, chopped (1 cup)
3/4	cup chopped onions
1/2	cup all-purpose flour
1	teaspoon salt
1/4	teaspoon white pepper

1	quart half-and-half (4 cups)
1	quart milk (4 cups)
2	cups frozen southern-style hash-brown potatoes (from 32 oz. pkg.)
1/2	teaspoon hot pepper sauce
1	cup chopped fresh spinach

special touch

If your children don't like the idea of oysters, why not call this dish Christmas Stew? When it's served with saltine or oyster crackers, little ones will be too busy having fun to worry about oysters.

1 Cut oysters in half; set aside. Melt butter in Dutch oven or large saucepan over medium heat. Add bell pepper and onions; cook and stir until tender. Stir in flour, salt and pepper. Cook 1 minute, stirring constantly.

2 Gradually stir in half-and-half, milk and reserved oyster liquid. Add potatoes and hot pepper sauce; mix well.

3 Cook over medium heat until stew is slightly thickened and potatoes are tender, stirring frequently. Stir in oysters and spinach. Cook until thoroughly heated, stirring frequently.

NUTRITIONAL INFORMATION PER SERVING: Calories 435 • Total Fat 25g • Saturated Fat 15g • Cholesterol 130mg • Sodium 710mg • Total Carbohydrate 34g • Dietary Fiber 1g • Sugars 13g • Protein 18g. DIETARY EXCHANGES: 2 Starch • 1-1/2 Lean Meat • 4 Fat • 2 Carbohydrate Choices.

orange-glazed roast chicken breasts
with sweet potatoes

spice and herb-roasted pork tenderloin

spice and herb-roasted pork tenderloin

PREP TIME: 15 Minutes ✳ READY IN: 50 Minutes ✳ SERVINGS: 6

1/2 teaspoon garlic-pepper blend	1/4 teaspoon salt
1/2 teaspoon dried rosemary leaves, crushed	2 (3/4 lb.) pork tenderloins
1/2 teaspoon dried thyme leaves, crushed	2 teaspoons olive or vegetable oil
1/2 teaspoon paprika	

1 Heat oven to 425°F. In small bowl, combine garlic-pepper blend, rosemary, thyme, paprika and salt; mix well.

2 Brush pork tenderloins with oil. Sprinkle with seasoning mixture; rub in with fingers. Place tenderloins in ungreased shallow baking pan.

3 Bake for 25 to 35 minutes or until meat thermometer inserted in center registers 160°F. Let stand 5 minutes before slicing.

NUTRITIONAL INFORMATION PER SERVING: Calories 160 • Total Fat 6g • Saturated Fat 2g • Cholesterol 70mg • Sodium 150mg • Total Carbohydrate 0g • Dietary Fiber 0g • Sugars 0g • Protein 26g. DIETARY EXCHANGES: 4 Very Lean Meat • 1/2 Fat • 0 Carbohydrate Choice.

special touch

For an eye-fetching presentation, slice this tenderloin on the diagonal before serving. Au gratin potatoes make a tasty side dish.

stuffed roast turkey and gravy

PREP TIME: 30 Minutes ✳ READY IN: 5 Hours ✳ SERVINGS: 12 to 16 Servings Turkey; 7 Cups Gravy

TURKEY	GRAVY
1 (12 to 16 lb.) whole turkey, thawed if frozen	Turkey pan drippings
1/2 teaspoon salt	2 (14 oz.) cans chicken broth
Stuffing of choice	1/3 cup all-purpose flour
1/3 cup butter or margarine, melted	Water

1 Heat oven to 325°F. Remove and discard neck and giblets from turkey. Rinse turkey inside and out with cold water; pat dry with paper towels. Sprinkle cavity of turkey with salt.

2 Spoon stuffing loosely into neck and body cavities of turkey. Place any remaining stuffing in lightly buttered casserole; cover and refrigerate to bake as side dish. Turn wings back and tuck tips over shoulder joints. Refasten drumsticks with metal piece or tuck under skin at tail. Fasten neck skin to back with skewers.

3 Place turkey, breast side up, in roasting pan. Insert ovenproof meat thermometer so bulb reaches center of thickest part of thigh, but does not rest on bone. Spoon melted butter over turkey. Do not add water or cover.

4 Bake for 3-1/2 to 4-1/4 hours or until thermometer registers 180°F to 185°F and leg joint moves easily. If necessary, cover turkey breast with tent of foil during last 1-1/2 to 2 hours of baking to prevent excessive browning.

5 Remove turkey from pan; let stand 15 minutes. Remove skewers from turkey. Remove stuffing; place in serving bowl.

6 Pour drippings from roasting pan into strainer over bowl. Spoon off fat that rises to top, reserving 1/2 cup fat. Pour drippings into measuring cup. Add broth and enough water to make 7 cups liquid. Set aside.

7 In large saucepan, combine reserved 1/2 cup fat and flour; mix well with wire whisk. Cook over medium heat for about 2 minutes or until mixture turns golden brown, stirring constantly with wire whisk.

8 Gradually stir drippings mixture into flour mixture. Cook over low heat until mixture boils and thickens, stirring constantly.

NUTRITIONAL INFORMATION PER SERVING: Calories 485 • Total Fat 27g • Saturated Fat 9g • Cholesterol 145mg • Sodium 450mg • Total Carbohydrate 16g • Dietary Fiber 0g • Sugars 0g • Protein 45g. DIETARY EXCHANGES: 1 Starch • 6 Lean Meat • 2 Fat • 1 Carbohydrate Choice.

special touch

When grocery shopping for your holiday feast, pick up some disposable food-storage containers. This way, you can pack up any extra food and send it home with your guests without worrying about getting your storage container back from them.

Joyful Entertaining

Casual gatherings…for two, a few or even more…help make the holidays special. Spend more time with your guests and less time in the kitchen with these simple delights.

p. 123

p. 124

p. 136

p. 134

p. 119

pork roast with cranberries p. 129

cook's notes

Slivered almonds or halved hazelnuts can be used in place of walnut pieces in this meal-in-one specialty.

chicken with basil cream sauce

READY IN: 25 Minutes ✳ SERVINGS: 4

1 tablespoon oil	1/4 cup water
1 lb. fresh chicken tenders	1/2 cup walnut pieces
1/4 teaspoon salt	1 (10 oz.) container refrigerated Alfredo sauce
1/4 teaspoon pepper	2 tablespoons chopped fresh basil
1 (16 oz.) package refrigerated fresh broccoli and carrots	

1 Heat oil in 12-inch skillet or Dutch oven over medium-high heat until hot. Add chicken; sprinkle with salt and pepper. Cook 4 to 5 minutes or until browned, stirring occasionally.

2 Add vegetables and water; cook 5 to 7 minutes or until chicken is no longer pink in center and vegetables are tender, stirring frequently.

3 Stir in all remaining ingredients. Cook 2 to 3 minutes or until thoroughly heated, stirring occasionally.

NUTRITIONAL INFORMATION PER SERVING: Calories 460 • Total Fat 28g • Saturated Fat 10g • Cholesterol 105mg • Sodium 730mg • Total Carbohydrate 18g • Dietary Fiber 5g • Sugars 3g • Protein 34g. DIETARY EXCHANGES: 1 Starch • 1 Other Carbohydrate • 1 Vegetable • 4 Very Lean Meat • 5 Fat.

chipotle-beef fajitas

READY IN: 20 Minutes ❉ SERVINGS: 2

- 2 tablespoons Old El Paso® taco seasoning mix (from 1.25 oz. package)
- 2 tablespoons lime juice
- 2 tablespoons finely chopped chipotle chiles in adobo sauce (from 7 or 11 oz. can)
- 1 teaspoon honey
- 1/2 lb. boneless beef sirloin steak, cut into thin bite-size strips

- 1 medium green or red bell pepper, cut into thin bite-size strips
- 1 medium red onion, cut into thin wedges
- 4 (8 inch) fat-free flour tortillas, heated
  Guacamole, sour cream, shredded lettuce and/or chopped tomatoes, if desired

cook's notes

If you have a smaller contact grill, cook half of the beef and vegetable mixture at a time. Keep the cooked portion warm by covering it with waxed paper.

1 Heat closed contact grill 5 minutes. In shallow nonmetal dish, mix taco seasoning mix, lime juice, chipotle chiles and honey. Add beef, bell pepper and onion; toss to coat.

2 When grill is heated, place beef and vegetables on bottom grill surface. Close grill; cook 4 to 6 minutes, turning mixture occasionally, until the beef is desired doneness and the vegetables are crisp-tender.

3 Spoon beef and vegetables evenly down center of each warm tortilla. Top with guacamole, sour cream, shredded lettuce and/or chopped tomatoes. Roll up each tortilla around filling.

NUTRITIONAL INFORMATION PER SERVING: Calories 410 • Total Fat 4g • Saturated Fat 1g • Cholesterol 60mg • Sodium 960mg • Total Carbohydrate 68g • Dietary Fiber 6g • Sugars 13g • Protein 32g. DIETARY EXCHANGES: 3 Starch • 3 Very Lean Meat • 1/2 Fat • 1 Other Carbohydrates.

roasted vegetable soup

roasted vegetable soup

PREP TIME: 25 Minutes ✳ READY IN: 1 Hour 5 Minutes ✳ SERVINGS: 3

2 tablespoons olive or vegetable oil	1 (8 oz.) package fresh whole mushrooms
1 teaspoon dried rosemary leaves, crushed	3 garlic cloves, minced
1/2 teaspoon salt	1 (14-1/2 oz.) can ready-to-serve chicken broth
1/4 teaspoon pepper	
2 cups sliced zucchini	3/4 cup whipping cream
1 sweet onion, halved lengthwise, sliced	2 tablespoons chopped fresh parsley
1 medium red bell pepper, coarsely chopped	

1 Heat oven to 475°F. In small bowl, combine oil, rosemary, salt and pepper; mix well. Set aside. In large resealable food storage plastic bag or bowl, combine zucchini, onion, bell pepper, mushrooms and garlic. Add oil mixture to bag; seal bag and mix well to coat vegetables. Remove vegetables from bag; place in single layer in ungreased 15x10x1-inch baking pan.

2 Bake for 30 minutes or until vegetables are golden brown and tender, stirring halfway through baking time.

3 In large saucepan, combine roasted vegetables, broth, cream and parsley; mix well. Cook and stir over medium heat for 8 to 10 minutes or until thoroughly heated.

NUTRITIONAL INFORMATION PER SERVING: Calories 390 • Total Fat 33g • Saturated Fat 15g • Cholesterol 80mg • Sodium 820mg • Total Carbohydrate 14g • Dietary Fiber 3g • Sugars 7g • Protein 8g. DIETARY EXCHANGES: 3 Vegetable • 7 Fat.

smoky southwestern shepherd's pie

SERVINGS: 6

1-1/2 lb. lean ground beef round	1 to 2 canned chipotle chiles in adobo sauce (from 11 oz. can), drained, seeded and chopped
1/2 cup chopped onion	
2 cups water	
3 tablespoons margarine or butter	1/2 teaspoon cumin
1/2 teaspoon salt	1/2 teaspoon dried oregano leaves
3/4 cup milk	1 (11 oz.) can vacuum-packed whole kernel corn with red and green peppers, drained
2 cups mashed potato flakes	
1 (4.5 oz.) can chopped green chiles	1/8 teaspoon paprika
1 cup shredded Mexican cheese blend (4 oz.)	1/3 cup sliced green onions
1 (10 oz.) can enchilada sauce	1 small tomato, cut into 6 wedges

1 Heat oven to 400°F. In large skillet, brown ground beef round with onion over medium-high heat for 8 to 10 minutes or until beef is thoroughly cooked, stirring frequently.

2 Meanwhile, in medium saucepan, combine water, margarine and salt. Bring to a boil. Remove from heat. Stir in milk and potato flakes. Cover; let stand 5 minutes. Stir in green chiles and 1/2 cup of the cheese.

3 Drain beef mixture. Add enchilada sauce, chipotle chiles, cumin and oregano; mix well. Bring to a boil. Remove from heat. Spread beef mixture in ungreased shallow 2-quart casserole. Top with corn. Spread potatoes evenly over corn. Sprinkle with remaining 1/2 cup cheese.

4 Bake for 13 to 17 minutes or until cheese is melted and filling is bubbly. Sprinkle with paprika and green onions. Arrange tomato wedges in center of casserole. Let stand 5 minutes before serving.

NUTRITIONAL INFORMATION PER SERVING: Calories 530 • Fat 29g • Sodium 930mg • Total Carbohydrate 37g • Protein 29g.

cook's notes

When roasting the vegetables, double the amount. The extra vegetables can be reheated for a side dish, served cold with a splash of vinaigrette dressing or warmed and tossed with hot rice for a vegetable pilaf.

KRISTINA VANNI
Libertyville, Illinois
Bake-Off® Contest 39, 2000

harvest chicken noodle soup

PREP TIME: 20 Minutes ✳ READY IN: 40 Minutes ✳ SERVINGS: 3

1/2 cup sliced celery	2 (14-1/2 oz.) cans ready-to-serve chicken broth
1/2 cup chopped carrot	
1/4 cup chopped onion	1/2 cup water
1 small zucchini, coarsely chopped	3 oz. (1-1/2 cups) uncooked medium egg noodles
1/2 teaspoon dried thyme leaves	1 cup cubed cooked chicken

1 In large saucepan, combine all ingredients except noodles and chicken; mix well. Bring to a boil. Stir in noodles and chicken. Reduce heat to low; simmer 15 to 20 minutes or until noodles and vegetables are tender.

NUTRITIONAL INFORMATION PER SERVING: Calories 250 • Total Fat 6g • Saturated Fat 2g • Cholesterol 70mg • Sodium 940mg • Total Carbohydrate 26g • Dietary Fiber 2g • Sugars 4g • Protein 24g. DIETARY EXCHANGES: 1-1/2 Starch • 1-1/2 Other Carbohydrate • 1 Vegetable • 2-1/2 Very Lean Meat • 1/2 Fat.

speedy sweet-and-sour chicken

READY IN: 20 Minutes ✳ SERVINGS: 3

1 (12 oz.) package frozen breaded cooked chicken nuggets	1-1/2 cups water
1-1/2 cups uncooked instant white rice	1 (1 lb. 5 oz.) package frozen stir fry vegetables and tangy sweet & sour sauce meal starter

1 Cook chicken nuggets as directed on package until thoroughly heated. Cook rice in water as directed on package.

2 Meanwhile, in large skillet, combine frozen vegetables, contents of pineapple pouch and frozen sauce from packet; mix well.

3 Cover; cook over medium-high heat for 7 to 10 minutes or until vegetables are crisp-tender, stirring frequently. Add cooked chicken; stir until well coated. Serve over rice. If desired, garnish with cashews.

NUTRITIONAL INFORMATION PER SERVING: Calories 680 • Total Fat 19g • Saturated Fat 4g • Cholesterol 20mg • Sodium 1350mg • Total Carbohydrate 108g • Dietary Fiber 7g • Sugars 29g • Protein 19g. DIETARY EXCHANGES: 3-1/2 Starch • 3 Fruit • 6-1/2 Other Carbohydrate • 1/2 High-Fat Meat • 2-1/2 Fat.

LOANNE CHIU
Fort Worth, Texas
Bake-Off® Contest 37, 1996
Prize Winner

southwest tortellini chowder

SERVINGS: 6

3 (10-1/2 oz.) cans condensed chicken broth	1 cup frozen corn (from 1 lb. pkg.)
1-1/2 cups mild chunky-style salsa or picante	1/2 cup coarsely chopped red bell pepper
1/2 teaspoon grated orange peel	1 (5 oz.) can evaporated milk
2 (9 oz.) packages refrigerated meat-filled or cheese-filled tortellini	Dash salt
2 cups frozen cut broccoli (from 1 lb. pkg.)	1/4 cup chopped fresh cilantro

1 In Dutch oven or large saucepan, combine broth, salsa and orange peel. Bring to a boil. Reduce heat to low; simmer 3 minutes.

2 Stir in tortellini and vegetables; cook over medium heat for 6 to 8 minutes or until tortellini and vegetables are tender.

3 Stir in milk and salt; cook 1 to 2 minutes or just until thoroughly heated, stirring occasionally. Do not boil. Top each serving of chowder with cilantro. Serve immediately.

NUTRITIONAL INFORMATION PER SERVING: Calories 400 • Fat 12g • Sodium 1750mg • Total Carbohydrate 52g • Protein 20g.

speedy sweet-and-sour chicken

hot turkey and gravy open-faced sandwiches

READY IN: 15 Minutes ✳ SERVINGS: 4

2 tablespoons margarine or butter

1 large onion, thinly sliced

3/4 lb. cooked turkey breast, cut into 1/8-inch-thick slices

1 (12 oz.) jar fat-free turkey gravy

4 slices bread

1 Melt margarine in large nonstick skillet over medium-high heat. Add onion; cover and cook 4 to 6 minutes or until onion is tender and lightly browned, stirring occasionally.

2 Add turkey and gravy; cook until thoroughly heated, stirring occasionally. To serve, place 1 slice of bread on each individual plate. Top bread with turkey and onion mixture.

NUTRITIONAL INFORMATION PER SERVING: Calories 270 • Total Fat 7g • Saturated Fat 1g • Cholesterol 70mg • Sodium 690mg • Total Carbohydrate 21g • Dietary Fiber 1g • Sugars 3g • Protein 30g. DIETARY EXCHANGES: 1-1/2 Starch • 1-1/2 Other Carbohydrate • 3-1/2 Very Lean Meat • 1/2 Fat.

cook's notes

Purchase cooked turkey for this recipe in the deli section of the grocery store, or use leftover turkey.

MADGE SAVAGE
Mount Vernon, Ohio
Bake-Off® Contest 30, 1994
Prize Winner

mexican fiesta biscuit bake

SERVINGS: 15

2 tablespoons margarine or butter

1 (1 lb. 0.3 oz.) can large refrigerated buttermilk biscuits

1 (10.8 oz.) can large refrigerated buttermilk biscuits

1 (16 oz.) jar medium thick and chunky salsa (1-3/4 cups)

3 cups shredded Monterey Jack cheese (12 oz.)

1/2 cup chopped green bell pepper

1/2 cup sliced green onions

1 (2-1/4 oz.) can sliced ripe olives, drained

1 cup picante salsa, if desired

1 Heat oven to 375°F. Melt margarine in oven in 13x9-inch (3-quart) glass baking dish or nonaluminum baking pan. Tilt to evenly coat dish. Separate dough into 13 biscuits; cut each biscuit into eighths. Place biscuit pieces in large bowl; toss with 1-3/4 cups salsa. Spoon evenly into margarine-coated dish. Sprinkle with cheese, bell pepper, green onions and ripe olives.

2 Bake for 35 to 45 minutes or until edges are deep golden brown and center is set. Let stand 15 minutes. Cut into squares; serve with 1 cup picante salsa.

NUTRITIONAL INFORMATION PER SERVING: Calories 280 • Fat 16g • Sodium 1050mg • Total Carbohydrate 25g • Protein 9g.

ham and fruit skillet

READY IN: 10 Minutes ✳ SERVINGS: 2

1 fully cooked hame slice (1/2 lb.)

1 (4 oz.) container refrigerated diced peaches, drained

2 tablespoons packed brown sugar

Dash ground cinnamon

1-1/2 teaspoons butter or margarine, cut into small pieces

1 In 8-inch nonstick skillet, brown ham on 1 side over medium heat. Turn ham; top with peaches. Sprinkle with brown sugar and cinnamon; dot with butter.

2 Cover; cook over medium heat about 2 minutes or until brown sugar and butter are melted and ham is browned.

NUTRITIONAL INFORMATION PER SERVING: Calories 290 • Total Fat 12g • Saturated Fat 5g • Cholesterol 65mg • Sodium 1470mg • Total Carbohydrate 25g • Dietary Fiber 0g • Sugars 23g • Protein 22g. DIETARY EXCHANGES: 3 Lean Meat • 1/2 Fat • 1-1/2 Other Carbohydrates.

cook's notes

If you'd prefer, use 2 smoked pork chops instead of the ham slice. Cooking time will be about the same.

beef au jus sandwiches

PREP TIME: 15 Minutes ✳ READY IN: 10 Hours 15 Minutes ✳ SERVINGS: 12

1 large sweet onion, sliced

1 (14 oz.) can beef broth

1 (4 lb.) boneless beef rump roast, trimmed of fat

2 tablespoons balsamic vinegar

1 (.7 oz.) envelope Italian salad dressing mix

1/2 teaspoon salt

1/4 teaspoon freshly ground black pepper

12 hoagie buns, split

1 large green bell pepper, thinly sliced

12 (1 oz.) slices provolone cheese, halved

1 Place onion slices and broth in 3-1/2- to 4-quart slow cooker. Brush all surfaces of beef roast with vinegar. Place on onions. Sprinkle with salad dressing mix, salt and pepper. Cover; cook on Low setting for 8 to 10 hours.

2 About 5 minutes before serving, remove beef from slow cooker; place on cutting board. Cut beef across grain into thin slices; return slices to slow cooker and mix well.

3 To assemble, spoon beef onto bottom halves of buns. Top with bell pepper, cheese and top halves of buns. Serve sandwiches with juices from slow cooker.

NUTRITIONAL INFORMATION PER SERVING: Calories 525 • Total Fat 15g • Saturated Fat 7g • Cholesterol 105mg • Sodium 1370mg • Total Carbohydrate 52g • Dietary Fiber 3g • Sugars 10g • Protein 46g. DIETARY EXCHANGES: 3-1/2 Starch • 3-1/2 Other Carbohydrate • 5 Lean Meat.

cook's notes

Serve the beefy sandwiches with horseradish, ketchup and mustard.

chicken and black bean tostizzas

chicken and black bean tostizzas

SERVINGS: 8

PIZZA

- 1 (1 lb. 1.3 oz.) can large refrigerated flaky biscuits
- 1/2 cup thick and chunky salsa
- 1 cup diced cooked chicken
- 1 cup canned black beans (from 15 oz. can), drained
- 1/4 cup chopped fresh cilantro
- 1/4 teaspoon cumin
- 2 green onions, chopped
- 1/2 cup green or red bell pepper strips (1-inch long)
- 1-1/2 cups shredded Cheddar cheese (6 oz.)

GARNISH, IF DESIRED

- 1/2 cup dairy sour cream
- 1/2 cup guacamole

1 Heat oven to 350°F. Separate dough into 8 biscuits. On ungreased cookie sheets, press or roll each biscuit into 5-1/2-inch circle. In medium bowl, combine salsa, chicken, black beans, cilantro and cumin; mix well. Spread evenly over biscuits to within 1/4 inch of edges. Top evenly with green onions, bell pepper strips and cheese.

2 Bake for 20 to 24 minutes or until biscuits are golden brown and cheese is melted. To serve, garnish with sour cream and guacamole.

NUTRITIONAL INFORMATION PER SERVING: Calories 400 • Fat 23g • Sodium 1010mg • Total Carbohydrate 32g • Protein 17g.

KAREN DURRETT
Portland, Oregon
Bake-Off® Contest 36, 1994

pork roast with cranberries

PREP TIME: 15 Minutes ❋ READY IN: 9 Hours 15 Minutes ❋ SERVINGS: 6

- 1 (2-1/2 lb.) boneless pork shoulder roast, trimmed of fat
- 1 cup sweetened dried cranberries
- 1/2 cup chicken broth
- 1 teaspoon shredded orange peel
- 1/2 cup cranberry juice cocktail
- 2 tablespoons cornstarch

1 Place pork roast in 3-1/2- to 4-quart slow cooker. In small bowl, combine cranberries, broth, orange peel and 1/4 cup of the cranberry juice cocktail; mix well. Pour over roast.

2 Cover; cook on Low setting for 7 to 9 hours. To serve, place the pork roast on serving platter; cover with foil to keep warm. Pour juices from the slow cooker into a medium saucepan; if necessary, skim off any fat.

3 In small bowl, combine remaining 1/4 cup cranberry juice cocktail and cornstarch; blend well. Stir into juices in saucepan. Cook and stir over medium heat until bubbly and thickened. Serve with pork roast. Garnish with shredded orange peel if desired.

NUTRITIONAL INFORMATION PER SERVING: Calories 330 • Total Fat 15g • Saturated Fat 5g • Cholesterol 85mg • Sodium 150mg • Total Carbohydrate 25g • Dietary Fiber 1g • Sugars 18g • Protein 24g. DIETARY EXCHANGES: 1/2 Starch • 1 Fruit • 1-1/2 Other Carbohydrate • 3 Medium-Fat Meat.

kitchen tip

Dried orange peel can be used in place of fresh orange peel. Look for dried peel near the seasonings at the grocery store.

Pillsbury
Bake-Off®

MARIE MICKELSON
Columbia Heights, Minnesota
Bake-Off® Contest 34, 1990
Prize Winner

cook's notes

Cut the pizza into small slices

for an excellent appetizer.

polynesian pork ribs

PREP TIME: 10 Minutes ✳ READY IN: 10 Hours 40 Minutes ✳ SERVINGS: 6

RIBS

2	lb. boneless country-style pork loin ribs
1	garlic clove, minced
1	small onion, sliced
1	(8 oz.) can crushed pineapple in unsweetened juice, undrained

SAUCE

3/4	cup ketchup
3	tablespoons brown sugar
3	tablespoons hoisin sauce
1	teaspoon grated gingerroot

1   Spray 3-1/2- to 4-quart slow cooker with nonstick cooking spray. Place pork ribs, garlic and onion in sprayed slow cooker. Spoon about half of the pineapple with some of the juice over ribs. Reserve remaining pineapple and juice. Cover; cook on Low setting for 8 to 10 hours.

2   About 35 minutes before serving, drain and discard cooking juices from slow cooker; wipe edge of slow cooker clean. In small bowl, combine ketchup, brown sugar, hoisin sauce, gingerroot and remaining pineapple with juice; mix well. Spoon or pour evenly over ribs. Increase heat setting to high; cover and cook an additional 25 to 30 minutes or until ribs are glazed.

NUTRITIONAL INFORMATION PER SERVING: Calories 395 • Total Fat 18g • Saturated Fat 6g • Cholesterol 95mg • Sodium 540mg • Total Carbohydrate 26g • Dietary Fiber 1g • Sugars 23g • Protein 32g. DIETARY EXCHANGES: 1/2 Starch • 1-1/2 Fruit • 2 Other Carbohydrate • 4 Medium-Fat Meat.

hearty reuben pizza

SERVINGS: 8

1	(10 oz.) can refrigerated pizza crust
1	cup sliced onions
1	to 2 tablespoons margarine or butter
1/2	cup salad dressing or mayonnaise
4-1/2	teaspoons Dijon or Viennese mustard

2	cups shredded Swiss cheese (8 oz.)
8	oz. thinly sliced deli corned beef
1	cup sauerkraut, drained, squeezed dry
1/2	to 1 teaspoon caraway seed
1	dill pickle, cut crosswise into thin slices

1   Heat oven to 425°F. Lightly grease 12-inch pizza pan or 13x9-inch pan. Unroll dough; place in greased pan. Starting at center, press out with hands. Bake for 9 to 12 minutes or until golden brown.

2   In large skillet, cook onions in margarine until tender. In small bowl, combine salad dressing and mustard; blend well. Spread 1/4 cup dressing mixture over partially baked crust. Sprinkle with 1/2 cup of the Swiss cheese. Overlap corned beef slices over cheese and dressing, covering completely. Spread remaining dressing mixture over corned beef. Top evenly with cooked onion slices, sauerkraut and remaining 1-1/2 cups Swiss cheese. Sprinkle with caraway seed. Bake at 425°F for an additional 10 minutes or until thoroughly heated and cheese is melted. Garnish with dill pickle slices.

NUTRITIONAL INFORMATION PER SERVING: Calories 360 • Fat 22g • Sodium 1040mg • Total Carbohydrate 23g • Protein 17g.

roasted chicken and cranberry croissants

READY IN: 15 Minutes ✳ SERVINGS: 4

1/2 cup whipped cream cheese spread (from 8 oz. tub)

1/2 teaspoon grated orange peel

4 croissants, split

4 leaves Bibb lettuce

3/4 lb. thinly sliced roasted chicken (from deli)

1/2 cup whole berry cranberry sauce (from 16 oz. can)

1 In small bowl, combine cream cheese and orange peel; blend well. Spread cream cheese mixture on cut sides of croissants.

2 Layer bottom halves of croissants with lettuce and chicken. Top chicken with cranberry sauce. Cover with top halves of croissants.

NUTRITIONAL INFORMATION PER SERVING: Calories 450 • Total Fat 21g • Saturated Fat 13g • Cholesterol 105mg • Sodium 1160mg • Total Carbohydrate 40g • Dietary Fiber 2g • Sugars 17g • Protein 25g. DIETARY EXCHANGES: 2 Starch • 1/2 Fruit • 2-1/2 Other Carbohydrate • 2-1/2 Very Lean Meat • 3-1/2 Fat.

cook's notes

If desired, the cranberry sauce can be pulsed in a food processor to make a spreadable fruit.

Yuletide Brunch Buffet

Share the joy of Christmas morning with a hearty meal. It's easy to greet the most memorable day of the year with these heartwarming dishes, each sure to garner smiles.

p. 155

p. 149

p. 159

p. 157

p. 146

puff pancake with caramelized fruit p. 159

sausage and egg brunch bake

sausage and egg brunch bake

PREP TIME: 40 Minutes ✳ READY IN: 9 Hours 50 Minutes ✳ SERVINGS: 12

EGG BAKE

- 1-1/2 lb. bulk Italian pork sausage
- 5 cups frozen country-style shredded hash-brown potatoes (from 30 oz. pkg.)
- 1/2 cup sliced green onions
- 2 (4.5 oz.) jars sliced mushrooms, drained
- 1 (2-1/4 oz.) can sliced ripe olives, drained
- 1 tablespoon chopped fresh basil
- 3 cups shredded colby-Monterey Jack cheese blend (12 oz.)
- 8 eggs
- 1-1/2 cups milk
- 1/2 teaspoon salt

TOPPING

- 1 tablespoon olive or vegetable oil
- 1 garlic clove, minced
- 6 Italian plum tomatoes, chopped (about 2 cups)
- 1/4 teaspoon salt
- 2 tablespoons chopped fresh basil

1 Spray 13x9-inch (3-quart) glass baking dish and 16x12-inch sheet of foil with nonstick cooking spray. In large skillet, cook sausage over medium-high heat until no longer pink, stirring occasionally. Remove sausage from skillet; drain on paper towels.

2 In large bowl, mix potatoes, onions, mushrooms, olives, 1 tablespoon basil and 2 cups of the cheese. Add cooked sausage; stir gently to mix. Spoon evenly into baking dish. Sprinkle with remaining 1 cup cheese.

3 Beat eggs in same large bowl. Add milk and 1/2 teaspoon salt; beat well. Pour over potato mixture in baking dish. Cover with foil, sprayed side down. Refrigerate at least 8 hours or overnight.

4 To serve, heat oven to 350°F. Bake covered 45 minutes. Uncover baking dish; bake 20 to 25 minutes longer or until center is set. Let stand 10 minutes before serving.

5 Meanwhile, in medium skillet, heat oil over medium heat until hot. Add garlic; cook and stir 1 minute. Add tomatoes and 1/4 teaspoon salt; cook about 5 minutes or until tomatoes are tender, stirring occasionally. Stir in 2 tablespoons basil. To serve, cut egg bake into squares. Serve with warm topping.

NUTRITIONAL INFORMATION PER SERVING: Calories 320 • Total Fat 19g • Saturated Fat 9g • Trans Fat 0g • Cholesterol 180mg • Sodium 650mg • Total Carbohydrate 22g • Dietary Fiber 3g • Sugars 4g • Protein 17g. DIETARY EXCHANGES: 1-1/2 Starch • 2 High-Fat Meat • 1/2 Fat.

cook's notes

Try this egg bake with shredded hot pepper Monterey Jack or mozzarella cheese instead of the colby-Monterey Jack cheese blend the recipe calls for. Serve the hearty casserole with Sunrise Mimosas (see recipe below).

sunrise mimosas

READY IN: 10 Minutes ✳ SERVINGS: 12

- 1 (10 oz.) package frozen strawberries in syrup, thawed, undrained
- 3 cups 100% tangerine juice (made from frozen concentrate)
- 2 (750 ml) bottles champagne or 7 cups club soda, chilled
- 6 strawberries with stems, halved, if desired

1 Place strainer over medium bowl; pour strawberries with syrup into strainer. Press berries with back of spoon through strainer to remove seeds; discard seeds.

2 In nonmetal bowl or pitcher, combine strawberry puree, tangerine juice and sparkling wine; stir gently. Serve over ice in stemmed goblets. Garnish each glass with strawberry half.

NUTRITIONAL INFORMATION PER SERVING: Calories 140 • Total Fat 0g • Saturated Fat 0g • Cholesterol 0mg • Sodium 0mg • Total Carbohydrate 16g • Dietary Fiber 1g • Sugars 12g • Protein 0g. DIETARY EXCHANGES: 1 Fruit • 1 Other Carbohydrate • 1-1/2 Fat.

waffles with peach-berry topping

READY IN: 15 Minutes ✳ SERVINGS: 4

8 frozen homestyle or buttermilk waffles	1 tablespoon fresh lemon juice
3 peaches or nectarines, pitted, sliced	1 cup fresh blueberries
1/2 teaspoon grated lemon peel	3/4 cup purchased blueberry syrup

1 Heat waffles as directed on package. Meanwhile, in medium nonmetal bowl, combine peaches, lemon peel and lemon juice; mix gently to coat. Add blueberries and syrup; stir gently.

2 Place 2 waffles on each of four breakfast plates. Top each serving with the fruit and the berry mixture.

NUTRITIONAL INFORMATION PER SERVING: Calories 380 • Total Fat 6g • Saturated Fat 2g • Cholesterol 0mg • Sodium 540mg • Total Carbohydrate 78g • Dietary Fiber 3g • Sugars 49g • Protein 4g. DIETARY EXCHANGES: 1-1/2 Starch • 3-1/2 Fruit • 5 Other Carbohydrate • 1 Fat.

seafood and cheese brunch bake

PREP TIME: 30 Minutes ✳ READY IN: 9 Hours 10 Minutes ✳ SERVINGS: 12

2 tablespoons butter or margarine	1 (6 oz.) can crabmeat, drained
1 (8 oz.) package sliced fresh mushrooms (3 cups)	1 (14 oz.) can quartered artichoke hearts, drained
1/3 cup sliced green onions	6 eggs
1/2 lb. shelled deveined uncooked medium shrimp, tails removed	1-1/2 cups milk
6 slices white bread	1/2 teaspoon salt
3 tablespoons purchased pesto	1/8 teaspoon ground red pepper (cayenne)
2 cups shredded Swiss cheese (8 oz.)	Fresh thyme sprigs, if desired

1 Spray 13x9-inch (3-quart) glass baking dish with nonstick cooking spray. Melt butter in large skillet over medium heat. Add mushrooms and onions; cook 5 to 7 minutes or until tender, stirring frequently. Add shrimp; cook until shrimp turn pink, stirring occasionally.

2 Spread 3 slices of bread with pesto. Top each with 1 plain bread slice, pressing firmly together. Cut sandwiches into 1/2-inch cubes. Layer half of bread cubes in sprayed baking dish. Sprinkle with half of the cheese. Top with all of the mushroom mixture, crabmeat and artichoke hearts. Top with remaining half of bread cubes and cheese.

3 Beat eggs in large bowl. Add milk, salt and ground red pepper; beat well. Pour over bread, pushing bread into milk mixture to moisten completely. Cover with foil. Refrigerate at least 8 hours or overnight.

4 To serve, heat oven to 350°F. Uncover baking dish; bake 35 to 40 minutes or until knife inserted in center comes out clean. Let stand 5 minutes before serving. Cut into squares to serve. Garnish with thyme sprigs.

NUTRITIONAL INFORMATION PER SERVING: Calories 245 • Total Fat 13g • Saturated Fat 6g • Cholesterol 170mg • Sodium 480mg • Total Carbohydrate 13g • Dietary Fiber 2g • Sugars 3g • Protein 19g. DIETARY EXCHANGES: 1 Starch • 2-1/2 Very Lean Meat • 2 Fat • 1 Carbohydrate Choice.

waffles with peach-berry topping

cranberry fluff fruit dip with fruit wreath

READY IN: 30 Minutes ❋ SERVINGS: 12

Dip

- 1 (7 oz.) jar marshmallow creme
- 1 (8 oz.) package cream cheese, softened
- 1/4 cup frozen cranberry-orange sauce, thawed

Fruit Wreath

- 1 bunch curly endive
- 2 red apples, cored, sliced

- 2 tablespoons lemon juice
- 3 small clusters seedless red grapes
- 3 small clusters seedless green grapes
- 5 or 6 strawberries
- 1 star fruit, sliced, if desired
- 2 tablespoons pomegranate seeds, if desired

1 In small bowl, beat marshmallow creme and cream cheese until smooth. Stir in cranberry sauce. Line large platter with endive leaves. Place bowl of dip in center.

2 Dip apple slices in lemon juice; arrange in circle about 1 inch from edge of plate, overlapping slices. Arrange grapes and strawberries on apples randomly around dip. Tuck slices of star fruit among other fruit. Sprinkle pomegranate seeds over endive leaves.

NUTRITIONAL INFORMATION PER SERVING: Calories 170 • Total Fat 7g • Saturated Fat 4g • Cholesterol 20mg • Sodium 75mg • Total Carbohydrate 25g • Dietary Fiber 3g • Sugars 21g • Protein 2g. DIETARY EXCHANGES: 1-1/2 Fruit • 1-1/2 Other Carbohydrate • 1-1/2 Fat.

florentine omelets

READY IN: 20 Minutes ✳ SERVINGS: 4

1 (9 oz.) package frozen spinach, thawed, squeezed to drain

1 (4.5 oz.) jar sliced mushrooms, drained

1/2 teaspoon salt

1/4 teaspoon nutmeg

2 (8 oz.) cartons refrigerated or frozen fat-free egg product, thawed (2 cups)

1 cup shredded reduced-fat Swiss cheese (4 oz.)

Coarse ground black pepper

1 Spray large nonstick skillet with nonstick cooking spray. Heat over medium heat until hot. Add spinach, mushrooms, salt and nutmeg; cook 2 to 3 minutes or until thoroughly heated, stirring occasionally. Remove mixture from skillet; set aside.

2 Let skillet cool 1 minute. Wipe skillet clean with paper towel. Spray skillet again with cooking spray; return to medium heat. Pour half of egg product into skillet; cook 3 to 4 minutes or until set but still moist on top, lifting edges occasionally to allow uncooked egg product to flow to bottom of skillet.

3 Top 1 side of cooked egg product with half of the spinach mixture and half of the cheese. With pancake turner, loosen edge of omelet and fold other half over filling. Cover skillet; cook 1 minute. Remove omelet from skillet.

4 Repeat with remaining egg product, spinach mixture and cheese. Sprinkle each omelet with pepper. To serve, cut each omelet in half.

NUTRITIONAL INFORMATION PER SERVING: Calories 160 • Total Fat 4g • Saturated Fat 3g • Cholesterol 15mg • Sodium 620mg • Total Carbohydrate 7g • Dietary Fiber 2g • Sugars 3g • Protein 24g. DIETARY EXCHANGES: 1 Vegetable • 3 Very Lean Meat • 1/2 Fat.

kitchen tip

To quickly thaw frozen spinach, cut a small slit in the center of the pouch; microwave spinach on High for 2 to 3 minutes or until thawed. Remove spinach from pouch; squeeze dry with paper towels.

BARBARA S. GIBSON
Ft. Wayne, Indiana
Bake-Off® Contest 26, 1975
Grand Prize Winner

easy crescent danish rolls

SERVINGS: 8

1 (8 oz.) package cream cheese, softened
1/2 cup sugar
1 tablespoon lemon juice
2 (8 oz.) cans refrigerated crescent dinner rolls
4 teaspoons preserves or jam

GLAZE
1/2 cup powdered sugar
1 teaspoon vanilla
2 to 3 teaspoons milk

1 Heat oven to 350°F. In small bowl, combine cream cheese, sugar and lemon juice; beat until smooth. Separate dough into 8 rectangles; firmly press perforations to seal. Spread each rectangle with about 2 tablespoons cream cheese mixture. Starting at longer side, roll up each rectangle, firmly pinching edges and ends to seal. Gently stretch each roll to about 10 inches. Coil each roll into a spiral with seam on the inside, tucking end under. Make deep indentation in center of each roll; fill with 1/2 teaspoon preserves. Place on ungreased large cookie sheet.

2 Bake for 20 to 25 minutes or until deep golden brown. In small bowl, blend all glaze ingredients, adding enough milk for desired drizzling consistency. Drizzle over warm rolls.

NUTRITIONAL INFORMATION PER SERVING: Calories 390 • Fat 21g • Sodium 550mg • Total Carbohydrate 45g • Protein 6g.

overnight maple french toast

PREP TIME: 15 Minutes ✳ READY IN: 8 Hours 50 Minutes ✳ SERVINGS: 5

2/3 cup firmly packed brown sugar	1-1/2 cups skim milk
1/2 cup maple-flavored syrup	1 teaspoon vanilla
1 tablespoon margarine or butter	1/8 teaspoon salt
10 (1-inch-thick) slices French bread	1-1/4 cups sliced strawberries
4 eggs	1 to 2 tablespoons powdered sugar

1 Spray 13x9-inch pan with nonstick cooking spray. In medium saucepan, combine brown sugar, syrup and margarine. Bring to a boil over medium heat, stirring constantly. Boil 1 minute.

2 Pour syrup mixture evenly in bottom of sprayed pan. Arrange bread slices in even layer over syrup mixture. Set aside.

3 In large bowl, combine eggs, milk, vanilla and salt; beat with wire whisk until smooth. Pour evenly over bread in pan. Cover; refrigerate at least 8 hours or overnight.

4 To bake, heat oven to 350°F. Uncover pan; bake 30 to 35 minutes or until lightly browned. To serve, top each serving with 1/4 cup sliced strawberries; sprinkle with powdered sugar.

NUTRITIONAL INFORMATION PER SERVING: Calories 530 • Total Fat 10g • Saturated Fat 3g • Cholesterol 175mg • Sodium 700mg • Total Carbohydrate 96g • Dietary Fiber 3g • Sugars 52g • Protein 14g. DIETARY EXCHANGES: 2 Starch • 4-1/2 Fruit • 6-1/2 Other Carbohydrate • 1 Medium-Fat Meat • 1/2 Fat.

cook's notes

Because of the need to prepare this recipe a day in advance, it makes a great dish when hosting overnight guests. While it's baking, accompaniments such as hash browns and bacon can be cooked on the stove so everything will be hot and ready at the same time.

magic marshmallow crescent puffs

magic marshmallow crescent puffs

SERVINGS: 16 Puffs

PUFFS
- 1/4 cup sugar
- 2 tablespoons all-purpose flour
- 1 teaspoon cinnamon
- 2 (8 oz.) cans refrigerated crescent dinner rolls
- 16 large marshmallows
- 1/4 cup margarine or butter, melted

GLAZE
- 1/2 cup powdered sugar
- 1/2 teaspoon vanilla
- 2 to 3 teaspoons milk
- 1/4 cup chopped nuts, if desired

1 Heat oven to 375°F. Spray 16 muffin cups with nonstick cooking spray. In small bowl, combine sugar, flour and cinnamon. Separate dough into 16 triangles. Dip 1 marshmallow in margarine; roll in sugar mixture. Place marshmallow on shortest side of triangle. Roll up starting at shortest side of triangle and rolling to opposite point. Completely cover marshmallow with dough; firmly pinch edges to seal. Dip 1 end in remaining margarine; place margarine side down in sprayed muffin cup. Repeat with remaining marshmallows.

2 Bake for 12 to 15 minutes or until golden brown. (Place foil or cookie sheet on rack below muffin cups to guard against spills.) Remove from oven; cool 1 minute. Remove from muffin cups; place on wire racks set over waxed paper. In small bowl, blend powdered sugar, vanilla and enough milk for desired drizzling consistency. Drizzle over warm rolls. Sprinkle with nuts.

NUTRITIONAL INFORMATION PER SERVING: Calories 200 • Fat 10g • Sodium 250mg • Total Carbohydrate 25g • Protein 2g.

EDNA (HOLMGREN) WALKER
Hopkins, Minnesota
Bake-Off® Contest 20, 1969
Grand Prize Winner

cook's notes

Consider these puffs the little black dress of your recipe collection. The sweet bites are perfect on a brunch buffet, as a party appetizer or even an after-dinner dessert.

bagel 'n brie brunch strata

PREP TIME: 10 Minutes ❄ READY IN: 9 Hours 5 Minutes ❄ SERVINGS: 8

- 6 eggs
- 1-1/4 cups milk
- 3 plain bagels, split, cut into 1/2-inch pieces
- 1 (8 oz.) round Brie cheese, rind removed, cut into 1/2-inch pieces
- 1 (16 oz.) bag frozen bell pepper and onion stir fry, thawed, patted dry with paper towels
- 1 teaspoon dried basil leaves
- 1/2 teaspoon salt
- 1/4 teaspoon pepper

1 Spray 13x9-inch (3-quart) glass baking dish with cooking spray. In large bowl, beat eggs and milk. Beat in all remaining ingredients until well blended. Pour into baking dish. Cover; refrigerate 8 hours or overnight.

2 Heat oven to 350°F. Uncover dish; bake 50 to 55 minutes or until strata is golden brown and center is set.

NUTRITIONAL INFORMATION PER SERVING: Calories 260 • Total Fat 13g • Saturated Fat 7g • Cholesterol 190mg • Sodium 530mg • Total Carbohydrate 20g • Dietary Fiber 2g • Sugars 5g • Protein 15g. DIETARY EXCHANGES: 1 Starch • 1 Other Carbohydrate • 1 Vegetable • 1-1/2 High-Fat Meat.

peach-banana smoothie

READY IN: 5 Minutes ❄ SERVINGS: 2

- 1 medium banana, cut up
- 1 ripe medium peach, pitted, sliced
- 1 (6 oz.) container low-fat peach yogurt
- 1/4 cup orange juice
- 1 teaspoon honey
- 1 cup small ice cubes

1 Combine all ingredients in blender container. Blend mixture for 1 to 2 minutes or until smooth and frothy.

NUTRITIONAL INFORMATION PER SERVING: Calories 190 • Total Fat 1g • Saturated Fat 1g • Cholesterol 4mg • Sodium 50mg • Total Carbohydrate 41g • Dietary Fiber 2g • Sugars 31g • Protein 5g. DIETARY EXCHANGES: 1/2 Starch • 2 Fruit • 3 Other Carbohydrate • 1/2 Low-Fat Milk.

FRAN NEAVOLL
Salem, Oregon
Bake-Off® Contest 37, 1996
Prize Winner

kitchen tip

The secret to preparing baked

goods that raise high in the

oven is starting with room tem-

perature ingredients. To take

the chill from the eggs, place

unbroken eggs in warm water.

Let them stand for several min-

utes. Milk can be microwaved

for a minute or so.

orange-glazed tropical fruit scones

SERVINGS: 8

SCONES
- 2 cups all-purpose flour
- 2 tablespoons sugar
- 3 teaspoons baking powder
- 1 teaspoon salt
- 1-1/2 teaspoons grated orange peel
- 1/4 cup butter or margarine
- 1/3 cup milk
- 2 eggs, beaten
- 1 cup tropical medley dried fruit or dried fruit bits
- 1/2 cup white vanilla chips

GLAZE
- 1 cup powdered sugar
- 2 to 3 tablespoons orange juice

SPREAD
- 1/3 cup apricot-pineapple or apricot preserves

1 Heat oven to 400°F. In large bowl, combine flour, sugar, baking powder, salt and orange peel; mix well. With pastry blender or fork, cut in butter until mixture resembles coarse crumbs. Add milk and eggs; blend well. Stir in dried fruit and white vanilla chips until well mixed.

2 On lightly floured surface, knead dough 6 or 7 times until smooth. Divide dough in half. Pat each half into a 6-inch circle. With floured knife, cut each circle into 4 wedges. Place wedges 2 inches apart on ungreased cookie sheet. Bake for 12 to 16 minutes or until golden brown. Cool 1 minute.

3 Meanwhile, in small bowl, combine powdered sugar and enough orange juice for desired drizzling consistency; blend until smooth. Drizzle mixture over top and sides of each scone. Cool 5 minutes. If desired, split each scone and spread with 2 teaspoons preserves, or serve preserves with scones. Serve warm.

HIGH ALTITUDE (3500-6500 FT): Increase flour to 2 cups plus 2 tablespoons. Bake at 400°F for 14 to 19 minutes or until golden brown.

NUTRITIONAL INFORMATION PER SERVING: Calories 430 • Fat 14g • Sodium 550mg • Total Carbohydrate 70g • Protein 7g.

cook's notes

Bake Mini Cheddar Popovers

early in the day. Loosely cover

the completely cooled popovers

and simply store them at room

temperature. Reheat them at

425°F for 5 minutes before

serving time.

mini cheddar popovers

READY IN: 30 Minutes ✳ SERVINGS: 24 Popovers

- 3 teaspoons oil
- 3/4 cup milk
- 1 egg
- 1 egg white
- 3/4 cup all-purpose flour
- 1/3 cup shredded Cheddar cheese (1-1/3 oz.)

1 Heat oven to 425°F. Spray 24 miniature muffin cups with nonstick cooking spray. Place muffin pans on cookie sheet. Add 1/8 teaspoon oil to bottom of each cup.

2 In small bowl, combine milk, egg and egg white; beat well with wire whisk. Lightly spoon flour into measuring cup; level off. Add flour; beat until smooth. Stir in cheese.

3 Place pans on cookie sheet in oven for several minutes to heat. Remove cookie sheet from oven; quickly divide batter evenly into hot muffin cups, filling each cup about 2/3 full.

4 Bake for 18 to 20 minutes or until popovers are puffed and deep golden brown. Immediately remove from muffin cups. Serve warm.

HIGH ALTITUDE (3500-6500 FT): Do not place muffin pan on cookie sheet; do not add oil to muffin cups. Do not preheat pan. If using dark pan, reduce oven temperature to 400°F.

NUTRITIONAL INFORMATION PER SERVING: Calories 25 • Total Fat 1g • Saturated Fat 1g • Cholesterol 10mg • Sodium 20mg • Total Carbohydrate 3g • Dietary Fiber 0g • Sugars 0g • Protein 1g. DIETARY EXCHANGES: 1/2 Starch • 1/2 Other Carbohydrate.

orange-glazed tropical fruit scones

orange pineapple muffin cake
raspberry-filled jelly doughnuts

orange pineapple muffin cake

SERVINGS: 12

CAKE

1-1/2	cups all-purpose flour
1	cup whole wheat flour
1/3	cup firmly packed brown sugar
3	teaspoons baking powder
1/2	teaspoon baking soda
1/4	teaspoon salt
1	(8-1/4 oz.) can crushed pineapple, drained
1/2	cup orange juice
1/3	cup margarine or butter, melted
1/2	to 1 teaspoon grated orange peel
1	egg, slightly beaten

GLAZE

1/2	cup powdered sugar
1/2	teaspoon grated orange peel
1	to 2 tablespoons orange juice

GARNISH

Fresh orange slices

Mint leaves

1 Heat oven to 400°F. Grease bottom only of 9-inch springform pan or 9-inch round cake pan. In large bowl, combine all-purpose flour, whole wheat flour, brown sugar, baking powder, baking soda and salt; mix well. In medium bowl, combine all remaining cake ingredients; blend well. Add to dry ingredients all at once; stir just until dry ingredients are moistened. Spread dough in greased pan.

2 Bake for 22 to 27 minutes or until light golden brown and toothpick inserted in center comes out clean. Cool 1 minute; remove from pan. In small bowl, combine all glaze ingredients, adding enough orange juice for desired drizzling consistency. Drizzle over warm cake. Garnish with orange slices and mint leaves. Serve warm.

HIGH ALTITUDE (3500-6500 FT): Decrease baking powder to 2 teaspoons. Bake as directed above.

NUTRITIONAL INFORMATION PER SERVING: Calories 200 • Fat 6g • Sodium 230mg • Total Carbohydrate 34g • Protein 4g.

NANCY LABRIE
Rye, New Hampshire
Bake-Off® Contest 34, 1990

cook's notes

Whole wheat flour is a great way to add a little texture and wholesomeness to items such as this citrus-flavored muffin cake. Try it with hot cups of coffee or tea.

raspberry-filled jelly doughnuts

SERVINGS: 10 Doughnuts

6	tablespoons margarine or butter, melted
3/4	cup sugar
3/4	teaspoon cinnamon
1/2	cup raspberry jelly
1	(12 oz.) can refrigerated buttermilk fluffy biscuits

1 Heat oven to 375°F. Place melted margarine in small bowl. In another small bowl, combine sugar and cinnamon; set aside. Stir jelly until smooth. Seal tip of large baster with foil. Remove rubber bulb. Spoon jelly into baster; replace bulb.

2 Prepare and bake biscuits according to package directions. Immediately dip each hot biscuit in melted margarine, coating all sides. Roll in sugar mixture, heavily coating all sides of each biscuit. Remove foil from tip of baster. Insert baster in side of each biscuit; squeeze small amount of jelly into center. (Refill baster as needed.) Serve warm or cold.

NUTRITIONAL INFORMATION PER SERVING: Calories 260 • Fat 12g • Sodium 430mg • Total Carbohydrate 36g • Protein 2g.

TED VIVEIROS
Sunnyvale, California
Bake-Off® Contest 34, 1990

cook's notes

To reheat doughnuts, wrap loosely in foil; heat at 350°F for 5 to 10 minutes.

ELLEN BURR
Truro, Massachusetts
Bake-Off® Contest 34, 1990

Kitchen tip

To toast sesame seed, spread

on baking pan; bake at 400°F

for 3 to 5 minutes or until light

golden brown.

dotted swiss and spinach quiche

SERVINGS: 8

1 refrigerated pie crust (from 15 oz. pkg.)	1/2 cup finely chopped prosciutto ham
2 teaspoons honey mustard or sweet hot mustard	1/2 teaspoon dried thyme leaves
1 teaspoon half-and-half or milk	1/4 cup all-purpose flour
1 tablespoon sesame seed	1/8 teaspoon white pepper or pepper
FILLING	1/8 teaspoon mace or nutmeg
1 tablespoon margarine or butter	1 cup whipping cream
1/4 cup chopped green onions	3 eggs
1 cup frozen cut leaf spinach (from 1-lb. pkg.), thawed, well drained	1 cup shredded Swiss cheese (4 oz.)
	2 tablespoons sesame seed, toasted

1   Prepare pie crust according to package directions for one-crust filled pie using 9-inch pie pan. Brush mustard over bottom of crust. Brush edge of crust with half-and-half. Press 1 tablespoon sesame seed onto crust edge. Place oven rack at lowest position. Heat oven to 400°F.

2   Melt margarine in medium skillet over medium heat. Add green onions; cook until crisp-tender, stirring frequently. Stir in spinach, ham and thyme. Reduce heat; simmer until spinach is thoroughly heated. Remove from heat. Spread spinach mixture over mustard in bottom of crust.

3   In small bowl using wire whisk, combine flour, white pepper, mace, whipping cream and eggs until well blended. Pour egg mixture over spinach layer. Sprinkle with cheese and 2 tablespoons toasted sesame seed.

4   Bake on lowest oven rack for 35 to 40 minutes or until knife inserted in center comes out clean and edges of crust are deep golden brown. Cover edge of pie crust with strips of foil after 15 to 20 minutes of baking to prevent excessive browning. Let stand 5 minutes before serving.

NUTRITIONAL INFORMATION PER SERVING: Calories 380 • Fat 28g • Sodium 340mg • Total Carbohydrate 19g • Protein 12g.

blueberry poppy seed brunch cake

SERVINGS: 8

2/3 cup sugar

1/2 cup margarine or butter, softened

2 teaspoons grated lemon peel

1 egg

1-1/2 cups all-purpose flour

2 tablespoons poppy seed

1/2 teaspoon baking soda

1/4 teaspoon salt

1/2 cup dairy sour cream

FILLING

2 cups fresh or frozen blueberries, thawed, drained on paper towels

1/3 cup sugar

2 teaspoons all-purpose flour

1/4 teaspoon nutmeg

GLAZE

1/3 cup powdered sugar

1 to 2 teaspoons milk

LINDA RAHMAN
Petaluma, California
Bake-Off® Contest 34, 1990
Grand Prize Winner

cook's notes

If you don't have any nutmeg on hand for the cake's filling, try using an equal amount of cinnamon. A tiny dash of lemon peel adds extra flair to the filling, too.

1 Heat oven to 350°F. Grease and flour bottom and sides of 9- or 10-inch springform pan. In large bowl, beat 2/3 cup sugar and margarine until light and fluffy. Add lemon peel and egg; beat 2 minutes at medium speed. In medium bowl, combine 1-1/2 cups flour, poppy seed, baking soda and salt; add to margarine mixture alternately with sour cream. Spread batter over bottom and 1 inch up sides of greased and floured pan, making sure batter on sides is 1/4 inch thick.

2 In medium bowl, combine all filling ingredients; spoon over batter. Bake for 45 to 55 minutes or until crust is golden brown. Cool slightly. Remove sides of pan.

3 In small bowl, combine powdered sugar and enough milk for desired drizzling consistency. Drizzle over warm cake. Serve warm or cool.

HIGH ALTITUDE (3500-6500 FT): Increase flour in cake to 1-3/4 cups. Bake as directed above.

NUTRITIONAL INFORMATION PER SERVING: Calories 380 • Fat 17g • Sodium 300mg • Total Carbohydrate 55g • Protein 5g.

puff pancake with caramelized fruit

puff pancake with caramelized fruit

READY IN: 40 Minutes ✳ SERVINGS: 4

PANCAKE
- 1/2 cup all-purpose flour
- 1/8 teaspoon salt
- 1/2 cup skim milk
- 4 egg whites
- 1 tablespoon margarine or butter

FRUIT MIXTURE
- 1 tablespoon margarine or butter
- 3 medium apples, peeled, cut into 1/4-inch-thick slices
- 2 medium pears, peeled, cut into 1/4-inch-thick slices
- 3/4 cup firmly packed brown sugar
- 1/2 cup sweetened dried cranberries
- 2 teaspoons lemon juice

1 Heat oven to 425°F. Lightly spoon flour into measuring cup; level off. In medium bowl, combine flour, salt, milk and egg whites; beat with wire whisk until smooth.

2 Place 1 tablespoon margarine in 9-inch glass pie pan. Heat in oven for 2 to 4 minutes or just until margarine sizzles. Remove pan from oven; tilt pan to coat bottom with melted margarine. Immediately pour batter into hot pan. Bake for 14 to 18 minutes or until puffed and golden brown.

3 Meanwhile, melt 1 tablespoon margarine in 12-inch nonstick skillet over medium heat. Add apples and pears; cook 2 minutes, stirring occasionally.

4 Add brown sugar, cranberries and lemon juice; mix well. Cook 8 to 10 minutes or until fruit is tender. To serve, pour fruit mixture into pancake. Serve immediately.

NUTRITIONAL INFORMATION PER SERVING: Calories 480 • Total Fat 7g • Saturated Fat 1g • Cholesterol 0mg • Sodium 220mg • Total Carbohydrate 96g • Dietary Fiber 5g • Sugars 73g • Protein 7g. DIETARY EXCHANGES: 2 Starch • 4-1/2 Fruit • 6-1/2 Other Carbohydrate • 1 Fat.

cook's notes

Consider preparing the puff pancake with Anjou pears. Anjou pears are soft, juicy and sweet, making them a perfect choice for caramelizing. When cooking with pears of any kind, choose those that are firm yet ripe.

raspberry-peach iced tea smoothies

READY IN: 5 Minutes ✳ SERVINGS: 4

- 1 cup frozen whole raspberries without syrup (about 4-1/2 oz.)
- 3/4 cup milk
- 2 tablespoons sugar-free low-calorie peach iced tea mix
- 1 (6 oz.) container Yoplait® Original 99% Fat-Free White Chocolate Raspberry Yogurt
- 1 (16 oz.) package frozen peach slices without syrup, reserving and thawing 2 slices for garnish

1 In blender container, combine raspberries, milk, tea mix and yogurt. Cover; blend on high speed until smooth.

2 Add half of the peach slices; cover and blend on high speed until smooth. Add remaining peaches; cover and blend until smooth.

3 Pour mixture into glasses. Cut reserved thawed peach slices in half crosswise. Garnish glasses with peach pieces.

NUTRITIONAL INFORMATION PER SERVING: Calories 120 • Total Fat 2g • Saturated Fat 1g • Cholesterol 5mg • Sodium 55mg • Total Carbohydrate 26g • Dietary Fiber 5g • Sugars 21g • Protein 5g. DIETARY EXCHANGE: 1-1/2 Starch.

JENNIFER PETERSON
Lincoln City, Oregon
Bake-Off® Contest 38, 1998

cook's notes

For additional citrus flavor,

substitute the lemon juice with

orange juice in the coffee cake's

delicious glaze.

lemon-pecan sunburst coffee cake

SERVINGS: 8

COFFEE CAKE
- 1 (1 lb. 1.3 oz.) can large refrigerated flaky biscuits
- 1/4 cup finely chopped pecans
- 1/4 cup sugar
- 2 teaspoons grated lemon peel
- 2 tablespoons butter or margarine, melted

GLAZE
- 1/2 cup powdered sugar
- 1-1/2 oz. cream cheese (from 3-oz. pkg.), softened
- 2-1/2 to 3 teaspoons lemon juice

1 Heat oven to 375°F. Grease 9- or 8-inch round cake pan. Separate dough into 8 biscuits. Place 1 biscuit in center of greased pan. Cut remaining biscuits in half, forming 14 half rounds. Arrange pieces around center biscuit in sunburst pattern with cut sides facing same direction.

2 In small bowl, combine pecans, sugar and lemon peel; mix well. Brush butter over top of biscuits; sprinkle with pecan mixture. Bake for 20 to 25 minutes or until golden brown.

3 Meanwhile, in small bowl, combine all glaze ingredients, adding enough lemon juice for desired drizzling consistency; blend until smooth. Drizzle over the warm coffee cake. Cool 10 minutes. Serve warm.

NUTRITIONAL INFORMATION PER SERVING: Calories 320 • Fat 16g • Sodium 620mg • Total Carbohydrate 40g • Protein 5g.

stuffed blueberry french toast

PREP TIME: 20 Minutes ✳ READY IN: 8 Hours 55 Minutes ✳ SERVINGS: 6

FRENCH TOAST

- 1 (1 lb.) loaf soft French bread (about 18 inches long)
- 1/2 cup honey-walnut cream cheese spread (from 8 oz. container)
- 1/2 cup blueberry preserves
- 4 eggs
- 3/4 cup milk
- 2 tablespoons sugar
- 1/4 teaspoon salt
- 2 tablespoons butter or margarine, melted

TOPPING

- 1/2 cup water
- 2 tablespoons sugar
- 2 teaspoons cornstarch
- 3 cups fresh blueberries

1 Spray 13x9-inch (3-quart) glass baking dish with nonstick cooking spray. Cut bread into 24 (3/4-inch-thick) slices. Spread 12 slices with cream cheese and preserves. Top with remaining bread slices to make 12 sandwiches. Arrange in baking dish, pressing together if necessary to fit.

2 In medium bowl, beat eggs, milk, 2 tablespoons sugar and the salt until well blended. Pour over bread in dish. Let stand 5 minutes. Cover tightly with foil; refrigerate 8 hours or overnight.

3 Heat oven to 400°F. Uncover dish; drizzle with butter. Cover with foil; bake 10 minutes. Uncover dish; bake 15 to 20 minutes longer or until golden brown.

4 Meanwhile, in 2-quart saucepan, mix water, 2 tablespoons sugar and the cornstarch. Stir in 1 cup of the blueberries.

5 Heat to boiling over medium-high heat, stirring constantly. Reduce heat to medium; simmer uncovered 1 to 2 minutes, stirring constantly, until slightly thickened. Remove from heat. Stir in remaining 2 cups blueberries. Serve topping over French toast.

HIGH ALTITUDE (3500-6500 FT): Heat oven to 425°F. In Step 4, simmer cornstarch mixture with 1 cup blueberries 3 to 4 minutes; continue as directed. If using frozen blueberries, when the remaining 2 cups blueberries are stir in, heat 3 to 4 minutes before serving.

NUTRITIONAL INFORMATION PER SERVING: Calories 520 • Total Fat 17g • Saturated Fat 8g • Trans Fat 1 g • Cholesterol 170mg • Sodium 770mg • Total Carbohydrate 78g • Dietary Fiber 4g • Sugars 30g • Protein 14g. DIETARY EXCHANGES: 3 Starch • 1/2 Fruit • 1-1/2 Other Carbohydrate • 1/2 Medium-Fat Meat • 2-1/2 Fat.

cook's notes

Frozen berries can be substituted for the fresh in this recipe. When the remaining 2 cups frozen berries are stirred in, let the mixture stand 3 to 5 minutes to let the berries thaw before serving.

egg and asparagus club sandwiches

egg and asparagus club sandwiches

READY IN: 45 Minutes ✳ SERVINGS: 2

2 eggs	6 (1/2-inch-thick) slices Italian bread
6 oz. fresh asparagus spears	4 slices tomato
2 tablespoons mayonnaise or salad dressing	1 (1-1/2 oz.) slice Swiss cheese, halved
1 tablespoon Dijon mustard	2 leaves leaf lettuce
2 teaspoons chopped fresh dill	

1 Place eggs in small saucepan; add enough cold water to cover eggs by 1 inch. Bring to a boil. Immediately remove from heat; cover and let stand 15 minutes. Drain; rinse with cold water. Place eggs in bowl of ice water; let stand 10 minutes. Peel eggs; slice. Set aside.

2 Meanwhile, wash asparagus; snap off tough stem ends. In large skillet, bring 1 inch lightly salted water to a boil. Arrange asparagus spears evenly in skillet. Cover; cook 4 to 5 minutes or until asparagus is crisp-tender. Drain; rinse with cold water to cool.

3 In small bowl, combine mayonnaise, mustard and dill; blend well. Spread mixture on 1 side of each bread slice. On 2 bread slices, spread side up, layer egg slices and asparagus; top each with second bread slice. Layer tomato slices, cheese and lettuce on each sandwich; top with remaining bread slices, spread side down. If desired, place 2 decorative toothpicks in each sandwich.

NUTRITIONAL INFORMATION PER SERVING: Calories 530 • Total Fat 26g • Saturated Fat 8g • Cholesterol 240mg • Sodium 920mg • Total Carbohydrate 52g • Dietary Fiber 4g • Sugars 7g • Protein 23g. DIETARY EXCHANGES: 3 Starch • 3 Other Carbohydrate • 1 Vegetable • 1-1/2 Medium-Fat Meat • 3-1/2 Fat.

crème caramel chai smoothie

READY IN: 10 Minutes ✳ SERVINGS: 4

SMOOTHIES

2 (6 oz.) containers crème caramel thick & creamy lowfat yogurt	1/2 cup milk
	1 tablespoon caramel-flavored sundae syrup
1 (1.1 oz.) package chai tea latte mix	1-1/2 cups crushed ice
1 ripe medium banana, cut into 1/2-inch-thick slices	**GARNISH**
	4 tablespoons whipped cream topping
	4 teaspoons caramel-flavored sundae syrup

1 In 5-cup blender, place all smoothie ingredients. Cover; blend on Low speed 10 seconds. Scrape down sides of blender. Blend on Medium speed an additional 20 to 30 seconds or until mixture is smooth.

2 Divide mixture evenly into 4 (8 oz.) glasses. Garnish each serving with 1 tablespoon whipped cream topping; drizzle each with 1 teaspoon sundae syrup. Serve immediately.

NUTRITIONAL INFORMATION PER SERVING: Calories 205 • Total Fat 3g • Saturated Fat 2g • Cholesterol 5mg • Sodium 160mg • Total Carbohydrate 39g • Dietary Fiber 1g • Sugars 31g • Protein 6g. DIETARY EXCHANGES: 2 Starch • 1/2 Other Carbohydrate • 1/2 Fat.

sugar-crusted almond pastries

SERVINGS: 24

2 (8 oz.) cans refrigerated crescent dinner rolls	2 cups slivered almonds
1/2 cup butter	1-1/3 cups sugar

1 Heat oven to 375°F. Unroll dough into 2 large rectangles. Place in ungreased 15x10x1-inch baking pan; press over bottom to form crust. Seal perforations.

2 Melt butter in medium saucepan over low heat. Cook and stir 4 to 5 minutes or until light golden brown. Add almonds and sugar; stir to coat. Spoon and spread mixture evenly over dough.

3 Bake for 11 to 16 minutes or until crust is deep golden brown. Cool 30 minutes. Cut into squares. Serve warm or cool.

NUTRITIONAL INFORMATION PER SERVING: Calories 210 • Fat 13g • Sodium 180mg • Total Carbohydrate 20g • Protein 3g.

KARLA KUNOFF
Bloomington, Indiana
Bake-Off® Contest 37, 1996
Prize Winner

Gifts from the Kitchen

Warm hearts this season with a delightful treat you prepared yourself. Cute cookies, fun candies and savory party mixes are just some of the treasures offered here.

p. 172

p. 180

p. 185

p. 177

p. 166

caramel candy bars p. 175
white chocolate thumbprints p. 175
peppermint bark hearts p. 174

holiday spiced nuts

PREP TIME: 30 Minutes ✳ READY IN: 50 Minutes ✳ SERVINGS: 32

1/3 cup butter, cut into pieces	1/4 teaspoon salt
1/3 cup light corn syrup	1-1/2 cups pecan halves
1 teaspoon cardamom	1 cup salted or unsalted whole cashews
1 teaspoon nutmeg	2/3 cup blanched whole almonds

1 Heat oven to 375°F. Line 15x10x1-inch baking pan with heavy-duty foil. Place butter in foil-lined pan. Place pan in oven for 4 to 5 minutes or until butter is melted.

2 Remove pan from oven. Add corn syrup, cardamom, nutmeg and salt; mix well. Add pecans, cashews and almonds; stir to coat. Spread in single layer in pan.

3 Bake at 375°F for 10 to 15 minutes or until nuts are golden brown. Remove from oven; immediately stir mixture. Cool 20 minutes or until completely cooled. Store in tightly covered container.

HIGH ALTITUDE (3500-6500 FT): Decrease butter to 3 tablespoons. Bake as directed above.

NUTRITIONAL INFORMATION PER SERVING: Calories 110 • Total Fat 9g • Saturated Fat 2g • Cholesterol 5mg • Sodium 70mg • Total Carbohydrate 5g • Dietary Fiber 1g • Sugars 2g • Protein 2g. DIETARY EXCHANGES: 1/2 Starch • 1/2 Other Carbohydrate • 1-1/2 Fat.

cherry-almond cups

PREP TIME: 40 Minutes ✳ READY IN: 2 Hours 30 Minutes ✳ SERVINGS: 48 Cups

CRUST

1	cup butter, softened
1/2	cup sugar
1	teaspoon almond extract
1	egg
2	cups all-purpose flour
1/4	teaspoon salt

FILLING

1/2	cup almond paste, chopped
1/4	cup sugar
1	egg

TOPPING

1/4	cup sliced almonds
24	red candied cherries, halved

1 In large bowl, mix butter and 1/2 cup sugar until well blended. Stir in almond extract and 1 egg. Stir in flour and salt until well mixed. Cover; refrigerate 1 hour if necessary for easier handling.

2 Heat oven to 350°F. In small microwavable bowl, microwave almond paste on High 15 to 20 seconds or until warm. Stir in 1/4 cup sugar until well mixed. Add 1 egg; mix well. (Mixture may be lumpy.)

3 Divide crust dough into 4 pieces; divide each into 12 pieces. Roll each piece into ball. Place 1 ball in each of 48 ungreased miniature muffin cups; press in bottom and up sides of each cup.

4 Spoon about 1 teaspoon filling into each cup. Sprinkle or arrange several almond slices and 1 cherry half on top of each cookie.

5 Bake 17 to 22 minutes or until centers are puffed and edges are light golden brown. Cool in pans 5 minutes. With tip of knife, lift cookies from cups. Cool completely, about 10 minutes.

NUTRITIONAL INFORMATION PER SERVING: Calories 90 • Total Fat 5g • Saturated Fat 3g • Cholesterol 20mg • Sodium 60mg • Total Carbohydrate 11g • Dietary Fiber 0g • Sugars 6g • Protein 1g. DIETARY EXCHANGES: 1/2 Starch • 1/2 Other Carbohydrate • 1 Fat.

special touch

A serving platter decorated with a holiday theme makes a great gift, particularly when it comes complete with Cherry-Almond Cups.

cook's notes

If you're multitasking and don't have time to stir the candy coating, try the melting method. Heat the oven to 200°F. After a few minutes, turn the oven off and place the cut-up coating in a heat-resistant bowl in the oven. Periodically, stir the candy coating until it has melted completely.

kitchen tip

Toast walnuts to bring out their best flavor. Spread the nuts in a single layer on a cookie sheet and bake them at 350°F for about 7 minutes or until they are fragrant and golden. Shake the pan once or twice during toasting. Let the nuts cool completely before use.

cranberry and macadamia nut bark

PREP TIME: 10 Minutes ✳ READY IN: 55 Minutes ✳ SERVINGS: 36 Pieces

1 (1 to 1-1/4-lb.) package vanilla-flavored candy coating or almond bark, cut into pieces	1 (3.25 oz.) jar macadamia nuts, coarsely chopped
1/2 cup sweetened dried cranberries or dried cherries	

1 Line cookie sheet with foil. Melt candy coating in medium saucepan over low heat, stirring constantly. Remove from heat.

2 Stir in cranberries and nuts. Spread on foil-lined cookie sheet. Cool 45 minutes or until completely cooled. Break bark into 1-1/2-inch pieces. Store in tightly covered container.

NUTRITIONAL INFORMATION PER SERVING: Calories 110 • Total Fat 7g • Saturated Fat 3g • Cholesterol 3mg • Sodium 15mg • Carbohydrate 11 g • Dietary Fiber 0g • Sugars 11g • Protein 1g. DIETARY EXCHANGES: 1/2 Starch • 1/2 Cholesterol • 1 Other Carbohydrate • 1 Fat.

spiced walnut brittle

PREP TIME: 15 Minutes ✳ READY IN: 45 Minutes ✳ SERVINGS: 20 Pieces

1 cup sugar	1 teaspoon butter
1/2 cup light corn syrup	1 teaspoon vanilla
1 cup coarsely chopped walnuts	1 teaspoon baking soda
1/2 teaspoon cinnamon	

1 Butter cookie sheet. In 8-cup microwavable measuring cup or medium microwavable bowl, combine sugar and corn syrup; mix well. Microwave on High for 4 minutes. Stir; microwave on High for an additional 3 to 5 minutes or until mixture turns light brown.

2 Add the chopped walnuts, cinnamon, butter and vanilla; blend well. Microwave on High for an additional 1 minute.

3 Add baking soda; stir until light and foamy. Pour onto buttered cookie sheet. Cool 30 minutes or until firm. Break brittle into 2-inch pieces. Store in tightly covered container.

NUTRITIONAL INFORMATION PER SERVING: Calories 110 • Total Fat 4g • Saturated Fat 0g • Cholesterol 0mg • Sodium 75mg • Total Carbohydrate 17g • Dietary Fiber 0g • Sugars 13g • Protein 1g. DIETARY EXCHANGES: 1 Fat • 1 Other Carbohydrate • 1 Carbohydrate Choice.

cranberry mustard

READY IN: 10 Minutes ✳ SERVINGS: 24

1/2 cup finely chopped sweetened dried cranberries

2 tablespoons honey

1 (8 oz.) jar Dijon mustard

1 In small microwavable bowl, combine cranberries, honey and 1 tablespoon of the mustard; mix well. Microwave on High for 45 to 60 seconds or until hot. Cool 2 minutes. Add remaining mustard; mix well. Store in refrigerator for up to 1 month.

NUTRITIONAL INFORMATION PER SERVING: Calories 25 • Total Fat 1g • Saturated Fat 0g • Cholesterol 0mg • Sodium 240mg • Total Carbohydrate 4g • Dietary Fiber 0g • Sugars 3g • Protein 0g. DIETARY EXCHANGES: Free • 0 Carbohydrate Choice.

cranberry and macadamia nut bark
spiced walnut brittle

spiced pear chutney
jalapeño cranberry relish

jalapeño cranberry relish

PREP TIME: 35 Minutes ✳ READY IN: 1 Hour 35 Minutes ✳ SERVINGS: 32

1 (12 oz.) bag fresh or frozen cranberries	2/3 cup sugar
1 to 2 jalapeño chiles, quartered, seeded	1/3 cup pomegranate seeds
1 tart apple, peeled, finely chopped	1/3 cup chopped fresh cilantro
1/2 cup finely chopped peeled jicama	1 tablespoon lemon juice
1/2 cup orange marmalade	1 tablespoon Dijon mustard

1 In food processor bowl with metal blade or blender container, coarsely grind cranberries and chiles.

2 In large bowl, mix all remaining ingredients. Stir in cranberry mixture until well blended. Refrigerate at least 1 hour or until chilled.

3 Spoon mixture into decorative crock or jar. Attach a tag to the jar that indicates that the relish may be stored in refrigerator for up to 1 week.

NUTRITIONAL INFORMATION PER SERVING: Calories 40 • Total Fat 0g • Saturated Fat 0g • Cholesterol 0mg • Sodium 15mg • Total Carbohydrate 10g • Dietary Fiber 1g • Sugars 8g • Protein 0g. DIETARY EXCHANGES: 1/2 Cholesterol • 1/2 Other Carbohydrate.

cook's notes

For less mess, peel and seed the juicy pomegranate under a gentle flow of water in the kitchen sink. Remember to attach a tag to your gift of relish, indicating that it must be refrigerated.

spiced pear chutney

PREP TIME: 25 Minutes ✳ READY IN: 4 Hours 10 Minutes ✳ SERVINGS: 32

3/4 cup packed brown sugar	1/4 cup golden or dark raisins
3/4 cup cider vinegar	1 tablespoon grated gingerroot
3 firm large pears, chopped (1-1/2 lb.)	1/2 teaspoon ground cinnamon
1/2 cup chopped onion (1 medium)	1/2 teaspoon ground coriander
1/2 cup chopped red bell pepper	

1 In large saucepan, mix brown sugar and vinegar until well blended. Heat to boiling over medium-high heat. Reduce heat to low; simmer 10 minutes.

2 Stir in all remaining ingredients. Return to a boil. Reduce heat; simmer 45 minutes or until thickened, stirring occasionally. Cool slightly. Refrigerate at least 3 hours or until chilled. Store in tightly covered container in refrigerator for up to 2 weeks.

NUTRITIONAL INFORMATION PER SERVING: Calories 20 • Total Fat 0g • Saturated Fat 0g • Trans Fat 0g • Cholesterol 0mg • Sodium 0mg • Total Carbohydrate 5g • Dietary Fiber 0g • Sugars 4g • Protein 0g. DIETARY EXCHANGE: Free.

cook's notes

A spiced chutney or relish makes a wonderful condiment when served alongside a meaty beef roast or turkey, pork or even lamb.

orange-spice coffee mix

READY IN: 5 Minutes ✳ SERVINGS: 8 to 16

1/2 cup instant espresso coffee granules, or instant coffee granules or crystals	3 teaspoons dried orange peel
1/4 cup sugar	3 teaspoons cinnamon
1/4 cup nondairy creamer	1 teaspoon nutmeg

1 In small bowl, combine all ingredients; mix well. Store in tightly covered container or resealable food storage plastic bag. Write directions (at right) on decorative card; attach to container.

NUTRITIONAL INFORMATION PER SERVING (1 CUP PREPARED COFFEE): Calories 20 • Total Fat 0g • Saturated Fat 0g • Cholesterol 0mg • Sodium 0mg • Total Carbohydrate 5g • Dietary Fiber 0g • Sugars 3g • Protein 0g. DIETARY EXCHANGES: Free • 0 Carbohydrate.

recipe

ORANGE-SPICE COFFEE
Spoon 1 to 2 tablespoons mix into a cup. Add 3/4 cup boiling water; stir until dissolved. If desired, garnish with whipped cream and dash of nutmeg or cinnamon. Serve immediately.

cherry-chocolate truffles

Prep: 40 Minutes ✷ READY IN: 2 Hours 10 Minutes ✷ SERVINGS: 48 Truffles

8 oz. semisweet chocolate, chopped	1/4 cup cherry-flavored brandy or liqueur
4 oz. bittersweet chocolate, chopped	2-1/2 oz. white chocolate baking bar, finely grated
1/4 cup half-and-half	Cocoa, if desired
1 cup butter, softened	48 small (1 inch) paper or foil candy cups
1 cup finely chopped dried red tart cherries	

1 In medium saucepan, combine semisweet chocolate, bittersweet chocolate and half-and-half. Cook over low heat until chocolate is melted, stirring frequently. Remove from heat. Cool for 10 minutes.

2 With wire whisk, beat butter, 1 tablespoon at a time, into chocolate until smooth and creamy. Beat in cherries and liqueur. Cover; refrigerate 1-1/2 hours, stirring twice, or until mixture is thick and can be molded.

3 Spread grated baking bar on sheet of waxed paper. Drop teaspoonfuls of chocolate mixture over grated baking bar; roll each to coat and shape into rough ball. For variety, roll some of the chocolate mixture in cocoa. Place truffles in candy cups. Refrigerate until serving.

NUTRITIONAL INFORMATION PER SERVING: Calories 95 • Total Fat 7g • Saturated Fat 4g • Cholesterol 10mg • Sodium 30mg • Total Carbohydrate 7g • Dietary Fiber 0g • Sugars 6g • Protein 1g. DIETARY EXCHANGES: 1/2 Starch • 1-1/2 Fat.

chocolate shortbread holiday trees

READY IN: 1 Hour 30 Minutes ✷ SERVINGS: 36 Cookies

COOKIES

1	cup powdered sugar
1	cup butter or margarine, softened
2	cups all-purpose flour
1/2	cup unsweetened baking cocoa
1	teaspoon vanilla

TOPPING

1-1/2	cups white vanilla baking chips
2	tablespoons shortening
1/2	cup coarsely chopped round peppermint candies (about 20)

1 Heat oven to 350°F. In large bowl, beat powdered sugar and butter until light and fluffy. Beat in flour, cocoa and vanilla until well blended.

2 On lightly floured surface, roll out dough to 3/8-inch thickness. Cut with floured 1-1/4-inch triangular cookie cutter or cut by hand with sharp knife. Place 1/2 inches apart on ungreased cookie sheets.

3 Bake 10 to 13 minutes or until firm to the touch. Immediately remove from cookie sheets. Line cooled cookie sheets with waxed paper.

4 In small saucepan, place the vanilla baking chips and the shortening; cook and stir over low heat until melted and smooth.

5 To make each tree, dip 1 edge of 1 cookie triangle into melted chip mixture; place on cookie sheet. Dip 1 edge of second triangle into melted chip mixture; place uncoated corner over coated edge of first triangle. Dip 1 edge of third triangle into melted chip mixture; place uncoated corner over coated edge of second triangle to form tree. Repeat with remaining cookie triangles. Drizzle remaining coating over completed trees; sprinkle with chopped candy.

NUTRITIONAL INFORMATION PER SERVING: Calories 140 • Total Fat 8g • Saturated Fat 3g • Cholesterol 0mg • Sodium 65mg • Total Carbohydrate 16g • Dietary Fiber 1g • Sugars 9g • Protein 1g. DIETARY EXCHANGES: 1/2 Starch • 1/2 Cholesterol • 1 Other Carbohydrate • 1-1/2 Fat.

cherry-chocolate truffles

caramel candy bars
white chocolate thumbprints
peppermint bark hearts

peppermint bark hearts

PREP TIME: 20 Minutes ❋ READY IN: 50 Minutes ❋ SERVINGS: 9 Pieces

18 (2-1/2-inch) peppermint candy canes, unwrapped

5 oz. vanilla-flavored candy coating or almond bark, chopped

2 teaspoons crushed peppermint candy canes

1 Line cookie sheet with waxed paper. Arrange candy canes on waxed paper in groups of 2 with ends touching to form heart shapes.

2 Place candy coating in 2-cup microwavable measuring cup. Microwave on Medium for 2 to 3 minutes, stirring once halfway through melting time. Stir until melted and smooth.

3 Spoon or pipe candy coating into centers of hearts to fill spaces. Sprinkle with crushed candy. Cool 30 minutes or until set.

NUTRITIONAL INFORMATION PER SERVING: Calories 190 • Total Fat 5g • Saturated Fat 3g • Cholesterol 3mg • Sodium 25mg • Total Carbohydrate 35g • Dietary Fiber 0g • Sugars 26g • Protein 1g. DIETARY EXCHANGES: 2-1/2 Cholesterol • 2-1/2 Other Carbohydrate • 1 Fat.

white chocolate thumbprints

PREP TIME: 1 Hour 10 Minutes ✳ SERVINGS: 60 Cookies

COOKIES
- 6 oz. white chocolate baking bar, chopped
- 1/2 cup firmly packed dark brown sugar
- 1/2 cup butter, softened
- 1/2 teaspoon vanilla
- 1 egg
- 2 cups all-purpose flour
- 1 teaspoon baking soda
- 1/4 teaspoon salt
- 2/3 cup currant jelly

GLAZE
- 4 oz. white chocolate baking bar
- 1/2 teaspoon shortening

1. Heat oven to 375°F. Spray cookie sheets with nonstick cooking spray. Melt 6 oz. white chocolate baking bar as directed on package. Cool 5 minutes or until slightly cooled.

2. In large bowl, combine brown sugar and butter; beat until light and fluffy. Add vanilla and egg; beat well. Add melted chocolate; mix until well combined. Add flour, baking soda and salt; mix well.

3. Shape dough into 1-inch balls. Place 2 inches apart on sprayed cookie sheets. With thumb or handle of wooden spoon, make indentation in center of each cookie. Spoon jelly into small bowl, stir until smooth. Place 1/2 teaspoon jelly in each indentation. (Cookies will look full.)

4. Bake at 375°F for 5 to 8 minutes or until edges are very light golden brown. Do not overbake. Cool 1 minute; remove from cookie sheets. Cool 10 minutes or until completely cooled.

5. Melt 4 oz. white chocolate baking bar with shortening as directed on package. Cool 5 minutes or until slightly cooled. Place mixture in resealable food storage plastic bag; seal bag. Cut small hole in bottom corner of bag. Squeeze bag to drizzle glaze over cooled cookies.

NUTRITIONAL INFORMATION PER SERVING: Calories 70 • Total Fat 3g • Saturated Fat 2g • Cholesterol 10mg • Sodium 50mg • Total Carbohydrate 10g • Dietary Fiber 0g • Sugars 6g • Protein 1g. DIETARY EXCHANGES: 1/2 Starch • 1/2 Other Carbohydrate • 1/2 Fat.

caramel candy bars

PREP TIME: 35 Minutes ✳ READY IN: 2 Hours ✳ SERVINGS: 32 Bars

BASE AND TOPPING
- 1-1/2 cups firmly packed brown sugar
- 1-1/2 cups butter, softened
- 1 cup quick-cooking rolled oats
- 1 cup crisp rice cereal
- 2 cups all-purpose flour
- 1 teaspoon baking soda
- 1/2 teaspoon salt

FILLING
- 35 vanilla caramels, unwrapped
- 1/3 cup milk

ADDITIONAL TOPPING
- 1 (14 oz.) package red and green candy-coated milk chocolate pieces

1. Heat oven to 350°F. Spray 13x9-inch pan with nonstick cooking spray. In large bowl, combine brown sugar and butter; beat until smooth. Stir in oats and cereal. Add flour, baking soda and salt; mix until well blended. Reserve 3 cups oat mixture for topping. Press remaining mixture in bottom of sprayed pan. Bake at 350°F for 10 minutes.

2. Meanwhile, in small saucepan, combine caramels and milk; heat over low heat until caramels are melted and mixture is smooth, stirring constantly.

3. Remove partially baked base from oven. Sprinkle with 1 cup of the chocolate pieces. Drizzle with caramel mixture, being careful not to let caramel touch sides of pan. Drop reserved oat mixture by heaping teaspoons over caramel mixture. Sprinkle with remaining chocolate pieces.

4. Return to oven; bake an additional 20 to 24 minutes or until center is set and top is golden brown. Cool 1 hour or until completely cooled. Cut into bars.

HIGH ALTITUDE (3500-6500 FT): Decrease butter to 1-1/4 cups. When melting caramels, increase heat to medium-low. Bake bars at 350°F for 26 to 30 minutes.

NUTRITIONAL INFORMATION PER SERVING: Calories 260 • Total Fat 12g • Saturated Fat 8g • Cholesterol 25mg • Sodium 210mg • Total Carbohydrate 36g • Dietary Fiber 1g • Sugars 26g • Protein 2g. DIETARY EXCHANGES: 1 Starch • 1-1/2 Fruit • 2 Fat or 2-1/2 Carbohydrate • 2 Fat.

special touch

Cookie tins are wonderful ways to share White Chocolate Thumbprints with friends and loved ones. Just be sure to separate layers of cookies with a sheet of waxed paper so they don't stick together.

Kitchen tip

To cut neat bars, line the entire pan with foil, leaving a few inches extending over the sides. Grasp the foil and lift cooled bars from the pan; move them to a cutting board. Loosen the foil and use a long serrated knife, sprayed with nonstick cooking spray, to cut uniform bars.

crispy chocolate treats in a jar

READY IN: 10 Minutes ✻ SERVINGS: 20 Cookies

2/3 cup miniature candy-coated semisweet chocolate baking bits	1/2 cup raisins
1 (1-quart) glass jar with cover	1/2 cup peanuts
1 cup Wheat Chex® Cereal	1/3 cup butterscotch chips

1 Place 1/3 cup of the baking bits in resealable food storage plastic bag or wrap in sheet of plastic wrap. Place in bottom of jar, hiding zipper section underneath bag.

2 Layer with 1/2 cup of the cereal squares, the raisins, peanuts, remaining 1/2 cup cereal squares, remaining 1/3 cup baking bits and the butterscotch chips. Press down gently while layering to make sure all ingredients fit. Cover; decorate glass jar as desired. Write directions (at left) on decorative card; attach to glass jar.

NUTRITIONAL INFORMATION PER SERVING: Calories 70 • Total Fat 4g • Saturated Fat 1g • Cholesterol 0mg • Sodium 60mg • Total Carbohydrate /g • Dietary Fiber 1g • Sugars 3g • Protein 2g. DIETARY EXCHANGES: 1/2 Starch • 1/2 Fat • 1/2 Carbohydrate Choice.

nutty holiday popcorn

PREP TIME: 45 Minutes ✻ READY IN: 1 Hour 15 Minutes ✻ SERVINGS: 18

16 cups popped popcorn (4 quarts)	1 (3 oz.) package red or green gelatin
2 cups salted peanuts	3 tablespoons water
1/3 cup butter or margarine	1 tablespoon light corn syrup
1/3 cup sugar	

1 Heat oven to 250°F. Cut two 8x12-inch sheets of foil. Place popcorn and peanuts in 2 ungreased 15x10x1-inch baking pans.

2 In medium saucepan, combine butter, sugar, gelatin, water and corn syrup. Cook over medium-low heat until sugar and gelatin are dissolved, stirring constantly. Using candy thermometer, continue cooking to 255°F (hard-ball stage), stirring constantly. Pour syrup over popcorn and peanuts; stir to coat. (Mixture will be hot.)

3 Bake for 15 minutes. Stir mixture; bake an additional 10 minutes. Remove from oven; immediately turn mixture out of pans onto foil. Cool 30 minutes or until completely cooled. Break into small pieces. Store in tightly covered container.

NUTRITIONAL INFORMATION PER SERVING: Calories 290 • Total Fat 20g • Saturated Fat 6g • Cholesterol 20mg • Sodium 130mg • Total Carbohydrate 21g • Dietary Fiber 3g • Sugars 13g • Protein 6g. DIETARY EXCHANGES: 1-1/2 Starch • 4 Fat • 1-1/2 Carbohydrate Choices.

caramel pecan sauce

PREP TIME: 15 Minutes ✻ READY IN: 30 Minutes ✻ SERVINGS: 21

1 cup firmly packed brown sugar	1/4 cup light corn syrup
1/2 cup chopped pecans	2 tablespoons butter or margarine
1/2 cup whipping cream	1/2 teaspoon vanilla

1 In medium saucepan, combine all ingredients except vanilla; mix well. Bring to a boil over medium heat, stirring occasionally. Boil 3 to 4 minutes, stirring occasionally. Remove from heat.

2 Stir in the vanilla. Cool about 15 minutes or until the Caramel Pecan Sauce is thickened. Store in the refrigerator.

NUTRITIONAL INFORMATION PER SERVING: Calories 80 • Total Fat 4g • Saturated Fat 2g • Cholesterol 8mg • Sodium 15mg • Total Carbohydrate 11g • Dietary Fiber 0g • Sugars 10g • Protein 0g. DIETARY EXCHANGES: 1/2 Fat • 1 Other Carbohydrate • 1 Carbohydrate Choice.

cook's notes

Leave out the pecans in this sweet ice cream topping and consider using walnuts or cashews instead.

layered mint-chocolate fudge

PREP TIME: 50 Minutes ✳ READY IN: 2 Hours 50 Minutes ✳ SERVINGS: 72 Candies

4-1/2 cups sugar
  1/2 cup butter
    1 (12 oz.) can evaporated milk
4-1/2 cups miniature marshmallows
    3 cups semisweet chocolate chips
    2 oz. unsweetened chocolate, cut into pieces

    1 teaspoon vanilla
    1 (6 oz.) package white chocolate baking bar, cut into pieces
  1/8 teaspoon peppermint extract
  1/8 teaspoon green paste icing color
    2 tablespoons chocolate sprinkles

1 Line 15x10x1-inch baking pan with foil so foil extends over sides of pan. Grease foil. In large saucepan, combine sugar, butter and evaporated milk; cook and stir over medium heat until sugar is dissolved. Bring to a full boil, stirring constantly. Boil 5 minutes over medium heat without stirring.

2 Remove from heat. Add marshmallows, stirring constantly until mixture is smooth. Remove 2 cups mixture; place in medium saucepan. Set aside.

3 To mixture in large saucepan, add chocolate chips, unsweetened chocolate and vanilla; stir until chocolate is melted and mixture is smooth. Quickly spread mixture in greased foil-lined pan.

4 Add white chocolate, peppermint extract and green icing color to reserved mixture in saucepan; stir until chocolate is melted and mixture is smooth. Pour evenly over fudge in pan; spread gently to cover. Sprinkle with chocolate sprinkles. Refrigerate 2 hours or until firm. Remove fudge from pan by lifting foil. Cut into squares.

NUTRITIONAL INFORMATION PER SERVING: Calories 140 • Total Fat 5g • Saturated Fat 3g • Cholesterol 5mg • Sodium 25mg • Total Carbohydrate 22g • Dietary Fiber 1g • Sugars 20g • Protein 1g. DIETARY EXCHANGES: 1-1/2 Cholesterol • 1-1/2 Other Carbohydrate • 1 Fat.

Kitchen tip

You can seal cooled fudge in heavy-duty foil or an airtight container and freeze it for up to 2 months. Bring fudge to room temperature before you need to unwrap it.

A Gift For You

Merry Ginger Muffin Mix

Recipes

merry ginger muffin mix
merry ginger muffins

instant chai mix

READY IN: 5 Minutes ✳ SERVINGS: 10

1/2	cup sugar	1	teaspoon coriander
2/3	cup instant tea mix	1/2	teaspoon cloves
2	teaspoons cinnamon		
1	teaspoon nutmeg		

1 In medium bowl, combine all ingredients; mix well. Carefully pour mixture into a decorative, 1-pint food storage container.

2 Write directions for Instant Chai (see recipe below) on a decorative card; attach directions to the storage container.

instant chai

READY IN: 5 Minutes ✳ SERVINGS: 1

2	tablespoons Instant Chai Mix (see recipe above)	1/2	cup boiling water
		1/4	cup warm milk

1 Spoon the Instant Chai Mix into a coffee cup or mug. Pour boiling water over mix; stir to blend. Stir in the warm milk.

NUTRITIONAL INFORMATION PER SERVING: Calories 75 • Total Fat 1g • Saturated Fat 1g • Cholesterol 5mg • Sodium 35mg • Total Carbohydrate 15g • Dietary Fiber 0g • Sugars 14g • Protein 2g. DIETARY EXCHANGE: 1 Other Carbohydrate.

cook's notes

Chai is a sweet, spiced hot tea,

flavored with milk, coriander,

cinnamon, cloves and nutmeg.

merry ginger muffin mix

READY IN: 10 Minutes ✳ SERVINGS: 48 Muffins

6	cups all-purpose flour	3	teaspoons baking powder
2	cups sugar	2	teaspoons salt
1/3	cup instant nonfat dry milk	1	teaspoon ground ginger
1/3	cup finely chopped crystallized ginger	1/3	teaspoon baking soda

1 In large bowl, combine all ingredients; mix well. Store in tightly covered container or resealable food storage plastic bag at room temperature or in a cool, dry place.

2 For gift giving, measure 2 cups of mix by dipping cup into mix and leveling off; place in tightly covered container or resealable food storage plastic bag. Write directions (at right) on decorative card; attach to gift container.

NUTRITIONAL INFORMATION PER SERVING: Calories 165 • Total Fat 7g • Saturated Fat 1g • Cholesterol 20mg • Sodium 115mg • Total Carbohydrate 22g • Dietary Fiber 0g • Sugars 10g • Protein 3g. DIETARY EXCHANGES: 1 Starch • 1 Fat • 1/2 Other Carbohydrate • 1-1/2 Carbohydrate Choices.

recipe

MERRY GINGER MUFFINS

Heat oven to 400°F. Line 12 medium muffin cups with paper baking cups. Combine muffin mix from container, 2/3 cup water, 1/3 cup oil and 1 slightly beaten egg in medium bowl; stir just until dry ingredients are moistened. Do not overmix. Divide evenly into paper-lined muffin cups. Bake 15 to 17 minutes or until toothpick inserted in center comes out clean. Immediately remove from pan. Serve warm.

Christmas Cookies & Bars

Santa's favorite treats could not be more delectable than those found in this classic collection. Enjoy a few over coffee or share them at friendly get-togethers.

p. 198

p. 213

p. 197

p. 206

p. 199

pistachio shortbread trees p. 218

white chocolate-raspberry bars

PREP TIME: 20 Minutes ✳ READY IN: 2 Hours ✳ SERVINGS: 48 Bars

1   (16.5 oz.) roll refrigerated sugar cookie dough

1-1/4 cups white chocolate chunks or white vanilla chips

1   (12 oz.) jar raspberry jam or preserves (3/4 cup)

1   teaspoon vegetable oil

1 Heat oven to 350°F. Break up cookie dough into ungreased 13x9-inch pan. With floured fingers, press dough evenly in bottom of pan to form crust. Sprinkle 1 cup of the white chocolate chunks over crust; press firmly into dough. Bake for 16 to 20 minutes or until light golden brown.

2 Remove partially baked crust from oven. Spread jam evenly over crust. Return to oven; bake an additional 10 minutes. Cool 1 hour or until completely cooled.

3 In small resealable plastic bag, combine remaining 1/4 cup white chocolate chunks and the oil; partially seal bag. Microwave on High for 30 seconds. Squeeze bag until chunks are smooth. If necessary, microwave an additional 15 to 30 seconds.

4 Cut small hole in bottom corner of bag. Squeeze bag gently to drizzle white chocolate over bars. Refrigerate about 20 minutes or until chocolate is set. Cut into bars. Serve at room temperature.

NUTRITIONAL INFORMATION PER SERVING: Calories 105 • Total Fat 4g • Saturated Fat 2g • Cholesterol 0mg • Sodium 45mg • Total Carbohydrate 16g • Dietary Fiber 0g • Sugars 12g • Protein 1g. DIETARY EXCHANGES: 1 Fat • 1 Other Carbohydrate • 1 Carbohydrate Choice.

meringue-topped chocolate chip bars

PREP TIME: 20 Minutes ✳ READY IN: 1 Hour 10 Minutes ✳ SERVINGS: 36 Bars

1 (16.5 oz.) roll refrigerated chocolate chip cookie dough

3 egg whites

1 teaspoon vanilla

1/2 cup packed brown sugar

1/2 cup finely chopped nuts

1 Heat oven to 350°F. In ungreased 13x9-inch pan, break up cookie dough; press evenly in pan to form crust. Bake 10 to 12 minutes or until golden brown.

2 Meanwhile, in large bowl with electric mixer, beat egg whites and vanilla on High speed until foamy. Gradually beat in brown sugar until stiff peaks form.

3 Remove partially baked crust from oven. Spread meringue over warm crust, sealing to edge of pan. Sprinkle nuts evenly over meringue.

4 Return to oven; bake 10 to 15 minutes longer or until meringue is golden brown. Cool completely on wire rack, about 30 minutes. Cut into bars. Store in refrigerator.

HIGH ALTITUDE (3500-6500 FT): Increase first bake time to 12 to 14 minutes at 350°F. Increase second bake time to 15 to 20 minutes.

NUTRITIONAL INFORMATION PER SERVING: Calories 95 • Total Fat 4g • Saturated Fat 1g • Cholesterol 0mg • Sodium 60mg • Total Carbohydrate 13g • Dietary Fiber 0g • Sugars 8g • Protein 2g. DIETARY EXCHANGES: 1 Starch • 1/2 Fat.

kitchen tip

While meringue is typically made by beating granulated sugar into stiffly beaten egg whites, brown sugar lends a wonderful, caramelized flavor to meringue toppings.

christmas ornament cookies

READY IN: 1 Hour ✳ SERVINGS: 24 Cookies

1 (16.5 oz.) roll refrigerated sugar cookie dough	1 tablespoon red sugar
1 egg white, beaten	1 tablespoon green sugar
	12 small gumdrops, cut in half

1 Heat oven to 350°F. Cut cookie dough lengthwise into 3 long slices; separate slices on work surface with rounded sides down. Lightly brush all cut surfaces with beaten egg white.

2 Sprinkle egg white area of 1 rounded slice with red sugar. Place middle slice on top; sprinkle with green sugar. Place remaining rounded slice, egg white side down, on top; press firmly and if necessary, reshape into roll.

3 Cut roll into 24 slices; place 1 inch apart on ungreased cookie sheets. Bake 9 to 11 minutes or until edges are light golden brown.

4 Immediately press gumdrop half onto outer edge of each cookie to resemble ornament hanger; remove from cookie sheets.

NUTRITIONAL INFORMATION PER SERVING: Calories 100 • Total Fat 3g • Saturated Fat 1g • Cholesterol 0mg • Sodium 75mg • Total Carbohydrate 17g • Dietary Fiber 0g • Sugars 11g • Protein 1g. DIETARY EXCHANGES: 1 Other Carbohydrate • 1/2 Fat.

cook's notes

Place the long cookie slices on a waxed paper-lined counter to make cleanup easier.

chocolate mint brownies

PREP TIME: 25 Minutes ✳ READY IN: 3 Hours 25 Minutes ✳ SERVINGS: 36 Brownies

BROWNIES

1 (19.8 oz.) box fudge brownie mix	1/4 cup milk
Water, vegetable oil and eggs called for on brownie mix box	1 teaspoon vanilla
	1/4 teaspoon peppermint extract
	8 to 10 drops green food color

FILLING

4 cups powdered sugar
1 (3 oz.) package cream cheese, softened
1/4 cup butter or margarine, softened

FROSTING

1 cup semisweet chocolate chips (6 oz.)
1/4 cup butter or margarine, softened
1/4 cup whipping cream

1 Heat oven to 350°F. Grease bottom only of 13x9-inch pan with shortening or nonstick cooking spray. Make and bake brownie mix as directed on box for 13x9-inch pan using water, oil and eggs. Cool completely, about 1 hour.

2 In large bowl, beat all filling ingredients on Medium speed until smooth. Spread over cooled brownies. Refrigerate about 1 hour before frosting.

3 In small saucepan, melt chocolate chips, 1/4 cup butter and the cream over low heat, stirring constantly. Remove from heat; cool 10 minutes. Pour over filling. Refrigerate about 1 hour or until chocolate is set. Cut into bars. Store in refrigerator.

HIGH ALTITUDE (3500-6500 FT): Follow High Altitude brownie mix directions for 13x9-inch pan.

NUTRITIONAL INFORMATION PER SERVING: Calories 210 • Total Fat 10g • Saturated Fat 4g • Trans Fat 0g • Cholesterol 25mg • Sodium 80mg • Total Carbohydrate 29g • Dietary Fiber 0g • Sugars 24g • Protein 1g. DIETARY EXCHANGES: 1/2 Starch • 1-1/2 Other Carbohydrate • 2 Fat.

gingerbread cookie wreath

READY IN: 1 Hour 40 Minutes ✳ SERVINGS: 16 (1 Wreath)

4 tablespoons all-purpose flour
1 (16.5 oz.) roll refrigerated gingerbread cookie dough
2 cups powdered sugar

3 to 4 tablespoons water or milk
   Food color
   Assorted small candy sprinkles, edible glitter and/or decorator sugar

1   Heat oven to 350°F. Line cookie sheet with parchment paper. Draw 10-inch circle on paper. Turn paper over so mark is on underside; line will show through.

2   Sprinkle 2 tablespoons of the flour on work surface. Shape 1/3 of the cookie dough into ball; press into flour. Keep remaining dough refrigerated. Press dough to form 8-inch round, turning and coating with flour frequently. Place in center of circle on paper-lined cookie sheet. Roll to form 10-inch round, about 1/4 inch thick. If necessary, trim uneven edges. Cut 4-inch round from center; remove smaller dough round and set aside for cutout cookies.

3   Bake wreath for 7 to 9 minutes or until light golden brown. Remove from cookie sheet; place on wire rack. Cool 10 minutes or until completely cooled.

4   Meanwhile, roll half of remaining dough on floured surface to 1/4-inch thickness. With 1-1/2- to 3-inch Christmas cookie cutters, cut out shapes. Place on ungreased cookie sheets. Repeat with remaining half of dough, dough scraps and flour.

5   Bake shapes at 350°F for 7 to 9 minutes or until light golden brown. Remove from cookie sheets; place on wire racks. Cool 10 minutes or until completely cooled.

6   In small bowl, blend powdered sugar and enough water for desired spreading consistency. Divide frosting into small bowls; add food color as desired. Frost and decorate cookies as desired. With dabs of frosting, attach cutout cookies to cookie wreath, allowing 1 layer to set before adding another layer.

NUTRITIONAL INFORMATION PER SERVING: Calories 205 • Total Fat 7g • Saturated Fat 2g • Cholesterol 10mg • Sodium 105mg • Total Carbohydrate 34g • Dietary Fiber 0g • Sugars 23g • Protein 1g. DIETARY EXCHANGES: 2 Other Carbohydrate • 1-1/2 Fat.

raspberry-filled white chocolate bars

SERVINGS: 24 Bars

MARK BOCIANSKI
Wheaton, Illinois
Bake-Off® Contest 34, 1990

1/2 cup margarine or butter	1 cup all-purpose flour
1 (12 oz.) package white vanilla chips or 2 (6 oz.) packages white baking bars, chopped (2 cups)	1/2 teaspoon salt
	1 teaspoon amaretto or almond extract
2 eggs	1/2 cup raspberry spreadable fruit or jam
1/2 cup sugar	1/4 cup sliced almonds, toasted

1 Heat oven to 325°F. Grease and flour 9-inch square pan or 8-inch square baking dish. Melt margarine in small saucepan over low heat. Remove from heat. Add 1 cup of the white vanilla chips. Let stand; do not stir.

2 In large bowl, beat eggs until foamy. Gradually add sugar, beating at High speed until lemon-colored. Stir in white vanilla chip mixture. Add flour, salt and amaretto; mix at Low speed until just combined. Spread half (about 1 cup) of batter in greased and floured pan. Bake for 15 to 20 minutes or until light golden brown.

3 Stir remaining 1 cup white vanilla chips into remaining half of batter; set aside. Melt spreadable fruit in small saucepan over low heat. Spread evenly over warm, partially baked crust. Gently spoon teaspoonfuls of remaining batter over fruit spread. (Some fruit spread may show through batter.) Sprinkle with almonds.

4 Return to oven; bake an additional 25 to 35 minutes or until toothpick inserted in center comes out clean. Cool completely. Cut into bars.

NUTRITIONAL INFORMATION PER SERVING: Calories 180 • Fat 9g • Sodium 105mg • Total Carbohydrate 22g • Protein 2g.

maple nut goodie bars

PREP TIME: 50 Minutes ✸ READY IN: 4 Hours 20 Minutes ✸ SERVINGS: 64 Bars

- 1 (12 oz.) bag semisweet chocolate chips (2 cups)
- 1 (11.5 oz.) bag milk chocolate chips (2 cups)
- 2 cups butter or margarine
- 1 cup peanut butter
- 1 (12 oz.) can cocktail peanuts (2-1/2 cups)

- 1/2 cup evaporated milk
- 1 (4-serving size) box vanilla pudding and pie filling mix (not instant)
- 1 (2 lb.) bag powdered sugar (7-1/2 cups)
- 2 teaspoons maple flavor

1 Line 15x10x1-inch pan with foil. Butter or spray foil with nonstick cooking spray. In large saucepan, melt chocolate chips and 1 cup of the butter over low heat, stirring frequently. Remove saucepan from heat. Stir in peanut butter until well blended. Spread half of mixture into pan. Freeze 10 minutes or until set. Place pan in refrigerator.

2 Meanwhile, stir peanuts into remaining chocolate mixture. Set aside. Melt remaining 1 cup butter in large saucepan over low heat. Gradually stir in evaporated milk. Stir in pudding mix. Cook until mixture is slightly thickened, stirring constantly. Do not boil.

3 Remove saucepan from heat. Stir in powdered sugar and maple flavor until well blended. Cool slightly, about 10 minutes. Carefully spread pudding mixture over chilled chocolate layer. Refrigerate 30 minutes.

4 Stir reserved chocolate-peanut mixture. Drop by spoonfuls onto chilled pudding layer; spread to cover. Refrigerate at least 3 hours or until firm. For bars, cut into 8 rows by 8 rows. Store in refrigerator.

NUTRITIONAL INFORMATION PER SERVING: Calories 230 • Total Fat 14g • Saturated Fat 4g • Cholesterol 0mg • Sodium 125mg • Total Carbohydrate 24g • Dietary Fiber 1g • Sugars 21g • Protein 3g. DIETARY EXCHANGES: 1-1/2 Fruit • 1-1/2 Other Carbohydrate • 1/2 High-Fat Meat • 2 Fat.

snow-covered gingerbread stars

PREP TIME: 15 Minutes ✸ READY IN: 55 Minutes ✸ SERVINGS: 24 Cookies

- 1 (16.5 oz.) roll refrigerated gingerbread cookie dough
- 1/2 to 3/4 cup all-purpose flour

- 1 cup white vanilla chips
- 2 tablespoons shortening

1 Heat oven to 350°F. Remove half of cookie dough from wrapper; refrigerate remaining dough until needed.

2 Sprinkle about 1/4 cup of the flour onto work surface; coat sides of half of dough with flour. With rolling pin, roll out dough to 1/4-inch thickness, adding additional flour as needed to prevent sticking.

3 With floured 3-inch star-shaped cookie cutter, cut out dough stars. Gently brush excess flour from stars; place 2 inches apart on ungreased cookie sheet. Repeat with remaining half of dough.

4 Bake 7 to 9 minutes or until light golden brown. Cool 1 minute; remove from cookie sheet and place on wire racks. Cool completely, about 15 minutes.

5 In 1-quart saucepan, heat vanilla chips and shortening over low heat about 4 minutes, stirring occasionally, until chips are melted and smooth. Remove from heat. Dip half of each cookie into vanilla coating, allowing excess to drip off. Place cookies on waxed paper-lined cookie sheet; refrigerate until vanilla coating is set, about 30 minutes.

NUTRITIONAL INFORMATION PER SERVING: Calories 175 • Total Fat 9g • Saturated Fat 4g • Cholesterol 10mg • Sodium 80mg • Total Carbohydrate 21g • Dietary Fiber 0g • Sugars 13g • Protein 2g. DIETARY EXCHANGES: 1-1/2 Other Carbohydrate • 2 Fat.

maple nut goodie bars

chocolate-caramel tartlets

chocolate-caramel tartlets

READY IN: 1 Hour 5 Minutes ✳ SERVINGS: 24 Tartlets

CRUST
- 1/2 cup butter, softened
- 1 (3 oz.) package cream cheese, softened
- 1-1/4 cups all-purpose flour
- 1 tablespoon sugar

FILLING
- 1/2 cup sugar
- 4 teaspoons water
- 1 tablespoon butter
- 1/3 cup whipping cream
- 1/4 cup semisweet chocolate chips
- 1 oz. vanilla-flavored candy coating, if desired

1 Heat oven to 450°F. In large bowl, combine all crust ingredients; mix with electric mixer at Low speed until well combined. Divide dough into 24 equal pieces; roll into balls. Press each in bottom and up sides of ungreased miniature muffin cup.

2 Bake for 7 to 9 minutes or until edges are light golden brown. Remove crusts from pans; place on wire racks. Cool 15 minutes or until completely cooled.

3 In heavy 1-1/2-quart saucepan, combine 1/2 cup sugar and water; mix well. With pastry brush dipped in water, brush any sugar down sides of saucepan. Without stirring, cook over medium-high heat for 10 to 12 minutes or until mixture turns dark golden brown. (If sugar mixture is not cooking, gently swirl mixture in saucepan.) Remove from heat. While stirring constantly, add 1 tablespoon butter and whipping cream; stir until bubbling stops. Return saucepan to low heat; cook and stir until mixture is smooth.

4 Spoon 1/2 teaspoon caramel mixture into each cooled baked crust. Stir chocolate chips into remaining caramel mixture until melted and smooth. If mixture thickens, cook and stir over low heat until smooth. Spoon about 1 teaspoon chocolate filling into each crust.

5 Chop candy coating; place in microwavable small bowl. Microwave on High for 30 seconds; stir until melted and smooth. If necessary, microwave an additional 10 seconds. Place in heavy-duty food storage plastic bag; cut tiny hole in one corner. On waxed paper, pipe 24 (1-inch) tree shapes. Let stand until set. Garnish each tartlet with a tree.

HIGH ALTITUDE (3500-6500 FT): Bake at 450°F for 8 to 10 minutes.

NUTRITIONAL INFORMATION PER SERVING: Calories 110 • Total Fat 7g • Saturated Fat 4g • Cholesterol 19mg • Sodium 40mg • Total Carbohydrate 11g • Dietary Fiber 0g • Sugars 6g • Protein 1g. DIETARY EXCHANGES: 1 Other Carbohydrate • 1-1/2 Fat.

cook's notes

Feel free to pipe the candy coating into tiny star shapes instead of trees if you'd like.

candy bar brownies

SERVINGS: 25 Brownies

- 2 (1.9 oz.) chocolate-covered coconut candy bars
- 1/2 cup shortening
- 1 cup sugar
- 1 teaspoon vanilla
- 2 eggs
- 1 cup all-purpose flour
- 1/2 teaspoon salt
- 1/2 cup chopped nuts

1 Heat oven to 350°F. Grease 9-inch square pan. In medium saucepan over low heat, melt candy bars and shortening, stirring occasionally until chocolate and shortening are melted. Add sugar and vanilla; blend well. Add eggs 1 at a time, beating well after each addition. Stir in flour, salt and nuts; mix well. Spread in greased pan.

2 Bake for 25 to 35 minutes or until top springs back when touched lightly in center. Cool completely; cut into bars.

HIGH ALTITUDE (3500-6500 FT): Decrease sugar to 3/4 cup. Bake as directed above.

NUTRITIONAL INFORMATION PER SERVING: Calories 120 • Fat 7g • Sodium 55mg • Total Carbohydrate 14g • Protein 2g.

ELIZABETH SEDENSKY
Cleveland, Ohio
Bake-Off® Contest 6, 1954

cherry-raspberry swirls

PREP TIME: 1 Hour 15 Minutes ✳ READY IN: 5 Hours 10 Minutes ✳ SERVINGS: 32 Cookies

FILLING
- 1 cup dried cherries
- 1/2 cup seedless raspberry jam
- 1/4 cup water

COOKIES
- 3/4 cup firmly packed brown sugar

- 1/2 cup butter, softened
- 1 egg
- 1-3/4 cups all-purpose flour
- 1 teaspoon baking powder
- 1 teaspoon grated lemon peel
- 1/4 teaspoon salt

1. In small saucepan, combine all filling ingredients; mix well. Bring to a boil over medium heat. Cover; simmer 10 minutes. Place mixture in food processor bowl with metal blade or blender container; process until pureed. Refrigerate 1 hour or until thoroughly chilled.

2. Meanwhile, in large bowl, combine brown sugar, butter and egg; beat until light and fluffy. Add all remaining cookie ingredients; mix well. Cover with plastic wrap; refrigerate 1 hour for easier handling.

3. Roll dough on floured pastry cloth to form 16x10-inch rectangle. Spoon and spread cooled filling evenly over dough to within 1/2 inch of edges. Starting with 16-inch side, roll up jelly-roll fashion. Cut in half to form two 8-inch rolls. Wrap each roll in plastic wrap or waxed paper; freeze 2 hours or until firm.

4. Heat oven to 375°F. Generously spray cookie sheets with nonstick cooking spray. With sharp knife, cut each roll of dough into 16 slices, each about 1/2 inch thick. Place slices 2 inches apart on sprayed cookie sheets.

5. Bake for 9 to 13 minutes or until edges are light golden brown. Immediately remove from the cookie sheets.

HIGH ALTITUDE (3500-6500 FT): Bake at 375°F for 10 to 14 minutes.

NUTRITIONAL INFORMATION PER SERVING: Calories 100 • Total Fat 3g • Saturated Fat 2g • Cholesterol 15mg • Sodium 65mg • Total Carbohydrate 17g • Dietary Fiber 0g • Sugars 10g • Protein 1g. DIETARY EXCHANGES: 1/2 Starch • 1/2 Fruit • 1 Other Carbohydrate • 1/2 Fat.

trimmed tree cookies

PREP TIME: 2 Hours 30 Minutes ✳ READY IN: 3 Hours 30 Minutes ✳ SERVINGS: 48 Cookies

COOKIE DOUGH
- 2/3 cup sugar
- 2/3 cup butter, softened
- 1 teaspoon vanilla
- 1 egg
- 1-3/4 cups all-purpose flour
- 1 teaspoon baking powder
- 1/2 teaspoon salt

TOPPING DOUGH
- 1/4 cup powdered sugar
- 1/4 cup butter, softened
- 3/4 cup all-purpose flour
- 6 tablespoons milk
- Green, yellow and red food color

1 In large bowl, combine sugar, 2/3 cup butter, vanilla and egg; beat until light and fluffy. Add 1-3/4 cups flour, baking powder and salt; mix until well blended. Cover with plastic wrap; refrigerate 1 hour for easier handling.

2 Meanwhile, in small bowl, combine powdered sugar and 1/4 cup butter; mix well. Add 3/4 cup flour and milk; mix at Low speed just until blended. Add additional flour if necessary to reduce stickiness. To half of topping dough, add green food color; mix well. Divide remaining topping dough in half. Add yellow food color to one half; mix well. Add red food color to other half; mix well. Place 3 topping doughs in separate decorating bags fitted with desired tips or resealable food storage plastic bags with small hole cut in one bottom corner of each.

3 Heat oven to 375°F. On lightly flowered surface, roll out half of cookie dough at a time to 1/8-inch thickness. Keep remaining dough refrigerated. Cut with floured tree-shaped cookie cutter. Place 1 inch apart on ungreased cookie sheets. Decorate cookies as desired with the colored dough in bags.

4 Bake for 6 to 9 minutes or until firm and edges are light golden brown. Immediately remove from cookie sheets. Cool completely.

NUTRITIONAL INFORMATION PER SERVING: Calories 70 • Total Fat 4g • Saturated Fat 2g • Cholesterol 15mg • Sodium 70mg • Total Carbohydrate 8g • Dietary Fiber 0g • Sugars 4g • Protein 1g. DIETARY EXCHANGES: 1/2 Fruit • 1/2 Other Carbohydrate • 1 Fat.

cook's notes

To easily mix food color into dough, place the dough in a food storage plastic bag with the food color and knead it. To decorate the cookies, if you don't have pastry bags, you can snip away a corner of a food storage plastic bag and place a pastry tip in the corner of the bag.

iced lemon cookies

iced lemon cookies

PREP TIME: 1 Hour 20 Minutes ✹ READY IN: 3 Hours 20 Minutes ✹ SERVINGS: 60 Cookies

COOKIES
- 1/2 cup butter, softened
- 1/2 cup granulated sugar
- 1/2 cup powdered sugar
- 1 egg
- 1/2 cup vegetable oil
- 1 teaspoon grated lemon peel
- 2-1/4 cups all-purpose flour
- 1/2 teaspoon baking soda
- 1/2 teaspoon cream of tartar
- 1/4 teaspoon salt
- 3 tablespoons granulated sugar

TOPPING
- 2 cups powdered sugar
- 3 to 4 tablespoons fresh lemon juice
- 3/4 cup coarsely chopped shelled pistachios

1 In large bowl, beat butter, 1/2 cup granulated sugar and 1/2 cup powdered sugar until light and fluffy. Beat in egg, oil and lemon peel until well blended. Beat in flour, baking soda, cream of tartar and salt until well blended. Cover dough with plastic wrap; refrigerate 2 hours for easier handling.

2 Heat oven to 325°F. Shape dough into 1-inch balls. Place 2 inches apart on ungreased cookie sheets. Flatten cookies into 2-inch rounds with bottom of glass dipped in 3 tablespoons granulated sugar.

3 Bake 9 to 11 minutes or until edges begin to set and cookies are light golden brown. Cool 2 minutes. Remove from cookie sheets to cooling racks. Cool completely, about 10 minutes.

4 Meanwhile, in small bowl, blend 2 cups powdered sugar and enough lemon juice for desired spreading consistency. Spread the frosting on cooled cookies. Sprinkle pistachios on frosting before it sets.

NUTRITIONAL INFORMATION PER SERVING: Calories 80 • Total Fat 4g • Saturated Fat 1g • Cholesterol 10mg • Sodium 35mg • Total Carbohydrate 11g • Dietary Fiber 0g • Sugars 7g • Protein 1g. DIETARY EXCHANGES: 1/2 Fruit • 1/2 Other Carbohydrate • 1 Fat.

cook's notes

These delicate lemon cookies can be topped with chopped pecans instead of pistachios, but the pistachios add a nice green color.

chocolate chip fruitcake bars

PREP TIME: 10 Minutes ✹ READY IN: 1 Hour 40 Minutes ✹ SERVINGS: 24 Bars

- 1 (16.5 oz.) roll refrigerated chocolate chip cookie dough
- 1/2 cup diced mixed candied fruit
- 1 tablespoon all-purpose flour
- 1/4 cup seedless raspberry jam
- Powdered sugar, if desired

1 Heat oven to 350°F. Spray 8-inch square pan with nonstick cooking spray. Break up 2/3 of cookie dough into sprayed pan. With floured fingers, press dough evenly in bottom of pan to form crust.

2 Break up remaining 1/3 of dough into small bowl. Add candied fruit and flour; mix well. Spread jam over dough in pan. Sprinkle with candied fruit mixture; press lightly into jam.

3 Bake for 25 to 30 minutes or until deep golden brown. Cool 1 hour or until completely cooled. Lightly dust with powdered sugar. Cut into bars.

NUTRITIONAL INFORMATION PER SERVING: Calories 135 • Total Fat 5 • Saturated Fat 2g • Cholesterol 10mg • Sodium 95mg • Total Carbohydrate 20g • Dietary Fiber 0g • Sugars 8g • Protein 2g. DIETARY EXCHANGES: 1 Starch • 1 Fat • 1 Carbohydrate Choice.

cook's notes

Line the pan with foil, allowing enough foil to make the bars easy to lift and transfer to a flat surface for cutting.

orange-spice pumpkin bars with browned butter frosting

PREP TIME: 20 Minutes ✳ READY IN: 2 Hours 5 Minutes ✳ SERVINGS: 48 Bars

BARS

2	cups all-purpose flour
1-1/2	cups sugar
2	teaspoons baking powder
1	teaspoon baking soda
2	teaspoons pumpkin pie spice
2	teaspoons grated orange peel
1/4	teaspoon salt
1/2	cup oil
1/2	cup orange juice
1	(15 oz.) can pumpkin
2	eggs

FROSTING

1/3	cup butter (do not use margarine)
2	cups powdered sugar
1/2	teaspoon vanilla
2	to 4 tablespoons milk

1 Heat oven to 350°F. Grease and flour 15x10x1-inch baking pan. In large bowl, combine all bar ingredients; beat at Low speed until moistened. Beat 2 minutes at Medium speed. Spread in greased and floured pan.

2 Bake for 23 to 27 minutes or until toothpick inserted in center comes out clean. Cool 1 hour or until completely cooled.

3 Heat butter in medium saucepan over medium heat until light golden brown, stirring constantly. Remove from heat. Stir in powdered sugar, vanilla and enough milk for desired spreading consistency; blend until smooth. Immediately spread frosting over cooled bars. Refrigerate 15 minutes or until set. Cut into bars. If desired, garnish with orange peel strips.

NUTRITIONAL INFORMATION PER SERVING: Calories 100 • Total Fat 4g • Saturated Fat 1g • Cholesterol 15mg • Sodium 70mg • Total Carbohydrate 16g • Dietary Fiber 0g • Sugars 12g • Protein 1g. DIETARY EXCHANGES: 1/2 Starch • 1/2 Other Carbohydrate • 1/2 Fat.

gingerbread cutouts

PREP TIME: 1 Hour 50 Minutes ✳ READY IN: 2 Hours 50 Minutes ✳ SERVINGS: 120 Cookies

1-1/2	cups sugar
1	cup butter, softened
3	tablespoons molasses
1	egg
2	tablespoons water or milk
3-1/4	cups all-purpose flour
2	teaspoons baking soda
2	teaspoons ground cinnamon
1-1/2	teaspoons ground ginger

1/2	teaspoon salt
1/2	teaspoon ground cardamom
1/2	teaspoon ground cloves
	Dried currants, if desired
1/2	cup sugar
	Vanilla creamy ready-to-spread frosting, if desired
	Assorted candies, if desired

1 In a large bowl, beat 1-1/2 cups sugar, the butter and molasses until light and fluffy. Beat in egg and water. Stir in flour and next six ingredients to form a smooth dough. Cover with plastic wrap; refrigerate 1 hour for easier handling.

2 Heat oven to 350°F. On floured surface, roll out 1/3 of dough at a time to 1/8-inch thickness. (Keep remaining dough refrigerated.) Cut with floured 2-1/2-inch gingerbread boy or girl cookie cutter. Place 1 inch apart on ungreased cookie sheets. If desired, decorate cookie cutouts with currant for eyes and buttons.

3 Bake 9 to 11 minutes or until set. Immediately remove from cookie sheets to cooling racks. Sprinkle sugar over each cookie or cool completely and decorate with frosting and candies.

NUTRITIONAL INFORMATION PER SERVING: Calories 45 • Total Fat 2g • Saturated Fat 1g • Cholesterol 5mg • Sodium 45mg • Total Carbohydrate 7g • Dietary Fiber 0g • Sugars 4g • Protein 0g.

caramel swirl cheesecake brownies

SERVINGS: 24 Brownies

BASE
- 1 (1 lb. 3.5 oz.) package fudge brownie mix
- 1/2 cup butter or margarine, softened
- 1/4 cup creamy peanut butter
- 1 egg

FILLING
- 2 (8 oz.) packages cream cheese, softened
- 1/3 cup creamy peanut butter
- 1 cup sugar
- 3 tablespoons all-purpose flour
- 1/4 cup dairy sour cream
- 2 teaspoons vanilla
- 2 eggs

CARAMEL SAUCE
- 12 caramels, unwrapped
- 3 tablespoons whipping cream

GARNISH, IF DESIRED
- 1/2 cup whipping cream
- 1 tablespoon powdered sugar

REBECCA MOE
Carmichael, California
Bake-Off® Contest 36, 1994
Prize Winner

1 Heat oven to 325°F. Grease bottom of 13x9-inch pan. In large bowl, combine all base ingredients; beat until dough forms. Press lightly in bottom of greased pan.

2 In large bowl, combine cream cheese and 1/3 cup peanut butter; beat at Low speed until smooth. Add sugar, flour, sour cream and vanilla; beat until blended. Add 2 eggs, 1 at a time, beating just until blended. Pour filling over base.

3 In small heavy saucepan, combine caramels and 3 tablespoons whipping cream. Cook and stir over low heat until caramels are melted and mixture is smooth. Drop spoonfuls of caramel sauce randomly over filling. For swirl effect, pull knife through batter in wide curves; turn pan and repeat.

4 Bake for 35 to 45 minutes or until center is set and edges are light golden brown. Cool 30 minutes. Refrigerate 1 hour before serving.

5 Just before serving, in small bowl, combine 1/2 cup whipping cream and powdered sugar; beat until stiff peaks form. Pipe whipped cream rosettes or spoon dollops of whipped cream on each serving. Store in refrigerator.

HIGH ALTITUDE (ABOVE 3500 FT): Add 2 tablespoons flour to dry brownie mix. Bake as directed above.

NUTRITIONAL INFORMATION PER SERVING: Calories 330 • Fat 20g • Sodium 210mg • Total Carbohydrate 33g • Protein 5g.

mint-kissed meringues

mint-kissed meringues

PREP TIME: 25 Minutes ✹ READY IN: 2 Hours 25 Minutes ✹ SERVINGS: 48 Cookies

2 egg whites	1/4 teaspoon mint extract
1/4 teaspoon cream of tartar	3 to 5 drops green food color
1/8 teaspoon salt	Multicolored candy sprinkles, if desired
1/2 cup sugar	

1 Heat oven to 200°F. Grease 2 large cookie sheets. In small bowl, combine egg whites, cream of tartar and salt; beat with electric mixer at Medium speed until foamy.

2 Increase mixer speed to High; add sugar 1 tablespoon at a time, beating until meringue is very stiff and glossy, and sugar is dissolved. Beat in mint extract. Fold in food color 1 drop at a time until of desired color.

3 Use disposable decorating bag or gallon-sized food storage plastic bag with 1/2-inch hole cut in bottom corner of bag. If desired, fit large star tip in corner. Spoon meringue into bag; twist top of bag to seal. Squeeze bag to pipe meringue into 1-inch puffs on greased cookie sheets. Sprinkle each with candy sprinkles.

4 Place cookie sheets on center rack in oven. Bake for 2 hours. Immediately remove cookies from cookie sheets; place on wire racks. Cool 5 minutes or until completely cooled.

NUTRITIONAL INFORMATION PER SERVING: Calories 10 • Total Fat 0g • Saturated Fat 0g • Cholesterol 0mg • Sodium 10mg • Total Carbohydrate 2g • Dietary Fiber 0g • Sugars 2g • Protein 0g. DIETARY EXCHANGES: Free • 0 Carbohydrate Choice.

cook's notes

These minty meringues can be made up to 1 month ahead and frozen. For maximum freshness, store them in an airtight container.

truffle-topped amaretto brownies

SERVINGS: 54 Brownies

BROWNIES

1 (1 lb. 3.5 oz.) package fudge brownie mix	1/4 cup powdered sugar
1/2 cup oil	1 (6 oz.) package semisweet chocolate chips, melted (1 cup)
1/3 cup water	2 to 3 tablespoons amaretto or 1 teaspoon almond extract
2 tablespoons amaretto or 1 teaspoon almond extract	
1 egg	**TOPPING**
3/4 cup chopped almonds	1/2 cup semisweet chocolate chips
FILLING	1/4 cup whipping cream
1 (8 oz.) package cream cheese, softened	1/2 cup sliced almonds, toasted

ARLENE SCHLOTTER
El Cajon, California
Bake-Off® Contest 34, 1990

1 Heat oven to 350°F. Grease 13x9-inch pan. In large bowl, combine all brownie ingredients. Beat 50 strokes by hand. Spread batter in greased pan. Bake for 26 to 33 minutes or until set. Cool completely.

2 In small bowl, beat cream cheese and powdered sugar at Medium speed until smooth. Add melted chocolate chips and 2 to 3 tablespoons amaretto; beat until well blended. Spread filling mixture over top of cooled brownies. Refrigerate at least 1 hour or until firm.

3 In small saucepan over low heat, melt 1/2 cup chocolate chips with whipping cream, stirring constantly until smooth. Carefully spread topping mixture evenly over chilled filling. Sprinkle with sliced almonds. Refrigerate at least 1 hour or until set. Cut into bars. Store in refrigerator.

HIGH ALTITUDE (3500-6500 FT): Add 1/3 cup flour to the dry brownie mix. Bake at 350°F for 30 to 35 minutes.

NUTRITIONAL INFORMATION PER SERVING: Calories 130 • Fat 8g • Sodium 40mg • Total Carbohydrate 13g • Protein 2g.

cook's notes

If using almond extract instead of amaretto, increase water in brownies to 1/2 cup; use almond extract and 2 tablespoons milk in the filling.

festive coconut macaroons

READY IN: 55 Minutes ✳ SERVINGS: 24 Cookies

4	egg whites	1/2	teaspoon almond extract
2/3	cup sugar	4	cups coconut
1/4	cup all-purpose flour	1/4	cup chopped red candied cherries
1/8	teaspoon salt	1/4	cup chopped green candied cherries

1 Heat oven to 325°F. Grease and lightly flour cookie sheets. In large bowl, beat egg whites until foamy. Beat in sugar, flour, salt and almond extract until well blended. Stir in coconut and candied cherries. Drop dough by scant tablespoonfuls 2 inches apart onto cookie sheets.

2 Bake the macaroons 13 to 17 minutes or until they are set and lightly browned. Immediately remove from cookie sheets.

NUTRITIONAL INFORMATION PER SERVING: Calories 100 • Total Fat 4g • Saturated Fat 4g • Cholesterol 0mg • Sodium 60mg • Total Carbohydrate 15g • Dietary Fiber 1g • Sugars 12g • Protein 1g. DIETARY EXCHANGES: 1 Starch • 1 Other Carbohydrate • 1/2 Fat.

christmas cutouts

PREP TIME: 1 Hour 25 Minutes   ✳   READY IN: 2 Hours 25 Minutes   ✳   SERVINGS: 72 Cookies

1 cup sugar	3 cups all-purpose flour
1 cup butter or margarine, softened	1-1/2 teaspoons baking powder
3 tablespoons milk	1/2 teaspoon salt
1 teaspoon vanilla	Sugar or decorating icing, if desired
1 egg	

1 In large bowl, combine 1 cup sugar, butter, milk, vanilla and egg; blend well. Add flour, baking powder and salt; mix well. Cover with plastic wrap; refrigerate 1 hour for easier handling.

2 Heat oven to 400°F. On lightly floured surface, roll out 1/3 of dough at a time to 1/8-inch thickness. Keep remaining dough refrigerated. Cut with floured 2-inch cookie cutters; place 1 inch apart on ungreased cookie sheets. If desired, sprinkle with sugar.

3 Bake for 5 to 9 minutes or until edges are light golden brown. Immediately remove from cookie sheets. Decorate as desired.

NUTRITIONAL INFORMATION PER SERVING: Calories 60 • Total Fat 3g • Saturated Fat 2g • Cholesterol 10mg • Sodium 45mg • Total Carbohydrate 7g • Dietary Fiber 0g • Sugars 3g • Protein 1g. DIETARY EXCHANGES: 1/2 Fat • 1/2 Other Carbohydrate • 1/2 Carbohydrate Choice.

kitchen tip

Decorating cookies is great fun for children. Keep the mess to a minimum by setting frosted cookies in a shallow baking dish. When the kids add sprinkles to the cookies, the extras will fall in the dish and not on the floor.

CHOCOLATE SPRITZ

Add 2 ounces melted unsweet-ened chocolate to powdered sugar mixture.

EGGNOG SPRITZ

Substitute 1 teaspoon rum extract for vanilla and add 1/4 teaspoon nutmeg with flour.

spritz cookies

READY IN: 1 Hour ✷ SERVINGS: 60 Cookies

1	cup powdered sugar	1	egg
1	cup butter, softened	2-1/3	cups all-purpose flour
1/2	teaspoon vanilla	1/4	teaspoon salt

1 Heat oven to 400°F. In large bowl, beat powdered sugar, butter, vanilla and egg until light and fluffy. Beat in flour and salt until well blended.

2 Fit cookie press with desired template. Fill cookie press; press dough onto ungreased cookie sheets.

3 Bake 5 to 7 minutes or until edges are firm but not brown. Immediately remove from cookie sheets.

NUTRITIONAL INFORMATION PER SERVING: Calories 50 • Total Fat 3g • Saturated Fat 2g • Cholesterol 10mg • Sodium 40mg • Total Carbohydrate 6g • Dietary Fiber 0g • Sugars 2g • Protein 1g. DIETARY EXCHANGES: 1/2 Starch • 1/2 Other Carbohydrate • 1/2 Fat.

fresh ginger-pumpkin tassies

PREP TIME: 35 Minutes ❋ READY IN: 1 Hour 30 Minutes ❋ SERVINGS: 24 Tassies

CRUST
- 1-1/4 cups all-purpose flour
- 1/2 cup butter, softened
- 1 (3 oz.) package cream cheese, softened

FILLING
- 3/4 cup firmly packed brown sugar
- 1/2 cup canned pumpkin
- 3 tablespoons half-and-half
- 1 teaspoon grated gingerroot
- 1/2 teaspoon vanilla
- 1 egg

TOPPING
- 1/4 cup all-purpose flour
- 2 tablespoons brown sugar
- 1 tablespoon butter, softened

1 Heat oven to 350°F. In large bowl, combine all crust ingredients; beat until well blended. Shape dough into 24 (1-1/4-inch) balls. Place 1 ball in each of 24 ungreased miniature muffin cups; press in bottom and up sides of each cup, level with tops of cups.

2 In medium bowl, combine all filling ingredients; blend well. Spoon scant tablespoon filling into each crust-lined cup. In small bowl, combine all topping ingredients; mix until crumbly. Carefully sprinkle 1 teaspoon topping over each filled cup.

3 Bake for 18 to 22 minutes or until puffed and tip of knife inserted in center comes out clean. Immediately run knife around edges of cookies. Cool cookies in pans for 5 minutes. Carefully remove cookies from muffin cups; place on wire racks to cool. Cool 30 minutes or until completely cooled.

HIGH ALTITUDE (3500-6500 FT): Bake at 350°F for 18 to 24 minutes.

NUTRITIONAL INFORMATION PER SERVING: Calories 120 • Total Fat 6g • Saturated Fat 4g • Cholesterol 25mg • Sodium 45mg • Total Carbohydrate 14g • Dietary Fiber 0g • Sugars 8g • Protein 2g. DIETARY EXCHANGES: 1 Starch • 1 Fat.

espresso cheesecake bars

PREP TIME: 15 Minutes ❋ READY IN: 4 Hours 5 Minutes ❋ SERVINGS: 25 Bars

- 1-1/2 cups chocolate cookie crumbs
- 1 teaspoon instant espresso coffee powder
- 1/4 cup butter, melted
- 1 (8 oz.) package cream cheese, softened
- 1/4 cup sugar
- 1/2 teaspoon vanilla
- 1 egg

1 Heat oven to 350°F. In medium bowl, combine cookie crumbs, 1/2 teaspoon of the espresso coffee powder and melted butter; mix well. Reserve 1/4 cup mixture for topping. Press remaining mixture in bottom of ungreased 8-inch square pan.

2 Beat cream cheese in medium bowl at Medium speed until smooth and creamy. Add sugar, remaining 1/2 teaspoon espresso coffee powder, vanilla and egg; blend well. Pour over crust. Sprinkle with reserved crumb mixture.

3 Bake for 15 to 20 minutes or just until center is set. Cool 30 minutes or until completely cooled. Cover loosely; refrigerate 3 to 4 hours or until firm. With hot, wet knife, cut into bars. Store in refrigerator.

HIGH ALTITUDE (3500-6500 FT): Bake at 350°F for 20 to 25 minutes or until center is set.

NUTRITIONAL INFORMATION PER SERVING: Calories 85 • Total Fat 6g • Saturated Fat 3g • Cholesterol 25mg • Sodium 80mg • Total Carbohydrate 7g • Dietary Fiber 0g • Sugars 4g • Protein 1g. DIETARY EXCHANGES: 1/2 Starch • 1 Fat.

kitchen tip

Tightly wrap unpeeled ginger-root and refrigerate it for up to 3 weeks, or freeze it for up to 6 months. Just grate the frozen gingerroot and return it to the freezer.

cook's notes

You can replace the instant espresso coffee powder with instant coffee granules when preparing these rich cheesecake bars.

cranberry-orange cookies

READY IN: 1 Hour ✳ SERVINGS: 60 Cookies

COOKIES
- 1-1/2 cups firmly packed brown sugar
- 1 cup butter, softened
- 1 teaspoon vanilla
- 2 eggs
- 2-1/4 cups all-purpose flour
- 2 teaspoons baking powder
- 1 teaspoon baking soda
- 1/2 teaspoon salt
- 2 cups rolled oats
- 1 cup sweetened dried cranberries
- 1 cup chopped orange slice candies

GLAZE
- 3/4 cup powdered sugar
- 2 to 3 teaspoons orange juice

1. Heat oven to 350°F. In large bowl, combine brown sugar and butter; beat until light and fluffy. Add vanilla and eggs; blend well. Add flour, baking powder, baking soda and salt; mix well. Stir in oats, cranberries and chopped candies. Drop dough by rounded teaspoonfuls 2 inches apart onto ungreased cookie sheets.

2. Bake for 9 to 11 minutes or until golden brown. Cool 1 minute; remove from cookie sheets. Cool 15 minutes or until completely cooled.

3. In small bowl, combine glaze ingredients, adding enough orange juice for desired drizzling consistency. Drizzle glaze over cooled cookies.

NUTRITIONAL INFORMATION PER SERVING: Calories 100 • Total Fat 3g • Saturated Fat 2g • Cholesterol 15mg • Sodium 90mg • Total Carbohydrate 17g • Dietary Fiber 1g • Sugars 11g • Protein 1g. DIETARY EXCHANGES: 1/2 Starch • 1/2 Fruit • 1 Other Carbohydrate • 1/2 Fat.

apricot-cranberry-nut bars

PREP TIME: 20 Minutes ✳ READY IN: 1 Hour 55 Minutes ✳ SERVINGS: 20 Bars

BASE AND TOPPING
- 1 (15.6 oz.) package cranberry-orange quick bread mix
- 1/3 cup butter, softened
- 1 egg, slightly beaten

FILLING
- 1 (12 oz.) can apricot filling
- 1 (3 oz.) package cream cheese, cut into small pieces
- 1/2 cup chopped pecans

1. Heat oven to 350°F. Grease 9-inch square pan. Place bread mix in large bowl. With pastry blender or fork, cut in butter until mixture resembles coarse crumbs. Add egg; mix well. Reserve 1 cup mixture for topping. Press remaining mixture evenly in bottom of greased pan.

2. In small bowl, combine all filling ingredients; stir gently to mix (do not break up cream cheese). Spread filling evenly over base. With fingers, crumble reserved mixture and sprinkle evenly over filling; press lightly.

3. Bake for 30 to 35 minutes or until top is golden brown. Cool 1 hour or until completely cooled. Cut into bars. Store in refrigerator.

HIGH ALTITUDE (3500-6500 FT): Bake at 375°F for 30 to 35 minutes.

NUTRITIONAL INFORMATION PER SERVING: Calories 170 • Total Fat 8g • Saturated Fat 4g • Cholesterol 25mg • Sodium 140mg • Total Carbohydrate 23g • Dietary Fiber 1g • Sugars 13g • Protein 2g. DIETARY EXCHANGES: 1/2 Starch • 1 Fruit • 1-1/2 Other Carbohydrate • 1-1/2 Fat.

cranberry-orange cookies
apricot-cranberry-nut bars

almond-coconut candy bars

PREP TIME: 45 Minutes ✹ READY IN: 5 Hours 10 Minutes ✹ SERVINGS: 36 Bars

BASE
- 1 cup semisweet chocolate chips
- 1/4 cup butter
- 1/2 cup chocolate cookie crumbs

FILLING
- 3 egg whites
- 1 cup sugar
- 2 teaspoons vanilla
- 1/2 teaspoon almond extract
- 2-1/2 cups coconut
- 3/4 cup all-purpose flour
- 36 whole almonds

GLAZE
- 1/2 cup semisweet chocolate chips
- 3 tablespoons butter

1 Heat oven to 350°F. Line 13x9-inch pan with foil. Spray foil with nonstick cooking spray. In small saucepan, combine 1 cup chocolate chips and 1/4 cup butter; melt over low heat, stirring occasionally. Stir in cookie crumbs. Spread mixture evenly in bottom of sprayed foil-lined pan. Refrigerate 15 minutes or until set.

2 Meanwhile, in large bowl, beat egg whites until soft peaks form. Gradually add sugar, beating until stiff peaks form. Add vanilla and almond extract; blend well. Stir in coconut and flour until well mixed.

3 Spread filling evenly over base. Arrange almonds over bars in 6 rows of 6 each. Bake for 20 to 25 minutes or until lightly browned and center is set when lightly touched.

4 In small saucepan, melt glaze ingredients over low heat, stirring frequently until smooth. Drizzle glaze over bars. Cool at least 4 hours or until set. Cut into bars.

HIGH ALTITUDE (3500-6500 FT): Bake at 350°F for 25 to 30 minutes.

NUTRITIONAL INFORMATION PER SERVING: Calories 130 • Total Fat 7g • Saturated Fat 4g • Cholesterol 5mg • Sodium 50mg • Total Carbohydrate 16g • Dietary Fiber 1g • Sugars 12g • Protein 1g. DIETARY EXCHANGES: 1 Fruit • 1 Other Carbohydrate • 1-1/2 Fat.

chocolate-dipped toffee moons

READY IN: 2 Hours ✹ SERVINGS: 60 Cookies

COOKIES
- 1/2 cup powdered sugar
- 1 cup butter, softened
- 2 teaspoons vanilla
- 2 cups all-purpose flour
- 1 cup finely chopped or ground almonds
- 1/2 cup toffee bits
- 1/4 teaspoon salt

GLAZE
- 1/2 cup semisweet chocolate chips
- 2 teaspoons shortening

1 Heat oven to 325°F. In large bowl, combine 1/2 cup powdered sugar, butter and vanilla; beat until light and fluffy. Add flour, almonds, toffee bits and salt; mix until well blended.

2 Shape dough into 1-inch balls. Roll each ball into 2-inch-long log; bend into crescent shape. Place 1 inch apart on ungreased cookie sheets.

3 Bake for 13 to 15 minutes or until set and bottoms are golden brown. Immediately remove from cookie sheets; place on wire racks. Cool 30 minutes or until completely cooled.

4 In 1-cup microwavable measuring cup, combine glaze ingredients. Microwave on High for 45 to 60 seconds, stirring once halfway through melting. Stir until smooth. Dip 1 end of each cooled cookie halfway into melted chocolate, letting excess drip off. Place on waxed paper; let stand until set.

NUTRITIONAL INFORMATION PER SERVING: Calories 70 • Total Fat 5g • Saturated Fat 3g • Cholesterol 10mg • Sodium 50mg • Total Carbohydrate 6g • Dietary Fiber 0g • Sugars 3g • Protein 1g. DIETARY EXCHANGES: 1/2 Fruit • 1/2 Other Carbohydrate • 1 Fat.

almond-coconut candy bars
chocolate-dipped toffee moons

spritz candy cane cookies

spritz candy cane cookies

PREP TIME: 1 Hour 15 Minutes ✳ SERVINGS: 84 Cookies

3/4	cup sugar	2-1/4	cups all-purpose flour
1/2	cup shortening	1/2	teaspoon baking powder
1/2	cup butter, softened		Dash salt
1	teaspoon peppermint extract	6	drops red food color
1	egg	15	hard peppermint candies, finely crushed

1 Heat oven to 375°F. In large bowl, combine sugar, shortening and butter; beat until light and fluffy. Add peppermint extract and egg; beat until well combined. Add flour, baking powder and salt; mix well.

2 Divide dough in half. To 1 half, add food color; mix until well blended and uniform in color. Attach star template to cookie press. With press lying on its side, fill one side with half of white dough; fill other side with half of pink dough. Press dough onto ungreased cookie sheets, forming 4-inch strips. Bend tops of each strip to form cane shape. Repeat with remaining dough.

3 Bake for 4 to 7 minutes or until edges are light golden brown. Cool 1 minute; remove from cookie sheet. Immediately sprinkle warm cookies with crushed candy.

NUTRITIONAL INFORMATION PER SERVING: Calories 40 • Total Fat 2g • Saturated Fat 1g • Cholesterol 5mg • Sodium 15mg • Total Carbohydrate 5g • Dietary Fiber 0g • Sugars 2g • Protein 0g. DIETARY EXCHANGES: 1/2 Other Carbohydrate • 1/2 Fat.

cook's notes

To speed up the shaping process, press out a line of dough along the length of the cookie sheet near the edge. Cut the dough line into 4-inch pieces. Use toothpick to curve the top of each piece, forming the cane's handle. Continue process to fill the cookie sheet.

chocolate chip-jam strips

READY IN: 1 Hour ✳ SERVINGS: 48 Cookies

COOKIES

2/3	cup butter, softened	1/2	teaspoon baking powder
1/3	cup sugar	1/2	cup miniature semisweet chocolate chips
1	teaspoon almond extract	1/2	cup seedless raspberry jam
1	egg		**ICING**
2	cups all-purpose flour	1/3	cup miniature semisweet chocolate chips
		1	teaspoon shortening

1 Heat oven to 350°F. In large bowl, combine butter and sugar; beat until light and fluffy. Add almond extract and egg; blend well. Add flour and baking powder; mix well. Stir in 1/2 cup chocolate chips.

2 Divide dough into 4 equal parts. On lightly floured surface, shape each part into 12-inch roll. Place rolls about 3 inches apart on 2 ungreased cookie sheets. Using handle of wooden spoon or finger, make depression about 1/2 inch wide and 1/4 inch deep lengthwise down center of each roll. Fill each roll with 2 tablespoons jam.

3 Bake for 15 to 20 minutes or until light golden brown, switching cookie sheets halfway through baking time. Cool 5 minutes. Cut each baked roll diagonally into 12 cookies; place on wire racks. Cool 10 minutes or until completely cooled.

4 In small microwavable bowl, combine icing ingredients. Microwave on High for 30 seconds. Stir; continue microwaving, stirring every 10 seconds, until chocolate is melted and can be stirred smooth. Drizzle icing over cooled cookies. Let stand until icing is set before storing. Store in loosely covered container.

HIGH ALTITUDE (3500-6500 FT): Bake at 350°F for 17 to 22 minutes.

NUTRITIONAL INFORMATION PER SERVING: Calories 75 • Total Fat 4g • Saturated Fat 2g • Cholesterol 10mg • Sodium 25mg • Total Carbohydrate 10g • Dietary Fiber 0g • Sugars 5g • Protein 1g. DIETARY EXCHANGES: 1/2 Starch • 1 Fat.

pistachio shortbread trees

READY IN: 1 Hour 15 Minutes ✳ SERVINGS: 32 Cookies

COOKIES

1	cup butter, softened
1/2	cup sugar
1/2	cup finely chopped pistachios
2-1/4	cups all-purpose flour

1	teaspoon vanilla
16	pretzel spindles or sticks, broken in half

ICING

1	cup powdered sugar
1	to 3 tablespoons milk

1 Heat oven to 325°F. Spray 2 cookie sheets with nonstick cooking spray. In large bowl, combine butter and sugar; beat until light and fluffy. Reserve 2 tablespoons of the pistachios. Add remaining pistachios, flour and vanilla; mix well. Dough will be stiff.

2 Divide dough evenly into 4 pieces; shape into balls. On lightly floured surface, pat each to form 6-inch round. Place rounds on sprayed cookie sheets. With table knife, lightly make indentations on surface of dough, dividing each round into 8 wedges. In outside edge of each wedge, insert 1 pretzel half for tree trunk.

3 Bake for 16 to 21 minutes or until edges are light golden brown. Cool 2 minutes; remove from cookie sheets. Cut each round into 8 wedges; place on wire racks. Cool 15 minutes or until completely cooled.

4 Very finely chop reserved 2 tablespoons pistachios. In small bowl, blend icing ingredients, adding enough milk for desired drizzling consistency. Drizzle icing in zigzag design over each cookie. Before icing sets, sprinkle cookies with reserved pistachios.

NUTRITIONAL INFORMATION PER SERVING: Calories 125 • Total Fat 7g • Saturated Fat 4g • Cholesterol 15mg • Sodium 50mg • Total Carbohydrate 15g • Dietary Fiber 0g • Sugars 7g • Protein 1g. DIETARY EXCHANGES: 1 Other Carbohydrate • 1-1/2 Fat.

mint truffle cups

PREP TIME: 35 Minutes ✳ READY IN: 2 Hours 40 Minutes ✳ SERVINGS: 24 Cookies

CRUST

1/2	cup powdered sugar
1/2	cup butter, softened
1	egg
1	cup all-purpose flour
1/4	cup unsweetened cocoa

FILLING

2/3	cup semisweet chocolate chips
1/2	cup whipping cream
1/4	teaspoon peppermint extract

TOPPING

12	thin chocolate and green mints, unwrapped, coarsely chopped

1 In medium bowl, combine powdered sugar and butter; beat until light and fluffy. Add egg; blend well. Add flour and cocoa; mix well. Cover with plastic wrap; refrigerate 1 to 2 hours for easier handling.

2 Heat oven to 325°F. Divide dough into 24 equal pieces. Place 1 piece in each of 24 ungreased miniature muffin cups; press in bottom and up sides of each cup, level with tops of cups.

3 Bake for 13 to 16 minutes or until set. Cool in pans on wire racks for 20 minutes. Remove from pans.

4 Meanwhile, in medium saucepan, combine all filling ingredients. Heat over low heat until chocolate is melted and smooth, stirring constantly. Remove from heat. Cool 20 minutes or until filling thickens slightly.

5 Spoon about 2 teaspoons filling into each baked chocolate cup. Refrigerate at least 30 minutes or until filling is set. Sprinkle chopped mints on top of each cookie; press in lightly. Store in refrigerator. Remove from refrigerator about 30 minutes before serving.

HIGH ALTITUDE (3500-6500 FT): Bake at 325°F for 15 to 18 minutes.

NUTRITIONAL INFORMATION PER SERVING: Calories 120 • Total Fat 8g • Saturated Fat 5g • Cholesterol 25mg • Sodium 35mg • Total Carbohydrate 11g • Dietary Fiber 0g • Sugars 6g • Protein 1g. DIETARY EXCHANGES: 1/2 Starch • 1/2 Other Carbohydrate • 1-1/2 Fat.

pistachio shortbread trees

chocolate-cherry gems

PREP TIME: 30 Minutes ✳ READY IN: 1 Hour 30 Minutes ✳ SERVINGS: 36 Cookies

cook's notes

Because these cookies are very tender, it is necessary to bake them in the miniature paper or foil cups. Look for the cups in the baking aisle of the supermarket or wherever cake decorating supplies are sold.

COOKIES

1	(16.5 oz.) roll refrigerated sugar cookie dough
1/4	cup unsweetened baking cocoa
1/4	cup semisweet chocolate chips, melted, cooled
1	(10 oz.) jar maraschino cherries, drained, chopped (3/4 cup)

CUPS

36	miniature paper or foil baking cups (1-1/4-inch diameter)

ICING

1/2	cup semisweet chocolate chips
1/2	cup sweetened condensed milk (not evaporated)
1	tablespoon brandy or maraschino cherry liquid

1 Heat oven to 350°F (325°F for dark cookie sheet). In large bowl, break up cookie dough. Stir or knead in cocoa and melted chocolate until well blended. Stir in cherries. Cover; freeze dough 30 minutes for easier handling.

2 Place paper cups on ungreased large cookie sheet. Shape dough into 36 (1-inch) balls; place each in paper cup.

3 Bake 11 to 17 minutes or until puffy and surface loses its shine. Immediately remove cookies in cups from cookie sheet; place on wire racks. Cool completely, about 15 minutes.

4 In 1-quart saucepan, heat 1/2 cup chocolate chips and condensed milk over low heat about 3 minutes, stirring constantly, until chips are melted and smooth. Stir in brandy. Drizzle about 1 teaspoon icing over top of each cooled cookie.

HIGH ALTITUDE (3500-6500 FT): Bake at 350°F for 13 to 19 minutes. Continue as directed above.

NUTRITIONAL INFORMATION PER SERVING: Calories 90 • Total Fat 3g • Saturated Fat 1g • Cholesterol 0mg • Sodium 55mg • Total Carbohydrate 15g • Dietary Fiber 0g • Sugars 11g • Protein 1g. DIETARY EXCHANGES: 1 Other Carbohydrate • 1/2 Fat.

pistachio shortbread trees

white chocolate-cashew pretzel bars

white chocolate-cashew pretzel bars

PREP TIME: 25 Minutes ✳ READY IN: 1 Hour 30 Minutes ✳ SERVINGS: 36 Bars

- 1 (16.5 oz.) roll refrigerated sugar cookie dough
- 1 (12 oz.) package white chocolate chunks or white vanilla chips
- 1 cup coarsely chopped pretzel sticks or twists
- 1-1/2 cups semisweet chocolate chips
- 1/4 cup peanut butter
- 1 cup chopped cashews

1 Heat oven to 350°F. Spray 13x9-inch pan with nonstick cooking spray. Break up cookie dough into sprayed pan. With floured fingers, press dough evenly in bottom of pan to form crust. Sprinkle 1 cup of the white chocolate chunks and the pretzels over dough; press lightly into dough.

2 Bake for 16 to 20 minutes or until light golden brown. Cool 30 minutes or until completely cooled.

3 Place 1/4 cup of the white chocolate chunks in small microwavable bowl; set aside. In large microwavable bowl, combine chocolate chips and remaining white chocolate chunks. Microwave on High for 2 minutes, stirring every 30 seconds, until melted and smooth. If necessary, microwave an additional 30 seconds. Stir in peanut butter and cashews. Spread mixture evenly over cooled baked crust. Refrigerate 15 minutes to set chocolate.

4 Microwave reserved 1/4 cup white chocolate chunks on High for 30 seconds; stir until melted and smooth. If necessary, microwave an additional 10 seconds. Drizzle over bars. Let stand 10 minutes or until set. Cut into bars.

NUTRITIONAL INFORMATION PER SERVING: Calories 165 • Total Fat 9g • Saturated Fat 3g • Cholesterol 5mg • Sodium 125mg • Total Carbohydrate 19g • Dietary Fiber 0g • Sugars 13g • Protein 2g. DIETARY EXCHANGES: 1 Starch • 2 Fat.

cheery cherry cookies

PREP TIME: 1 Hour 15 Minutes ✳ READY IN: 1 Hour 45 Minutes ✳ SERVINGS: 60 Cookies

COOKIES
- 1 (16.5 oz.) roll refrigerated sugar cookie dough
- 1/2 cup chopped maraschino cherries, well drained on paper towels
- 1/3 cup sugar

ICING
- 1/2 cup semisweet chocolate chips
- 1 tablespoon shortening

1 Heat oven to 350°F. In large bowl, break up cookie dough. Stir or knead in cherries. Cover; freeze dough 30 minutes for easier handling.

2 Shape dough into balls, using 1 teaspoon dough for each, and roll in sugar; place 2 inches apart on ungreased cookie sheets.

3 Bake 9 to 12 minutes or until set and edges are light golden brown. Cool 1 minute; remove from cookie sheets and place on wire racks. Cool completely, about 10 minutes.

4 In small microwavable bowl, microwave chocolate chips and shortening on High 1 minute, stirring once halfway through microwaving, until melted. If necessary, continue to microwave on High in 15-second increments, stirring until smooth. Drizzle icing over cooled cookies.

NUTRITIONAL INFORMATION PER SERVING: Calories 50 • Total Fat 2g • Saturated Fat 1g • Cholesterol 0mg • Sodium 30mg • Total Carbohydrate 8g • Dietary Fiber 0g • Sugars 6g • Protein 0g. DIETARY EXCHANGES: 1/2 Other Carbohydrate • 1/2 Fat.

frosted irish cream brownies

PREP TIME: 15 Minutes ✳ READY IN: 2 Hours ✳ SERVINGS: 48 Brownies

BROWNIES
- 1 (19.8-oz.) package fudge brownie mix
- 1/2 cup oil
- 1/4 cup Irish cream liqueur
- 2 eggs

FROSTING
- 1/2 cup butter or margarine, softened
- 2 cups powdered sugar
- 2 tablespoons Irish cream liqueur
- 1/2 teaspoon vanilla
- 2 to 3 teaspoons milk

GLAZE
- 1 oz. semisweet chocolate, chopped
- 1 teaspoon butter or margarine

1 Heat oven to 350°F. Grease bottom only of 13x9-inch pan. In large bowl, combine all brownie ingredients; beat 50 strokes with spoon. Spread in greased pan.

2 Bake for 25 to 30 minutes or until brownies are set and begin to pull away from sides of pan. Do not overbake. Cool 45 minutes or until completely cooled.

3 Beat 1/2 cup butter in small bowl until light and fluffy. Beat in all remaining frosting ingredients; add enough milk for desired spreading consistency. Spread over cooled brownies.

4 Place glaze ingredients in small microwavable bowl. Microwave on High for 30 seconds; stir until melted and smooth. Drizzle over frosted brownies. Refrigerate 30 minutes or until firm. Cut into bars.

HIGH ALTITUDE (3500-6500 FT): Add 3 tablespoons flour to dry brownie mix; decrease oil to 1/4 cup. Bake as directed above.

NUTRITIONAL INFORMATION PER SERVING: Calories 115 • Total Fat 5g • Saturated Fat 2g • Cholesterol 15mg • Sodium 60mg • Total Carbohydrate 16g • Dietary Fiber 0g • Sugars 13g • Protein 1g. DIETARY EXCHANGES: 1 Other Carbohydrate • 1 Fat.

orange spritz

READY IN: 45 Minutes ✳ SERVINGS: 60 Cookies

- 1 cup butter or margarine, softened
- 1 cup powdered sugar
- 1/2 teaspoon vanilla
- 1 egg
- 2-1/3 cups all-purpose flour
- 1 tablespoon grated orange peel
- 1/4 teaspoon salt

1 Heat oven to 400°F. In large bowl, combine butter, powdered sugar, vanilla and egg; beat until light and fluffy. Add flour, orange peel and salt; mix well.

2 Place desired template in cookie press. Fill cookie press with dough. Press dough onto ungreased cookie sheets.

3 Bake for 4 to 7 minutes or until bottoms are light golden brown. Immediately remove from cookie sheets.

NUTRITIONAL INFORMATION PER SERVING: Calories 55 • Total Fat 3g • Saturated Fat 2g • Cholesterol 10mg • Sodium 30mg • Total Carbohydrate 6g • Dietary Fiber 0g • Sugars 2g • Protein 1g. DIETARY EXCHANGES: 1/2 Fat • 1/2 Other Carbohydrate • 1/2 Carbohydrate Choice.

frosted irish cream brownies

chocolate-cherry gems

PREP TIME: 30 Minutes ✳ READY IN: 1 Hour 30 Minutes ✳ SERVINGS: 36 Cookies

COOKIES

- 1 (16.5 oz.) roll refrigerated sugar cookie dough
- 1/4 cup unsweetened baking cocoa
- 1/4 cup semisweet chocolate chips, melted, cooled
- 1 (10 oz.) jar maraschino cherries, drained, chopped (3/4 cup)

CUPS

- 36 miniature paper or foil baking cups (1-1/4-inch diameter)

ICING

- 1/2 cup semisweet chocolate chips
- 1/2 cup sweetened condensed milk (not evaporated)
- 1 tablespoon brandy or maraschino cherry liquid

1 Heat oven to 350°F (325°F for dark cookie sheet). In large bowl, break up cookie dough. Stir or knead in cocoa and melted chocolate until well blended. Stir in cherries. Cover; freeze dough 30 minutes for easier handling.

2 Place paper cups on ungreased large cookie sheet. Shape dough into 36 (1-inch) balls; place each in paper cup.

3 Bake 11 to 17 minutes or until puffy and surface loses its shine. Immediately remove cookies in cups from cookie sheet; place on wire racks. Cool completely, about 15 minutes.

4 In 1-quart saucepan, heat 1/2 cup chocolate chips and condensed milk over low heat about 3 minutes, stirring constantly, until chips are melted and smooth. Stir in brandy. Drizzle about 1 teaspoon icing over top of each cooled cookie.

HIGH ALTITUDE (3500-6500 FT): Bake at 350°F for 13 to 19 minutes. Continue as directed above.

NUTRITIONAL INFORMATION PER SERVING: Calories 90 • Total Fat 3g • Saturated Fat 1g • Cholesterol 0mg • Sodium 55mg • Total Carbohydrate 15g • Dietary Fiber 0g • Sugars 11g • Protein 1g. DIETARY EXCHANGES: 1 Other Carbohydrate • 1/2 Fat.

black and white brownies

SERVINGS: 36 Brownies

PENELOPE WEISS
Pleasant Grove, Utah
Bake-Off® Contest 35, 1992

BROWNIES

- 1 (1 lb. 3.5 oz.) package fudge brownie mix
- 1/4 cup water
- 1/2 cup oil
- 2 eggs
- 1/2 cup chopped pecans
- 1 (6 oz.) package semisweet chocolate chips (1 cup)
- 1 (12 oz.) package white vanilla chips (2 cups)

FROSTING

- 2 cups powdered sugar
- 1/4 cup unsweetened cocoa
- 3 to 4 tablespoons hot water
- 1/4 cup margarine or butter, melted
- 1 teaspoon vanilla
- 1/2 to 1 cup pecan halves

1 Heat oven to 350°F. Grease bottom only of 13x9-inch pan. In large bowl, combine brownie mix, water, oil and eggs; beat 50 strokes with spoon. Add 1/2 cup pecans, chocolate chips and 1 cup of the vanilla chips; mix well. Spread in greased pan.

2 Bake for 28 to 34 minutes or until center is set. Remove from oven; immediately sprinkle with remaining 1 cup vanilla chips. Return to oven for 1 minute to soften chips; spread evenly over brownies with back of spoon. Cool.

3 In small bowl, combine all frosting ingredients except pecan halves; beat until smooth. (Mixture will be thin.) Spoon over melted white vanilla chips; spread to cover. Arrange pecan halves over frosting. Cool 1-1/2 hours or until completely cooled. Cut into bars.

HIGH ALTITUDE (3500-6500 FT): Add 1/3 cup flour to dry brownie mix. Increase water to 1/3 cup; decrease oil to 1/3 cup. Bake at 375°F for 30 to 35 minutes.

NUTRITIONAL INFORMATION PER SERVING: Calories 240 • Fat 13g • Sodium 70mg • Total Carbohydrate 29g • Protein 2g.

HELEN PEACH
Pensacola, Florida
Bake-Off® Contest 34, 1990
Prize Winner

chewy peanut brownie bars

SERVINGS: 50 Bars

CRUST
1   (1 lb. 3.5 oz.) package fudge brownie mix
1/2 cup margarine or butter, melted
1   egg

FILLING
1   cup light corn syrup
3/4 cup peanut butter
1   cup unsalted peanuts
1   tablespoon margarine or butter, melted

1/2 teaspoon vanilla

GLAZE
1   tablespoon margarine or butter
1   oz. unsweetened chocolate
7-1/2 teaspoons water
1   cup powdered sugar
1/2 teaspoon vanilla

1 Heat oven to 350°F. In large bowl, combine all crust ingredients; mix well. Press evenly in bottom of ungreased 15x10x1-inch baking pan.

2 In small bowl, beat corn syrup and peanut butter at Low speed until well blended. Stir in remaining filling ingredients. Spread filling evenly over crust to within 1/2 inch of edges.

3 Bake for 18 to 20 minutes or until edges are firm and center is just firm to the touch. Cool completely.

4 In small saucepan over low heat, heat 1 tablespoon margarine, chocolate and water, stirring constantly until mixture is smooth. Remove from heat. Stir in powdered sugar and 1/2 teaspoon vanilla; blend until smooth. Drizzle glaze over cooled brownies. Let stand until set. Cut into bars.

HIGH ALTITUDE (3500-6500 FT): Add 1/4 cup flour to dry brownie mix. Bake as directed above.

NUTRITIONAL INFORMATION PER SERVING: Calories 140 • Fat 7g • Sodium 85mg • Total Carbohydrate 18g • Protein 2g.

pistachio bars

PREP TIME: 25 Minutes ✳ READY IN: 2 Hours 20 Minutes ✳ SERVINGS: 25 Bars

BASE
1   cup all-purpose flour
1/4 cup sugar
1/2 cup butter

TOPPING
1   egg

1/4 cup sugar
1/4 cup corn syrup
1   tablespoon butter, melted
1/4 teaspoon vanilla
1   cup coarsely chopped pistachios
1/2 cup flaked coconut

1 Heat oven to 350°F. In medium bowl, combine flour and 1/4 cup sugar; mix well. With pastry blender or fork, cut in 1/2 cup butter until mixture resembles coarse crumbs. Press mixture in bottom of ungreased 8-inch square pan.

2 Bake for 20 to 25 minutes or until light golden brown. Cool 10 minutes.

3 Meanwhile, beat egg slightly in medium bowl. Add all remaining topping ingredients except pistachios and coconut; mix well. Stir in pistachios and coconut.

4 Remove pan from oven. Spoon and spread coconut mixture evenly over warm base. Return to oven; bake an additional 15 to 20 minutes or until edges are golden brown. Cool 1 hour 15 minutes or until completely cooled. Cut into bars.

NUTRITIONAL INFORMATION PER SERVING: Calories 120 • Total Fat 7g • Saturated Fat 3g • Cholesterol 20mg • Sodium 60mg • Total Carbohydrate 12g • Dietary Fiber 0g • Sugars 6g • Protein 2g. DIETARY EXCHANGES: 1/2 Starch • 1/2 Other Carbohydrate • 1-1/2 Fat.

special touch

Use red-dyed pistachios alone

or with natural green pistachios

for fun, Christmas flair.

pistachio bars

festive christmas tree cookies

festive christmas tree cookies

READY IN: 1 Hour ❋ SERVINGS: 24 Cookies

GREEN DOUGH

- 1/4 cup all-purpose flour
- 1/4 cup butter or margarine, softened
- 1 tablespoon green crème de menthe liqueur or crème de menthe syrup
- 2 drops green food color

Decorating bag fitted with small writing tip

COOKIES

- 1 (16.5 oz.) roll refrigerated sugar cookie dough

Star-shaped or confetti candy sprinkles

1 Heat oven to 350°F. In small bowl, mix all green dough ingredients until well blended. Place dough in decorating bag fitted with small writing tip; set aside.

2 Remove half of cookie dough from wrapper; refrigerate remaining dough until needed. On lightly floured surface with rolling pin, roll out dough to 1/4-inch thickness. With a 2-1/2- to 3-1/2-inch tree-shaped cookie cutter, cut out 24 dough trees; place 2 inches apart on ungreased cookie sheets.

3 Squeeze bag to pipe green dough around outer edge of each tree cookie; pipe dots randomly in center. Top each dot with candy sprinkles.

4 Bake 9 to 11 minutes or until cookies are light golden brown. Cool 1 minute; remove from cookie sheets.

NUTRITIONAL INFORMATION PER SERVING: Calories 115 • Total Fat 5g • Saturated Fat 2g • Cholesterol 5mg • Sodium 85mg • Total Carbohydrate 16g • Dietary Fiber 0g • Sugars 10g • Protein 1g. DIETARY EXCHANGES: 1 Other Carbohydrate • 1 Fat.

rum-pecan macaroons

READY IN: 1 Hour 15 Minutes ❋ SERVINGS: 48 Cookies

- 1 (16.5 oz.) roll refrigerated sugar cookie dough
- 1-1/2 cups flaked or shredded coconut
- 1 cup chopped pecans
- 1-1/2 teaspoons rum extract

Candied red and green cherry halves or pecan halves

1 Heat oven to 350°F. In large bowl, break up cookie dough. Stir in coconut, chopped pecans and rum extract (dough will be stiff).

2 Shape dough into 1-inch balls; place 2 inches apart on ungreased cookie sheets. Press cherry half in center of each cookie.

3 Bake 9 to 13 minutes or until macaroon edges are golden brown. Immediately remove from cookie sheets.

HIGH ALTITUDE (3500-6500 FT): Bake at 350°F for 10 to 14 minutes.

NUTRITIONAL INFORMATION PER SERVING: Calories 85 • Total Fat 4g • Saturated Fat 1g • Cholesterol 0mg • Sodium 60mg • Total Carbohydrate 11g • Dietary Fiber 0g • Sugars 7g • Protein 1g. DIETARY EXCHANGES: 1 Other Carbohydrate • 1/2 Fat.

cook's notes

A small resealable food-storage plastic bag can be used in place of the decorating bag. Place green dough in bag; seal. Cut small hole in bottom corner of bag. Squeeze bag to pipe dough as directed at left.

kitchen tip

Coconut stored for a long time can become dry. You may want to check what you have on hand before you begin. Buy a new can or package for the best results.

cashew-fudge bars

PREP TIME: 20 Minutes ❋ READY IN: 1 Hour 45 Minutes ❋ SERVINGS: 36 Bars

1-3/4 cups cashew halves
1 (16.5 oz.) roll refrigerated chocolate chip cookie dough
1/2 cup old-fashioned oats

1 can (14 oz.) sweetened condensed milk (not evaporated)
1 bag (12 oz.) semisweet chocolate chips
1 teaspoon vanilla

1 Heat oven to 350°F (325°F for dark pan). Chop 1 cup of the cashew halves. In large bowl, break up cookie dough. Stir in chopped cashews and oats. In ungreased 13x9-inch pan, press dough evenly to form crust. Bake 12 minutes.

2 Meanwhile, in 1-1/2-quart saucepan, cook condensed milk and chocolate chips over low heat about 6 minutes, stirring constantly, until chips are melted and smooth. Stir in vanilla.

3 Remove partially baked crust from oven. Spread chocolate mixture evenly over crust. Sprinkle with remaining 3/4 cup cashews; press gently into chocolate.

4 Return to oven; bake 18 to 23 minutes longer or until edges and center begin to crack. Cool completely on wire rack, about 1 hour. Cut into bars.

HIGH ALTITUDE (3500-6500 FT): Increase first bake time to 15 minutes at 350°F. Meanwhile, in saucepan, cook condensed milk and chocolate chips over medium-low heat. Increase second bake time to 20 to 25 minutes.

NUTRITIONAL INFORMATION PER SERVING: Calories 200 • Total Fat 10g • Saturated Fat 4g • Cholesterol 5mg • Sodium 90mg • Total Carbohydrate 24g • Dietary Fiber 1g • Sugars 16g • Protein 4g. DIETARY EXCHANGES: 1-1/2 Starch • 2 Fat.

cranberry-oatmeal cheesecake bars

PREP TIME: 20 Minutes ❋ READY IN: 2 Hours 30 Minutes ❋ SERVINGS: 36 Bars

1 (16.5 oz.) roll refrigerated sugar cookie dough
1 cup old-fashioned oats
1/4 cup packed brown sugar
1 (8 oz.) package cream cheese, softened

1/4 cup all-purpose flour
1/4 cup granulated sugar
2 eggs
1 (16 oz.) can whole berry cranberry sauce

1 Heat oven to 350°F. In large bowl, break up cookie dough. Stir in oats and brown sugar until crumbly (if necessary, knead with hands); reserve 1/2 cup mixture for topping. In ungreased 13x9-inch pan, press remaining mixture evenly to form crust. Bake 10 to 15 minutes or until light golden brown.

2 Meanwhile, in medium bowl with electric mixer, beat cream cheese, flour, granulated sugar and eggs on Medium speed until smooth.

3 Remove partially baked crust from oven. Spread cream cheese mixture evenly over crust. Drop cranberry sauce by small spoonfuls over cream cheese mixture. Crumble and sprinkle reserved cookie dough mixture over top.

4 Return to oven; bake 23 to 28 minutes longer or until edges are golden brown and filling is set. Cool completely on wire rack, about 1-1/2 hours. Cut into bars. Store in refrigerator.

HIGH ALTITUDE (3500-6500 FT): Heat oven to 375°F. Increase first bake time to 15 to 20 minutes. Increase second bake time to 25 to 30 minutes.

NUTRITIONAL INFORMATION PER SERVING: Calories 135 • Total Fat 5g • Saturated Fat 2g • Cholesterol 20mg • Sodium 75mg • Total Carbohydrate 20g • Dietary Fiber 0g • Sugars 14g • Protein 2g. DIETARY EXCHANGES: 1 Starch • 1 Fat.

cranberry-oatmeal cheesecake bars
cashew-fudge bars

chocolate-hazelnut biscotti

chocolate-hazelnut biscotti

PREP TIME: 1 Hour 15 Minutes ✳ READY IN: 1 Hour 40 Minutes ✳ SERVINGS: 36 Biscotti

1 cup sugar	1/4 cup unsweetened Dutch process cocoa
1/2 cup butter or margarine, softened	2 teaspoons baking powder
2 teaspoons vanilla	3/4 cup hazelnuts (filberts), toasted, chopped
3 eggs	1/2 cup miniature semisweet chocolate chips
2-2/3 cups all-purpose flour	2 oz. vanilla candy coating or almond bark, chopped

1 Heat oven to 350°F. Lightly grease cookie sheet. In large bowl, combine sugar and butter; beat until light and fluffy. Add vanilla and eggs; blend well. Add flour, cocoa and baking powder; mix well. Stir in toasted hazelnuts and chocolate chips.

2 Divide dough in half; shape each into 10-inch log. Place logs 5 inches apart on greased cookie sheet; flatten each until 3 inches wide.

3 Bake for 20 to 25 minutes or until firm when touched in center. Cool on cookie sheet for 10 minutes. With serrated knife, cut diagonally into 1/2-inch slices. Arrange slices, cut side down, on same cookie sheet.

4 Return to oven; bake 10 minutes. Turn slices over; bake an additional 5 to 10 minutes or until cut sides are lightly browned and crisp. Remove from cookie sheet; place on wire rack. Cool 10 minutes or until completely cooled.

5 Place candy coating in small microwavable bowl. Microwave on High for 45 seconds, stirring once, or until melted and smooth. If necessary, microwave an additional 20 seconds. Drizzle over biscotti.

NUTRITIONAL INFORMATION PER SERVING: Calories 125 • Total Fat 6g • Saturated Fat 3g • Cholesterol 25mg • Sodium 50mg • Total Carbohydrate 16g • Dietary Fiber 0g • Sugars 8g • Protein 2g. DIETARY EXCHANGES: 1 Starch • 1 Fat.

chocolaty caramel pecan bars

PREP TIME: 30 Minutes ✳ READY IN: 1 Hour 30 Minutes ✳ SERVINGS: 24 Bars

BASE

1/2 cup powdered sugar	1/3 cup whipping cream
1/2 cup butter or margarine, softened	2 cups pecan halves
1 tablespoon whipping cream	**TOPPING**
1 cup all-purpose flour	1 teaspoon butter or margarine
FILLING	1/2 cup milk chocolate chips
24 caramels, unwrapped	2 tablespoons whipping cream

1 Heat oven to 325°F. Grease 9-inch square pan. In medium bowl, mix powdered sugar, 1/2 cup butter and 1 tablespoon whipping cream until well blended. Add flour; mix until crumbly. With floured hands, press mixture evenly in pan. Bake 15 to 20 minutes or until firm to the touch.

2 Meanwhile, in medium saucepan, place caramels and 1/3 cup whipping cream. Cook over low heat, stirring frequently, until caramels are melted and mixture is smooth. Remove from heat. Add pecans; stir well to coat. Immediately spoon over baked base; spread carefully to cover.

3 In small saucepan over low heat, melt 1 teaspoon butter and the chocolate chips, stirring constantly. Stir in 2 tablespoons whipping cream. Drizzle over filling. Refrigerate 1 hour or until filling is firm. For bars, cut into 6 rows by 4 rows.

NUTRITIONAL INFORMATION PER SERVING: Calories 190 • Total Fat 13g • Saturated Fat 4g • Cholesterol 10mg • Sodium 70mg • Total Carbohydrate 17g • Dietary Fiber 1g • Sugars 10g • Protein 2g. DIETARY EXCHANGES: 1 Starch • 1 Other Carbohydrate • 2-1/2 Fat.

special touch

For a great gift, wrap up a few biscotti and present them with a Christmas coffee mug and a package of flavored coffee grounds.

Playful Childhood Treats

Laughter always fills the air when little ones help out in the kitchen. Invite a tiny baker to prepare these sweets with you, and you'll build memories that truly last a lifetime.

p. 251

p. 243

p. 248

p. 236

p. 250

santa claus cookies p. 248

special touch

With a variety of candies and

pretzels, you can make sure no

two snowmen look alike.

peanutty snowmen

PREP TIME: 40 Minutes ✳ READY IN: 1 Hour 20 Minutes ✳ SERVINGS: 32 Cookies

1 (16 oz.) package vanilla-flavored candy coating (almond bark)

1 (1 lb.) package peanut-shaped peanut butter-filled sandwich cookies

96 miniature semisweet chocolate chips (about 1 tablespoon)

Assorted candies, pretzel sticks and fruit roll snacks

1 Line cookie sheets with waxed paper. Place 1/4 of candy coating in small microwavable bowl. Microwave on High 30 seconds. Stir; continue to microwave in 15-second increments until coating can be stirred smooth.

2 Dip each side of 8 cookies into candy coating to coat; place on cookie sheets. Add chocolate chips for eyes.

3 Repeat with remaining candy coating and cookies. Decorate as desired with assorted candies. Let cookies stand at room temperature for 30 minutes or until coating is set.

NUTRITIONAL INFORMATION PER SERVING: Calories 150 • Total Fat 8g • Saturated Fat 3.5g • Trans Fat 0.5g • Cholesterol 0mg • Sodium 65mg • Total Carbohydrate 17g • Dietary Fiber 0g • Sugars 12g • Protein 2g. DIETARY EXCHANGES: 1/2 Starch • 1/2 Other Carbohydrate • 1-1/2 Fat.

peppermint spritz cookies

READY IN: 50 Minutes ✳ SERVINGS: 48 Cookies

1 roll (16.5 oz.) refrigerated sugar cookie dough
1/4 cup all-purpose flour

1/4 to 1/2 teaspoon peppermint extract
Red sugar

1 Heat oven to 350°F. In medium bowl, break up cookie dough. Stir or knead in flour until blended. Add peppermint extract; stir or knead dough until well blended.

2 Place about half of dough in cookie press fitted with star tip. Press dough into 5-inch strips on ungreased cookie sheets. With fingers, shape top of each to resemble candy cane. Sprinkle with red sugar. Repeat with remaining half of dough.

3 Bake 5 to 7 minutes or until the edges are light golden brown. Immediately remove from cookie sheets.

HIGH ALTITUDE (3500-6500 FT): Bake at 350°F for 7 to 9 minutes.

NUTRITIONAL INFORMATION PER SERVING: Calories 45 • Total Fat 1g • Saturated Fat 0g • Cholesterol 0mg • Sodium 35mg • Total Carbohydrate 8g • Dietary Fiber 0g • Sugars 4g • Protein 1g. DIETARY EXCHANGES: 1/2 Other Carbohydrate • 1/2 Fat.

kitchen tip

To give cookies a traditional peppermint stick flavor, be sure to use extract labeled "peppermint" and not "mint" or "spearmint."

easy cookie wreaths

READY IN: 1 Hour 10 Minutes ✳ SERVINGS: 32 Cookies

1 (16.5 oz.) roll refrigerated sugar cookie dough	Green food color
	Red food color
1-1/4 cups vanilla ready-to-spread frosting (from 16 oz. container)	Small candies or colored sugar

1 Heat oven to 350°F. Remove half of cookie dough from wrapper; refrigerate remaining dough until needed. Cut half of dough into 1/4-inch-thick slices; place 3 inches apart on ungreased cookie sheet.

2 With small (about 3/4-inch) cutter, cut out hole in center of each slice. Cut each cutout hole in half, forming 2 small semicircles; place semicircles on dough ring to form bow. Repeat with remaining half of dough.

3 Bake 7 to 10 minutes or until light golden brown. Cool 2 minutes; remove from cookie sheet and place on wire racks. Cool completely, about 15 minutes.

4 Meanwhile, in small bowl, mix 3/4 cup of the frosting and enough green food color until desired green color. In another small bowl, mix remaining 1/2 cup frosting and enough red food color until desired pink color.

5 Frost cooled wreaths with green frosting; frost bows with pink frosting. Decorate with small candies or colored sugar.

NUTRITIONAL INFORMATION PER SERVING: Calories 115 • Total Fat 4g • Saturated Fat 2g • Cholesterol 0mg • Sodium 55mg • Total Carbohydrate 20g • Dietary Fiber 0g • Sugars 16g • Protein 1g. DIETARY EXCHANGES: 1 Other Carbohydrate • 1 Fat.

crispy tree treats

READY IN: 30 Minutes ✳ SERVINGS: 16

1/4	cup butter or margarine	5	cups crisp rice cereal
1	(10 oz.) bag large marshmallows	1/2	cup small gummi candies
1/4	teaspoon green food color	16	small gumdrops, flattened

1 In large saucepan, melt butter and marshmallows over low heat, stirring until smooth. Remove from heat. Stir in food color. Add cereal and small gummi candies; stir until well coated.

2 With buttered hands, shape 1/4 cup mixture at a time into 3-dimensional cones resembling trees. Cut out small star shapes from gumdrops with 1/2-inch canapé cutter. Press star onto top of each tree.

NUTRITIONAL INFORMATION PER SERVING: Calories 150 • Total Fat 3g • Saturated Fat 1g • Cholesterol 0mg • Sodium 140mg • Total Carbohydrate 31g • Dietary Fiber 0g • Sugars 17g • Protein 1g. DIETARY EXCHANGES: 1/2 Starch • 1-1/2 Fruit • 2 Other Carbohydrate • 1/2 Fat.

special touch

Use the cute trees to accent homemade gingerbread houses.

santa's reindeer cookies

santa's reindeer cookies

READY IN: 1 Hour ❋ SERVINGS: 48 Cookies

1	(16.5 oz.) roll refrigerated sugar cookie dough, well chilled	4	cups (108) small pretzel twists
4	tablespoons all-purpose flour	14	candied red or green cherries, cut into quarters, or spice drop candies
1/3	cup vanilla ready-to-spread frosting (from 16 oz. can)	1/3	cup raisins

1 Heat oven to 350°F. Cut cookie dough in half; unwrap one half and refrigerate remaining half of dough until needed. Coat sides of dough with 2 tablespoons of the flour.

2 Roll out dough to form 9-inch square, using additional flour as needed to prevent sticking. Cut square into four 2-1/4-inch-wide strips; cut each strip into 6 equal triangles. Place on ungreased cookie sheet.

3 Bake for 6 to 8 minutes or until light golden brown. Cool 1 minute; remove from cookie sheet. Cool 10 minutes or until completely cooled. Repeat with remaining half of dough and flour.

4 Spread frosting over cookies. Press pretzels into top 2 corners of each cookie to resemble antlers. Place cherry piece at bottom to resemble nose. Place raisins on frosting for eyes. Let stand until frosting is set before storing.

NUTRITIONAL INFORMATION PER SERVING: Calories 130 • Total Fat 4g • Saturated Fat 3g • Cholesterol 0mg • Sodium 230mg • Total Carbohydrate 22g • Dietary Fiber 1g • Sugars 10g • Protein 2g. DIETARY EXCHANGES: 1 Starch • 1 Fat • 1/2 Other Carbohydrate • 1-1/2 Carbohydrate Choices.

special touch

Chocolate ready-to-spread frosting can be used in place of the vanilla frosting, and chocolate chips or white vanilla chips can be used instead of the raisins. Or mix and match so each cookie has a unique look.

giant snowy mitten

PREP TIME: 40 Minutes ❋ Ready in 1 Hour 10 Minutes ❋ SERVINGS: 8

1/2	(16.5 oz.) roll refrigerated sugar cookie dough	Green, red and blue food color
1	cup vanilla ready-to-spread frosting (from 16 oz. can)	

1 Place cookie dough in freezer for 30 minutes or until very firm. Heat oven to 350°F. Line cookie sheet with parchment paper.

2 Cut cookie dough into 16 slices. Arrange 15 slices, 1/4 inch apart, in shape of mitten on paper-lined cookie sheet. (See diagram at right.) Roll remaining slice of dough into log; place on side of mitten. Flatten to form oblong shape for thumb.

3 Bake for 14 to 15 minutes or until golden brown. Remove parchment paper with cookie from cookie sheet. Cool 15 minutes or until completely cooled. Remove cookie from paper.

4 Meanwhile, reserve 1/2 cup frosting to spread over cookie. Divide remaining 1/2 cup frosting into thirds; place in 3 small bowls. Add different food color to each bowl; blend well. Place each colored frosting in small resealable food storage plastic bag. Cut small hole in bottom corner of each bag.

5 Spread reserved white frosting evenly over cooled cookie. Pipe colored frostings into decorative pattern on mitten. To serve, cut cookie into pieces.

NUTRITIONAL INFORMATION PER SERVING: Calories 300 • Total Fat 10g • Saturated Fat 6g • Cholesterol 5mg • Sodium 110mg • Total Carbohydrate 51g • Dietary Fiber 0g • Sugars 41g • Protein 1g. DIETARY EXCHANGES: 2 Fat • 3-1/2 Other Carbohydrates • 3-1/2 Carbohydrate Choices.

north woods birdhouse cookies

READY IN: 1 Hour 10 Minutes ✳ SERVINGS: 12 Cookies

1 (16.5 oz.) roll refrigerated gingerbread cookie dough
   Vanilla ready-to-spread frosting (from 16 oz. container)
   Thin pretzel sticks

3 Tootsie Roll Midgees® candies, unwrapped
   White decorator icing
   Assorted colors of decorating gels
   Miniature candy-coated chocolate baking bits

1 Heat oven to 350°F. Remove half of cookie dough from wrapper; refrigerate remaining dough until needed. On lightly floured surface with rolling pin, roll half of dough to 1/4-inch thickness.

2 With 3- to 3-1/2-inch cookie cutters such as diamond, heart or star, cut out dough shapes for birdhouses (or cut desired shapes from dough with knife). Use 1-inch canapé cutter or sharp knife to make "door" in bottom half of each. If desired, use drinking straw to make hole in top of cookie for hanging. Place 3 inches apart on ungreased cookie sheet. Repeat with the remaining half of dough.

3 For decorations on birdhouses, roll scraps of dough and cut miniature shapes such as trees, stars and other small shapes; do not attach to birdhouses. Place miniature shapes on cookie sheets.

4 Bake 7 to 11 minutes or until set (bake small shapes about 7 minutes). Carefully remove from cookie sheet; place on wire racks. If necessary, re-poke holes for hanging. Cool completely, about 20 minutes.

5 To decorate cookies, use vanilla frosting to attach small baked shapes to birdhouses. Attach pretzels for roofs. Cut each unwrapped candy into 4 lengthwise pieces; attach 1 piece with frosting below door to resemble perch. Use vanilla frosting or decorator icing to make snow on roofs. Use decorating gels and baking bits to add decorations or words to birdhouses.

NUTRITIONAL INFORMATION PER SERVING: Calories 370 • Total Fat 15g • Saturated Fat 7g • Cholesterol 15mg • Sodium 250mg • Total Carbohydrate 57g • Dietary Fiber 0g • Sugars 39g • Protein 2g. DIETARY EXCHANGES: 4 Other Carbohydrate • 3 Fat.

christmas tree candy pops

READY IN: 35 Minutes ✳ SERVINGS: 24

1 (6-1/2 oz.) cup green candy melts or coating wafers
   Small candies and/or decorating icing

Flat wooden sticks with rounded ends
Plastic wrap

1 Line cookie sheets with foil. Melt candy melts as directed on package. Spoon melted candy into resealable food storage plastic bag or small plastic squeeze bottle; seal bag or cover bottle. If using bags, cut small hole in one bottom corner.

2 On foil-lined cookie sheets, squeeze out melted candy to create 3-inch tree shapes about 1/4 inch thick. Immediately decorate as desired with candies or icing.

3 Freeze 1 minute to set. When set, peel candy pops from foil. To attach shapes to wooden sticks, place small amount of melted coating on stick; gently press shape onto stick. Let stand 5 minutes or until set. Wrap each in plastic wrap.

NUTRITIONAL INFORMATION PER SERVING: Calories 75 • Total Fat 4g • Saturated Fat 3g • Cholesterol 5mg • Sodium 10mg • Total Carbohydrate 9g • Dietary Fiber 0g • Sugars 9g • Protein 1g. DIETARY EXCHANGES: 1 Fat • 1/2 Other Carbohydrate • 1/2 Carbohydrate Choice.

north woods
birdhouse cookies

fun with santa cookies

fun with santa cookies

READY IN: 1 Hour ✴ SERVINGS: 24 Cookies

1 roll (16.5 oz.) refrigerated sugar cookie dough	Red food color (liquid or paste)
1/2 cup vanilla ready-to-spread frosting (from 16 oz. container)	Miniature candy-coated chocolate baking bits and/or chocolate chips

1 Heat oven to 350°F. Remove half of cookie dough from wrapper; refrigerate remaining dough until needed. On lightly floured surface with rolling pin, roll out half of dough to 1/4-inch thickness.

2 With cookie cutters, cut dough into 2-1/2-inch circles, ovals, stars and half moon shapes (see shapes in photo at left); place 2 inches apart on ungreased cookie sheet. Repeat with remaining half of dough.

3 Bake 6 to 8 minutes or until light golden brown. Immediately remove from cookie sheet; place on wire racks. Cool completely, about 15 minutes.

4 In small bowl, mix vanilla frosting and red food color until well blended and desired red color. Decorate cookies as cleverly shaped Santas with red frosting and baking bits.

NUTRITIONAL INFORMATION PER SERVING: Calories 140 • Total Fat 4g • Saturated Fat 2g • Cholesterol 0mg • Sodium 75mg • Total Carbohydrate 25g • Dietary Fiber 0g • Sugars 19g • Protein 1g. DIETARY EXCHANGES: 1-1/2 Other Carbohydrate • 1 Fat.

roly-poly snowmen

PREP TIME: 1 Hour ✴ READY IN: 1 Hour 15 Minutes ✴ SERVINGS: 12 Cookies

1 (16.5 oz.) roll refrigerated sugar cookie dough	Decorator icing or decorating gel
1/4 cup all-purpose flour	Assorted miniature candies
	Orange gumdrops (cut into pieces for noses)

1 Heat oven to 350°F. Remove half of cookie dough from wrapper; refrigerate remaining dough until needed.

2 On lightly floured surface, knead 2 tablespoons of the flour into half of dough. Shape dough into 6 (3/4-inch), 6 (1-inch) and 6 (1-1/4-inch) balls. To form snowmen, place 1 ball of each size, 1/4 inch apart, on ungreased cookie sheet. Repeat with remaining half of dough.

3 Bake 12 to 16 minutes or until edges are light golden brown. Cool 1 minute; remove from cookie sheet and place on wire racks. Cool completely, about 15 minutes. Decorate each cookie with icing and candies.

HIGH ALTITUDE (3500-6500 FT): Bake at 350°F for 14 to 18 minutes. Continue as directed above.

NUTRITIONAL INFORMATION PER SERVING: Calories 305 • Total Fat 10g • Saturated Fat 5g • Cholesterol 5mg • Sodium 160mg • Total Carbohydrate 51g • Dietary Fiber 0g • Sugars 36g • Protein 3g. DIETARY EXCHANGES: 1 Starch • 2-1/2 Other Carbohydrate • 2 Fat.

kitchen tip

Paste colors can be found at baking supply stores or at craft stores among the cake decorating supplies. Since paste colors produce an intense deep color, start by using a small amount. Store paste colors at room temperature.

kitchen tip

These whimsical snowmen are perfect to use as holiday favors on your table. Wrap each cookie individually in plastic wrap or cellophane and tie with a bow to match the colors of your table.

Wintry Desserts

Impressive edibles are longtime hallmarks of the holiday season. Now you can bejewel your buffet table and deck out your dinner with these simply sweet sensations.

p. 258

p. 263

p. 295

p. 267

p. 308

strawberry pretzel delight p. 269

cook's notes

Cheesecakes without chocolate drizzle can be frozen in a tightly covered freezer container for up to 1 month. To thaw, refrigerate overnight or let stand at room temperature for 30 minutes.

cookies 'n cream mini cheesecakes

PREP TIME: 25 Minutes ✻ READY IN: 2 Hours 10 Minutes ✻ SERVINGS: 24

CRUST

16 creme-filled chocolate sandwich cookies, crushed (about 1-1/2 cups)

2 tablespoons butter, melted

FILLING

1 (8 oz.) package cream cheese, softened

1/4 cup milk

2 tablespoons sugar

1 teaspoon vanilla

1 egg

4 creme-filled chocolate sandwich cookies, cut into 1/4-inch pieces (about 1/2 cup)

CHOCOLATE TOPPING

3 tablespoons semisweet chocolate chips

1 teaspoon shortening

1 Heat oven to 325°F. Line 24 miniature muffin cups with paper baking cups. In small bowl, combine crushed cookies and butter; mix well. Press 1 teaspoon cookie mixture firmly in bottom of each paper-lined muffin cup.

2 In large bowl, combine cream cheese, milk and sugar; beat with electric mixer at medium speed until light and fluffy. Add vanilla and egg; beat well. Fold in cut-up cookies. Spoon 1 heaping tablespoon cream cheese mixture into each crust-lined muffin cup.

3 Bake for 12 to 14 minutes or until edges are set and centers are still soft. Cool in pan on wire rack for 30 minutes. Refrigerate at least 1 hour or up to 48 hours before serving.

4 Just before serving, in 1-cup microwavable measuring cup, combine chocolate chips and shortening. Microwave on High for 30 to 45 seconds or until melted, stirring once. Drizzle chocolate over tops of cheesecakes. Store in refrigerator.

NUTRITIONAL INFORMATION PER SERVING: Calories 105 • Total Fat 7g • Saturated Fat 4g • Cholesterol 20mg • Sodium 95mg • Total Carbohydrate 8g • Dietary Fiber 0g • Sugars 5g • Protein 2g. DIETARY EXCHANGES: 1/2 Starch • 1-1/2 Fat.

quick saucy cranberry cake

PREP TIME: 15 Minutes ✳ READY IN: 1 Hour 25 Minutes ✳ SERVINGS: 9

1 (15.6 oz.) package cranberry-orange quick bread mix

1/2 cup water

2 tablespoons oil

2 eggs

1 cup fresh cranberries

3/4 cup firmly packed brown sugar

1-1/4 cups boiling water

1 Heat oven to 350°F. Spray 8-inch square (2-quart) glass baking dish with nonstick cooking spray. In large bowl, combine bread mix, water, oil and eggs; stir 50 to 75 strokes with spoon until mix is moistened.

2 Sprinkle cranberries in sprayed baking dish. Spoon and spread batter evenly over cranberries. Sprinkle with brown sugar. Pour boiling water evenly over batter.

3 Bake for 35 to 40 minutes or until cake is golden brown and top springs back when touched lightly in center. Cool at least 30 minutes.

4 To serve, cut cake into squares. Invert squares onto individual dessert plates. If desired, top with sweetened whipped cream. Store in refrigerator.

HIGH ALTITUDE (3500-6500 FT): Bake at 375°F for 33 to 38 minutes.

NUTRITIONAL INFORMATION PER SERVING: Calories 340 • Total Fat 7g • Saturated Fat 3g • Cholesterol 25mg • Sodium 370mg • Total Carbohydrate 66g • Dietary Fiber 1g • Sugars 45g • Protein 4g. DIETARY EXCHANGES: 1 Starch • 3-1/2 Fruit • 4-1/2 Other Carbohydrate • 1 Fat.

chocolate-glazed fudge cake

chocolate-glazed fudge cake

PREP TIME: 30 Minutes ✳ READY IN: 2 Hours 10 Minutes ✳ SERVINGS: 16

CAKE
- 1 cup butter
- 16 oz. semisweet chocolate, chopped
- 2 teaspoons vanilla
- 6 eggs, lightly beaten

GLAZE
- 1/4 cup whipping cream
- 1 tablespoon light corn syrup
- 1 teaspoon vanilla
- 3 oz. semisweet chocolate, chopped

GARNISH
- 2 tablespoons chopped toasted hazelnuts (filberts)

1 Heat oven to 350°F. Grease 8-inch round cake pan. In medium saucepan, melt butter and 16 oz. chocolate over medium-low heat, stirring until smooth. Remove from heat. Stir in 2 teaspoons vanilla. Gently stir in eggs until well combined. Pour into greased pan. Place cake pan in 13x9-inch pan; add warm water until 1 inch deep.

2 Bake for 35 to 40 minutes or until center is set. Remove cake pan from water bath; place on wire rack. Cool 40 minutes.

3 Carefully run a knife around the edge of pan; invert cake onto wire rack. Cool an additional 20 minutes.

4 Meanwhile, in small saucepan, combine whipping cream, corn syrup and 1 teaspoon vanilla. Bring to a boil over medium heat, stirring occasionally. Remove from heat. Add 3 oz. chocolate; stir until melted and smooth.

5 Place cake on serving platter. Place pieces of waxed paper under cake to catch drips. Slowly pour glaze over top and sides of cake to cover. With narrow metal spatula, smooth glaze over cake. Sprinkle hazelnuts around top edge of cake. When the glaze is set, remove waxed paper. Store in the refrigerator.

HIGH ALTITUDE (3500-6500 FT): Bake at 350°F for 45 to 50 minutes.

NUTRITIONAL INFORMATION PER SERVING: Calories 335 • Total Fat 25g • Saturated Fat 15g • Cholesterol 115mg • Sodium 110mg • Total Carbohydrate 23g • Dietary Fiber 2g • Sugars 19g • Protein 4g. DIETARY EXCHANGES: 1-1/2 Starch • 5 Fat.

streusel-topped cranberry-pear tart

PREP TIME: 25 Minutes ✳ READY IN: 1 Hour 20 Minutes ✳ SERVINGS: 8

CRUST AND FILLING
- 1 refrigerated pie crust (from 15 oz. box), softened as directed on box
- 1/2 cup sugar
- 4 teaspoons cornstarch
- 2 teaspoons ground cinnamon
- 4 cups thinly sliced peeled pears
- 3/4 cup fresh or frozen cranberries

TOPPING
- 1/4 cup sugar
- 1/4 cup all-purpose flour
- 2 tablespoons butter or margarine, softened

1 Place cookie sheet in oven on middle oven rack. Heat oven to 375°F. Place crust in 9-inch tart pan with removable bottom as directed on box for One-Crust Filled Pie.

2 In large bowl, mix 1/2 cup sugar, the cornstarch and cinnamon. Add pears and cranberries; toss gently to coat. Spoon into crust-lined pan.

3 In small bowl, mix all of the topping ingredients with a fork until well blended. Sprinkle mixture over filling.

4 Place tart on cookie sheet in oven. Bake 45 to 55 minutes or until crust is deep golden brown and pears are tender. Serve warm or cool.

NUTRITIONAL INFORMATION PER SERVING: Calories 290 • Total Fat 10g • Saturated Fat 4.5g • Trans Fat 0g • Cholesterol 10mg • Sodium 130mg • Total Carbohydrate 50g • Dietary Fiber 3g • Sugars 27g • Protein 0g. DIETARY EXCHANGES: 1/2 Fruit • 3 Other Carbohydrate • 2 Fat.

kitchen tip

The superfine and powdered sugars in these meringue cookies ensure that they will be light in texture. To make superfine sugar, place granulated sugar in the bowl of a food processor fitted with a metal blade. Pulse sugar briefly until very fine.

A small amount of almond extract in nut-based recipes brightens and intensifies the nutty flavor, no matter which nut is used.

hazelnut meringues

PREP TIME: 45 Minutes ✳ READY IN: 2 Hours 30 Minutes ✳ SERVINGS: 24

1/4 cup hazelnuts (filberts)	1/4 teaspoon cream of tartar
1/4 cup powdered sugar	1/4 cup superfine sugar
2 egg whites	1/8 teaspoon almond extract

1 Heat oven to 350°F. Place hazelnuts in single layer on ungreased cookie sheet. Bake for 10 minutes or until skins begin to loosen and hazelnuts turn golden brown.

2 Remove hazelnuts from oven; place on towel. Wrap towel around hazelnuts; let stand 10 minutes. Rub hazelnuts with towel to remove as much skin as possible.

3 In food processor bowl with metal blade, combine hazelnuts and powdered sugar. Process until fine powder forms. Set aside.

4 Reduce oven temperature to 200°F. Line cookie sheets with parchment paper. In large bowl, beat egg whites with electric mixer at Medium speed until foamy. Beat in cream of tartar. Increase speed to High; beat until soft peaks form. Slowly beat in superfine sugar. Continue beating until egg whites are glossy and stiff. Beat in almond extract. Quickly fold in nut powder.

5 Place meringue mixture in large decorating bag or resealable gallon plastic bag fitted with 1/2-inch open star tip. Pipe meringue into star shapes onto paper-lined cookie sheets.

6 Bake at 200°F for 1-1/4 to 1-1/2 hours or until crisp. Cool on cookie sheet for 15 minutes or until completely cooled. Gently remove from parchment paper.

NUTRITIONAL INFORMATION PER SERVING: Calories 25 • Total Fat 1g • Saturated Fat 0g • Cholesterol 0mg • Sodium 0mg • Total Carbohydrate 4g • Dietary Fiber 0g • Sugars 3g • Protein 0g. DIETARY EXCHANGES: 1/2 Fruit • 1/2 Other Carbohydrate.

lemon sorbet with strawberry sauce

READY IN: 15 Minutes ✳ SERVINGS: 10

2 cups frozen whole strawberries	1/4 cup orange-flavored liqueur
1/4 cup sugar	2-1/2 pints lemon sorbet (5 cups)

1 In blender container or food processor bowl with metal blade, combine strawberries, sugar and liqueur; blend until smooth.

2 To serve, scoop sorbet into individual dessert dishes. Spoon about 2 tablespoons sauce over each. If desired, garnish with additional fresh berries.

NUTRITIONAL INFORMATION PER SERVING: Calories 170 • Total Fat 0g • Saturated Fat 0g • Cholesterol 0mg • Sodium 0mg • Total Carbohydrate 41g • Dietary Fiber 2g • Sugars 37g • Protein 0g. DIETARY EXCHANGES: 3 Fruit • 3 Other Carbohydrate.

cook's notes

Subtitute 1 teaspoon grated orange peel for the orange-flavored liqueur.

lemon sorbet with strawberry sauce
hazelnut meringues

cook's notes

Remember to first soften gelatin for 1 to 3 minutes in cold liquid before heating it to dissolve. The cool water swells the gelatin granules so they fully, easily and quickly dissolve in hot liquid without over-heating.

Remove the gelatin mixture from the heat as soon as all the granules have disappeared.

To keep the whole candies from melting into the topping, garnish the dessert squares just before serving.

creamy peppermint-topped brownie dessert

PREP TIME: 30 Minutes ✳ READY IN: 2 Hours 45 Minutes ✳ SERVINGS: 24

BROWNIE BASE
- 1 (19.8 oz.) package fudge brownie mix
- 1/2 cup oil
- 1/4 cup water
- 2 eggs

TOPPING
- 2 cups whipping cream
- 1 envelope unflavored gelatin
- 1 cup crushed round peppermint candies (about 40 candies)
- 24 round peppermint candies

1 Heat oven to 350°F. Line 13x9-inch pan with foil; spray bottom only with nonstick cooking spray. Prepare brownie mix as directed on package, using oil, water and eggs. Spread in sprayed foil-lined pan. Bake at 350°F for 28 to 30 minutes. Do not overbake. Cool in pan on wire rack for 1 hour.

2 While brownies are cooling, place 1/2 cup of the whipping cream in small saucepan. Sprinkle gelatin over cream; let stand 5 minutes to soften. Heat over low heat for 2 to 3 minutes or until gelatin has dissolved, stirring occasionally. Remove from heat. Stir in half of the crushed candies. Cool 20 to 25 minutes or until lukewarm, stirring occasionally. (Most of the candy will melt.)

3 Beat remaining 1-1/2 cups whipping cream in large bowl until stiff peaks form. Fold in remaining half of crushed candies. Working quickly, stir 1/4 of whipped cream mixture into gelatin mixture. Fold gelatin mixture into remaining whipped cream until blended.

4 Spread whipped cream mixture over cooled brownies. Cover; refrigerate at least 1 hour or until serving time.

5 To serve, using foil lift dessert from pan; cut into squares. Top each serving with whole peppermint candy.

HIGH ALTITUDE (3500-6500 FT): See brownie package for directions.

NUTRITIONAL INFORMATION PER SERVING: Calories 365 • Total Fat 21g • Saturated Fat 8g • Cholesterol 60mg • Sodium 65mg • Total Carbohydrate 43g • Dietary Fiber 2g • Sugars 35g • Protein 3g. DIETARY EXCHANGES: 1 Starch • 1-1/2 Fruit • 2-1/2 Other Carbohydrate • 4 Fat.

chocolate silk pecan pie

SERVINGS: 10

1 refrigerated pie crust (from 15 oz. pkg.)

PECAN FILLING

1/3 cup sugar

1/2 cup dark corn syrup

3 tablespoons margarine or butter, melted

1/8 teaspoon salt, if desired

2 eggs

1/2 cup chopped pecans

FILLING

1 cup hot milk

1/4 teaspoon vanilla

1-1/3 cups semisweet chocolate chips

TOPPING

1 cup whipping cream

2 tablespoons powdered sugar

1/4 teaspoon vanilla

Chocolate curls, if desired

LEONARD (LEN) THOMPSON
San Jose, California
Bake-Off® Contest 32, 1986
Prize Winner

1. Prepare pie crust according to package directions for one-crust filled pie using 9-inch pie pan. Heat oven to 350°F. In small bowl, combine sugar, corn syrup, margarine, salt and eggs; beat 1 minute at Medium speed. Stir in pecans. Pour into crust-lined pan. Bake for 40 to 55 minutes or until center of pie is puffed and golden brown. Cool 1 hour.

2. While filled crust is cooling, in blender container or food processor bowl with metal blade, combine all filling ingredients; blend 1 minute or until smooth. Refrigerate about 1-1/2 hours or until mixture is slightly thickened but not set. Gently stir; pour into cooled filled crust. Refrigerate until firm, about 1 hour.

3. In small bowl, beat topping ingredients until stiff peaks form. Spoon or pipe over filling. Garnish with chocolate curls. Store in refrigerator.

NUTRITIONAL INFORMATION PER SERVING: Calories 490 • Fat 32g • Sodium 240mg • Total Carbohydrate 46g • Protein 5g.

mocha cappuccino pudding cake

PREP TIME: 10 Minutes ✳ READY IN: 55 Minutes ✳ SERVINGS: 9

CAKE

1-1/4 cups all-purpose flour

3/4 cup sugar

2 tablespoons unsweetened baking cocoa

1 tablespoon instant espresso coffee granules

1-1/2 teaspoons baking powder

1/2 teaspoon salt

1/2 cup fat-free (skim) milk

2 tablespoons butter or margarine, melted

1 teaspoon vanilla

PUDDING

1 cup sugar

2 tablespoons unsweetened baking cocoa

1 teaspoon instant espresso coffee granules

1-1/2 cups very warm fat-free (skim) milk (120°F to 130°F)

Fat-free frozen yogurt, if desired

Fresh or frozen raspberries, if desired

cook's notes

Pudding cake is a magical dessert. It bakes like a cake, while creating its own pudding-like topping!

1. Heat oven to 350°F. In medium bowl, mix flour, 3/4 cup sugar, 2 tablespoons cocoa, 1 tablespoon espresso coffee, the baking powder and salt. Stir in all remaining cake ingredients until well blended; spread in ungreased 9-inch square pan.

2. In small bowl, mix all pudding ingredients except milk; sprinkle evenly over cake batter. Pour very warm milk over sugar mixture.

3. Bake 35 to 45 minutes or until center is set and firm to the touch. If desired, place foil or cookie sheet on lower oven rack under cake to catch any spills. To serve, spoon warm cake into dessert dishes. If desired, top with frozen yogurt and/or raspberries.

NUTRITIONAL INFORMATION PER SERVING: Calories 270 • Total Fat 3g • Saturated Fat 2g • Cholesterol 10mg • Sodium 260mg • Total Carbohydrate 57g • Dietary Fiber 1g • Sugars 42g • Protein 4g. DIETARY EXCHANGES: 1 Starch • 3 Other Carbohydrate • 1/2 Fat.

strawberry fudge pie

PREP TIME: 30 Minutes ❋ READY IN: 3 Hours 20 Minutes ❋ SERVINGS: 8

CRUST
- 1 refrigerated pie crust (from 15 oz. box), softened as directed on package

BROWNIE LAYER
- 1 (10.25 oz.) package fudge brownie mix
- 1/4 cup oil
- 2 tablespoons water
- 1 egg

CHEESECAKE LAYER
- 1 (8 oz.) package cream cheese, softened
- 1/4 cup sugar
- 1 teaspoon vanilla
- 1 egg

TOPPING
- 3 cups fresh strawberries, halved
- 2 tablespoons hot fudge ice cream topping

1 Heat oven to 350°F. Place pie crust in 9-inch glass pie plate as directed on package for one-crust filled pie.

2 In large bowl, combine all brownie layer ingredients; beat 50 strokes with spoon. Spread in bottom of crust-lined pan.

3 Bake for 30 to 35 minutes or until top is shiny and center is set. If necessary, cover edge of crust with strips of foil after 15 to 20 minutes of baking to prevent excessive browning.

4 Meanwhile, in small bowl, combine cream cheese, sugar, vanilla and 1 egg; beat until smooth. Working quickly, drop cream cheese mixture by small spoonfuls over partially baked brownies; carefully spread to cover brownie layer. Bake an additional 18 to 20 minutes or until cream cheese is set. Cool at least 1 hour.

5 Arrange strawberry halves, cut side down, over top of cream cheese layer. Refrigerate 1 hour or until serving time. Immediately before serving, place ice cream topping in small microwavable dish. Microwave on Defrost for 45 seconds. Spoon into small resealable plastic bag; seal bag. Cut small hole in bottom corner of bag; squeeze bag to drizzle topping over pie. Store in refrigerator.

HIGH ALTITUDE (3500-6500 FT): For brownie layer, see package for directions. Before baking, cover edge of crust with strips of foil to prevent excessive browning. Bake as directed above.

NUTRITIONAL INFORMATION PER SERVING: Calories 500 • Total Fat 27g • Saturated Fat 11g • Cholesterol 90mg • Sodium 360mg • Total Carbohydrate 58g • Dietary Fiber 3g • Sugars 34g • Protein 6g. DIETARY EXCHANGES: 2 Starch • 2 Fruit • 4 Other Carbohydrate • 5 Fat.

eggnog ice cream dessert

PREP TIME: 25 Minutes ❋ READY IN: 4 Hours 55 Minutes ❋ SERVINGS: 16

- 24 gingersnap cookies
- 1/2 cup chopped pecans
- 1/4 cup butter, melted
- 6 cups vanilla ice cream, softened (3 pints)
- 1-1/2 teaspoons nutmeg
- 1-1/2 teaspoons rum extract
- 16 pecan halves, toasted

1 Heat oven to 350°F. In food processor bowl with metal blade, process gingersnaps and chopped pecans until mixture is finely ground. Add butter; process until mixed. Press mixture in bottom and 1 inch up sides of ungreased 9-inch springform pan. Bake for 8 to 10 minutes or until edges are lightly browned. Cool 30 minutes or until completely cooled.

2 In large bowl, combine softened ice cream, nutmeg and rum extract; stir until blended. Spread evenly in crust-lined pan. Place pecan halves around top edge of torte. Cover dessert; freeze at least 4 hours or up to 2 weeks.

3 To serve, let dessert stand at room temperature for 15 minutes. Run knife around edge of dessert; remove sides of pan. Cut into wedges to serve.

NUTRITIONAL INFORMATION PER SERVING: Calories 210 • Total Fat 13g • Saturated Fat 6g • Cholesterol 30mg • Sodium 140mg • Total Carbohydrate 21g • Dietary Fiber 1g • Sugars 13g • Protein 3g. DIETARY EXCHANGES: 1 Starch • 1/2 Fruit • 1-1/2 Other Carbohydrate • 2-1/2 Fat.

strawberry fudge pie
eggnog ice cream dessert

cranberry-apple pie squares

PREP TIME: 40 Minutes ✳ READY IN: 2 Hours 40 Minutes ✳ SERVINGS: 12

CRUST
- 1-1/2 cups all-purpose flour
- 1 tablespoon sugar
- 1/4 teaspoon salt
- 1/2 cup butter or margarine
- 1 egg yolk
- 1/4 cup milk

FILLING
- 8-1/2 cups thinly sliced, peeled baking apples (3 lb.; about 9 medium)
- 1 cup sugar
- 1/4 cup all-purpose flour
- 2 teaspoons cinnamon
- 1/2 teaspoon salt
- 1 cup chopped fresh or frozen cranberries, thawed

TOPPING
- 1 cup all-purpose flour
- 1/2 cup firmly packed brown sugar
- 1/2 cup butter or margarine, softened
- 1 cup caramel ice cream topping, heated
  Vanilla or cinnamon ice cream, if desired

1 Heat oven to 375°F. In large bowl, combine 1-1/2 cups flour, sugar and 1/4 teaspoon salt; mix well. With pastry blender, cut in 1/2 cup butter until mixture resembles coarse crumbs.

2 In small bowl, combine egg yolk and milk; beat well. Add to flour mixture; stir just until dry ingredients are moistened.

3 On lightly floured surface, roll dough to form 15x11-inch rectangle. Place in ungreased 13x9-inch pan. Press in bottom and 1 inch up sides of pan.

4 Place apples in large microwave-safe bowl. Microwave on High for 6 to 8 minutes, stirring every 2 minutes, or until apples are fork-tender. Add 1 cup sugar, 1/4 cup flour, cinnamon and 1/2 teaspoon salt; mix well. Spoon apple mixture over crust. Sprinkle with cranberries.

5 In medium bowl, combine 1 cup flour, brown sugar and 1/2 cup butter; mix until crumbly. Sprinkle over fruit.

6 Bake for 45 to 60 minutes or until topping is deep golden brown, apples are tender and filling is bubbly. Cool 1 hour.

7 To serve, cut warm dessert into squares; place on individual dessert plates. Top each with caramel topping and ice cream.

HIGH ALTITUDE (3500-6500 FT): Increase flour in filling to 1/2 cup. Microwave apples on High for 8 to 10 minutes. Bake at 400°F for 45 to 60 minutes.

NUTRITIONAL INFORMATION PER SERVING: Calories 480 • Total Fat 16g • Saturated Fat 10g • Cholesterol 60mg • Sodium 350mg • Total Carbohydrate 80g • Dietary Fiber 3g • Sugars 50g • Protein 4g. DIETARY EXCHANGES: 1 Starch • 4 Other Carbohydrate • 3-1/2 Fat.

fudgy peppermint truffle chocolate cake

PREP TIME: 30 Minutes ✳ READY IN: 2 Hours 15 Minutes ✳ SERVINGS: 12

FILLING

- 1 (6 oz.) package semisweet chocolate chips (1 cup)
- 2/3 cup sweetened condensed milk (not evaporated)
- 1/2 teaspoon peppermint extract

CAKE

- 1 (18.25 oz.) package devil's food cake mix with pudding

- 1 (8 oz.) container nonfat sour cream
- 1/3 cup oil
- 3 eggs

ICING

- 3/4 cup powdered sugar
- 1-1/2 oz. cream cheese, softened
- 1 to 2 tablespoons milk
- 6 hard peppermint candies, finely crushed

1 Heat oven to 350°F. Grease and flour 12-cup fluted tube pan. In medium microwavable bowl, combine all filling ingredients. Microwave on High for 30 seconds; stir until melted and smooth. If necessary, microwave an additional 10 to 20 seconds. Set aside.

2 In large bowl, combine all cake ingredients; beat with electric mixer at Low speed until combined. Beat 2 minutes at Medium speed. Spoon into greased and floured pan. Drop spoonfuls of filling over batter, keeping filling away from sides of pan.

3 Bake for 35 to 45 minutes or until toothpick inserted near center comes out clean and edges begin to pull away from sides of pan. Cool in pan for 10 minutes. Invert cake onto wire rack. Cool 1 hour or until completely cooled. (Center of cake may sink slightly during cooling.)

4 In medium bowl, combine powdered sugar, cream cheese and 1 tablespoon of the milk; beat with wire whisk until smooth, adding additional milk until of desired drizzling consistency. Drizzle icing over cooled cake. Sprinkle with crushed candy. Store in refrigerator.

HIGH ALTITUDE (3500-6500 FT): For cake, add 2 tablespoons flour to dry cake mix; decrease oil to 2 tablespoons and increase eggs to 4. Bake at 375°F for 40 to 45 minutes.

NUTRITIONAL INFORMATION PER SERVING: Calories 445 • Total Fat 18g • Saturated Fat 6g • Cholesterol 65mg • Sodium 450mg • Total Carbohydrate 64g • Dietary Fiber 2g • Sugars 51g • Protein 7g. DIETARY EXCHANGES: 2 Starch • 2 Other Carbohydrate • 3-1/2 Fat.

cook's notes

Don't like peppermint? Omit the peppermint extract and garnish the cake with chocolate curls if you'd like.

raspberry-glazed double chocolate dessert

PREP TIME: 1 Hour ✱ READY IN: 4 Hours 15 Minutes ✱ SERVINGS: 16

CAKE
- 16 oz. semisweet chocolate
- 1 cup unsalted butter
- 6 eggs

WHITE CHOCOLATE GANACHE
- 8 oz. white chocolate baking bar, cut into small pieces
- 1/2 cup whipping cream
- 1 tablespoon unsalted butter

RASPBERRY GLAZE
- 1 (10 oz.) package frozen raspberries in syrup, thawed
- 1 tablespoon cornstarch

TOPPING
- 1 cup whipping cream
- 1 cup fresh raspberries

1 Heat oven to 400°F. Spray 9-inch springform pan with nonstick cooking spray. In medium saucepan, melt semisweet chocolate and 1 cup butter over medium-low heat, stirring constantly until smooth. Cool 35 minutes or until completely cooled.

2 Beat eggs in small bowl at High speed for 5 minutes or until light and lemon colored. Fold cooled chocolate into eggs until well blended. Pour into sprayed pan.

3 Bake for 15 minutes. Dessert will be soft in center. Cool in pan on wire rack for 1-1/2 hours or until completely cooled. Refrigerate 1-1/2 hours or until firm.

4 Meanwhile, place white chocolate baking bar in small bowl. In small saucepan, bring 1/2 cup whipping cream and 1 tablespoon butter just to a boil. Pour over chocolate; stir until smooth. Cool 5 minutes or until completely cooled. Refrigerate 1 hour or until chilled.

5 Place strainer over saucepan; pour raspberries into strainer. Press mixture with back of spoon through strainer to remove seeds; discard seeds. Stir in cornstarch. Cook over medium heat until mixture boils and thickens, stirring constantly. Cool 30 minutes or until completely cooled.

6 Spread white chocolate ganache on top of cooled dessert. Spread raspberry glaze over ganache. Refrigerate 30 minutes; serve or refrigerate until serving time.

7 To serve, let dessert stand at room temperature for 1 hour. In medium bowl, beat 1 cup whipping cream until stiff peaks form. Spoon whipped cream into pastry bag with large star tip. Pipe cream onto edge of dessert. Garnish with fresh raspberries.

HIGH ALTITUDE (3500-6500 FT): Spray 10-inch springform pan with nonstick cooking spray. Bake at 400°F for 20 minutes.

NUTRITIONAL INFORMATION PER SERVING: Calories 460 • Total Fat 34g • Saturated Fat 20g • Cholesterol 140mg • Sodium 50mg • Total Carbohydrate 33g • Dietary Fiber 3g • Sugars 30g • Protein 5g. DIETARY EXCHANGES: 1-1/2 Starch • 1 Fruit • 2-1/2 Other Carbohydrate • 6 Fat.

brandied cherry sauce over ice cream

READY IN: 10 Minutes ✱ SERVINGS: 8

- 1 (15.5 oz.) can pitted dark sweet (Bing) cherries
- Orange juice (about 1/4 cup)
- 1/4 cup sugar
- 1 tablespoon cornstarch
- 2 tablespoons brandy, if desired
- 1 quart vanilla ice cream (4 cups)

1 Drain cherry liquid into 1-cup measuring cup; add enough orange juice to make 1 cup. Set cherries aside.

2 In small saucepan, combine cherry liquid mixture, sugar and cornstarch; mix well. Cook over medium heat until mixture comes to a boil, stirring constantly. Remove from heat. Stir in brandy and cherries. Serve sauce warm or cold over individual servings of ice cream.

NUTRITIONAL INFORMATION PER SERVING: Calories 215 • Total Fat 7g • Saturated Fat 5g • Cholesterol 30mg • Sodium 55mg • Total Carbohydrate 35g • Dietary Fiber 0g • Sugars 29g • Protein 3g. DIETARY EXCHANGES: 1 Starch • 1 Fruit • 1-1/2 Fat.

raspberry-glazed double chocolate dessert

crème de menthe cheesecake

PREP TIME: 20 Minutes ✷ READY IN: 6 Hours ✷ SERVINGS: 16

CRUST
- 1-3/4 cups chocolate cookie crumbs (from 9 oz. pkg.)
- 1/4 cup butter, melted

FILLING
- 3 (8 oz.) packages cream cheese, softened
- 3/4 cup sugar
- 3 eggs
- 3/4 cup whipping cream
- 1/4 cup green crème de menthe

GARNISH
- 1/2 cup whipping cream
- 1 tablespoon powdered sugar
- 8 thin chocolate and green mints, coarsely chopped

1 Heat oven to 300°F. In medium bowl, combine crust ingredients; mix well. Press in bottom and up sides of ungreased 9-inch springform pan.

2 Beat cream cheese in large bowl with electric mixer at Medium speed until fluffy. Gradually add sugar, beating until smooth. Add eggs, 1 at a time, beating well after each addition. Stir in 3/4 cup whipping cream and crème de menthe until well blended. Pour into crust-lined pan.

3 Bake for 60 to 70 minutes or until edges are set but center still jiggles slightly when gently shaken. Turn oven off; open oven door at least 4 inches. Let cheesecake sit in oven for 30 minutes or until center is set.

4 Remove cheesecake from oven. Cool in pan on wire rack for 1 hour or until completely cooled. Cover; refrigerate at least 3 hours before serving.

5 Just before serving, carefully run knife around sides of pan to loosen; remove sides of pan. In small bowl, beat 1/2 cup whipping cream and powdered sugar until stiff peaks form. Pipe or spoon whipped cream around edge of cheesecake. Garnish with chopped mints. Store in refrigerator.

HIGH ALTITUDE (3500-6500 FT): To help prevent cracking, place pan filled with 1 to 1-1/2 inches water on oven rack below cheesecake during baking.

NUTRITIONAL INFORMATION PER SERVING: Calories 360 • Total Fat 27g • Saturated Fat 16g • Cholesterol 115mg • Sodium 240mg • Total Carbohydrate 23g • Dietary Fiber 0g • Sugars 17g • Protein 6g. DIETARY EXCHANGES: 1-1/2 Starch • 5-1/2 Fat.

overnight eggnog bread pudding with cherry-bourbon sauce

PREP TIME: 25 Minutes ❋ READY IN: 9 Hours 10 Minutes ❋ SERVINGS: 12

1	(1 lb.) loaf French bread, cut into 1-inch cubes	1	quart dairy eggnog (do not use canned) (4 cups)
1/4	cup sugar	2	tablespoons sugar
3/4	teaspoon nutmeg	1	(21 oz.) can cherry pie filling
4	eggs	1/4	cup butter
		2	tablespoons bourbon

1 Heat oven to 350°F. Spray 13x9-inch (3-quart) glass baking dish with nonstick cooking spray. Place bread cubes in sprayed baking dish.

2 In medium bowl, combine 1/4 cup sugar and nutmeg; mix well. Add eggs; beat well with wire whisk. Stir in eggnog. Pour over bread; stir gently to coat. Cover; refrigerate at least 8 hours or overnight.

3 Heat oven to 350°F. Uncover dish; sprinkle top with 2 tablespoons sugar. Place dish in larger baking pan; place in oven. Pour 1/2 inch water into larger pan. Bake for 40 to 45 minutes or until lightly browned and knife inserted in center comes out clean. Remove pan from water bath.

4 Meanwhile, in medium saucepan, combine pie filling and butter; cook over medium-high heat for about 10 minutes or until butter is melted and filling is bubbly, stirring frequently. Remove from heat; stir in bourbon.

5 To serve, cut bread pudding into squares; place on individual dessert plates. Serve warm with cherry sauce.

NUTRITIONAL INFORMATION PER SERVING: Calories 340 • Total Fat 13g • Saturated Fat 7g • Cholesterol 130mg • Sodium 310mg • Total Carbohydrate 49g • Dietary Fiber 2g • Sugars 28g • Protein 9g. DIETARY EXCHANGES: 2 Starch • 1 Fruit • 3 Other Carbohydrate • 3 Fat.

cook's notes

Prepare the bourbon sauce using another fruit ingredient instead of cherry pie filling. Try preserves, thawed raspberries or a commercial dessert sauce. Orange juice can be used in place of bourbon.

café latte crème brûlée

PREP TIME: 30 Minutes ❋ READY IN: 4 Hours 35 Minutes ❋ SERVINGS: 6

3	cups whipping cream	1/2	cup sugar
2	teaspoons instant coffee granules or crystals	1	teaspoon vanilla
5	egg yolks	6	tablespoons firmly packed brown sugar
2	eggs		

1 Heat oven to 325°F. Place six 6 oz. ramekins or custard cups in 15x10x1-inch baking pan. In medium saucepan, combine whipping cream and instant coffee granules; heat just to a simmer, stirring occasionally. Remove from heat.

2 In medium bowl, combine egg yolks and eggs; beat well. Stir in sugar until combined. With wire whisk, gradually stir in hot cream mixture until well blended. Stir in vanilla. Pour mixture evenly into ramekins.

3 Place pan with ramekins in oven; pour hot water into pan until 1/2 to 3/4 inch up sides of ramekins.

4 Bake for 30 to 35 minutes or until centers of custards are soft set. Carefully remove pan from oven. Place ramekins on wire rack. Cool 30 minutes. Refrigerate at least 3 hours or overnight.

5 Before serving, place ramekins in 15x10x1-inch baking pan. Top each with 1 tablespoon brown sugar. Broil 4 to 6 inches from heat for 1 to 2 minutes or until sugar is melted. (Watch closely.) Or, melt sugar with kitchen torch. Store in refrigerator.

HIGH ALTITUDE (3500-6500 FT): Bake at 325°F for 45 to 50 minutes.

NUTRITIONAL INFORMATION PER SERVING: Calories 610 • Total Fat 50g • Saturated Fat 29g • Cholesterol 415mg • Sodium 80mg • Total Carbohydrate 34g • Dietary Fiber 0g • Sugars 34g • Protein 7g. DIETARY EXCHANGES: 2-1/2 Fruit • 2-1/2 Other Carbohydrate • 1 Medium-Fat Meat • 9 Fat.

cook's notes

Bake the custards one day in advance. Let them cool, then cover the ramekins tightly with plastic wrap so the custards won't pick up flavors from other refrigerated foods. Just before serving, remove the custards from the refrigerator, unwrap, top with brown sugar and broil.

pomegranate tartlets

PREP TIME: 45 Minutes ❄ READY IN: 1 Hour 45 Minutes ❄ SERVINGS: 36 tartlets

CRUST
3   refrigerated pie crusts (from two 15 oz. boxes), softened as directed on package

TOPPING
1   pomegranate

FILLING
1   (3 oz.) package vanilla pudding and pie filling mix (not instant)

1-3/4   cups whipping cream

2   tablespoons dark rum

1   teaspoon powdered sugar

1   Heat oven to 450°F. Remove pie crusts from pouches. Unroll crusts. With 2-1/2-inch round cutter, cut crusts into 36 rounds. Press each round into miniature muffin cup. Bake for 7 to 9 minutes or until lightly browned. Remove tartlet shells from pan; place on wire racks. Cool 10 minutes.

2   Meanwhile, cut pomegranate in half; remove seeds. Set aside. In medium saucepan, combine pudding mix and whipping cream; stir with wire whisk to blend. Cook over medium heat for about 5 minutes or until mixture comes to a boil, stirring constantly. Remove from heat. Stir in rum.

3   Immediately spoon about 2 rounded teaspoons filling into each tartlet shell. Top each with about 1 teaspoon pomegranate seeds.

4   Cover loosely; refrigerate at least 1 hour or until serving time. Just before serving, sprinkle tartlets with powdered sugar.

NUTRITIONAL INFORMATION PER SERVING: Calories 225 • Total Fat 15g • Saturated Fat 5g • Cholesterol 15mg • Sodium 250mg • Total Carbohydrate 20g • Dietary Fiber 0g • Sugars 3g • Protein 3g. DIETARY EXCHANGES: 1 Starch • 1 Other Carbohydrate • 3 Fat.

orange crème dessert with ruby cranberry sauce

PREP TIME: 40 Minutes ✳ READY IN: 3 Hours 40 Minutes ✳ SERVINGS: 12

12 chocolate-covered graham crackers, finely crushed (about 1 cup)	1 envelope unflavored gelatin
2 cups fresh or frozen cranberries	1/4 cup orange juice
3/4 cup sugar	4 (6 oz.) containers orange crème fat-free yogurt (2 cups)
1 teaspoon cornstarch	2 teaspoons grated orange peel
3/4 cup water	2 cups frozen light whipped topping, thawed

1 Heat oven to 375°F. Spray 9-inch springform pan with cooking spray. Press cracker crumbs evenly in bottom of pan. Bake 7 minutes. Place in refrigerator or freezer until completely cooled.

2 Meanwhile, in medium saucepan, mix cranberries, sugar, cornstarch and water until smooth. Heat to boiling over medium heat, stirring constantly. Reduce heat to low; simmer 10 to 15 minutes or until cranberries pop, stirring occasionally. Cool 15 minutes. Refrigerate until serving.

3 In small saucepan, stir gelatin and orange juice; let stand 2 minutes. Place saucepan over low heat; stir until gelatin is dissolved.

4 In blender container, place yogurt and orange peel; blend until smooth. With blender running, add gelatin mixture. Cover; blend at High speed for 15 to 20 seconds or until combined. Spoon into medium bowl. Gently stir in whipped topping. Spoon and gently spread over cooled crust. Refrigerate 3 hours or until set.

5 To serve, run knife around edge of dessert; remove side of pan. Cut dessert into wedges; place on individual dessert plates. Top each with 2 tablespoons cranberry mixture.

NUTRITIONAL INFORMATION PER SERVING: Calories 190 • Total Fat 4g • Saturated Fat 3.5g • Trans Fat 0g • Cholesterol 0mg • Sodium 65mg • Total Carbohydrate 34g • Dietary Fiber 1g • Sugars 28g • Protein 4g. DIETARY EXCHANGES: 1 Starch • 1 Other Carbohydrate • 1 Fat.

special touch

Be sure to put a pot of coffee on when guests sit down for dinner. This way, the coffee is freshly brewed and ready for dessert time immediately after dinner.

chocolate praline layer cake

chocolate praline layer cake

SERVINGS: 16

CAKE
1/2 cup butter or margarine

1/4 cup whipping cream

1 cup firmly packed brown sugar

3/4 cup coarsely chopped pecans

1 (1 lb. 2.25 oz.) package devil's food cake mix with pudding

1-1/4 cups water

1/3 cup oil

3 eggs

TOPPING
1-3/4 cups whipping cream

1/4 cup powdered sugar

1/4 teaspoon vanilla

12 to 16 whole pecans, if desired

12 to 16 chocolate curls, if desired

JULIE KONECNE
Bemidji, Minnesota
Bake-Off® Contest 33, 1988
Grand Prize Winner

1 Heat oven to 325°F. In small heavy saucepan, combine butter, 1/4 cup whipping cream and brown sugar. Cook over low heat just until butter is melted, stirring occasionally. Pour into two 9- or 8-inch round cake pans; sprinkle evenly with chopped pecans.

2 In large bowl, combine cake mix, water, oil and eggs at Low speed until moistened; beat 2 minutes at High speed. Carefully spoon batter over pecan mixture.

3 Bake for 35 to 45 minutes or until cake springs back when touched lightly in center. Cool 5 minutes. Remove from pans. Cool completely.

4 In small bowl, beat 1-3/4 cups whipping cream until soft peaks form. Blend in powdered sugar and vanilla; beat until stiff peaks form.

5 To assemble cake, place 1 layer on serving plate, praline side up. Spread with half of whipped cream. Top with second layer, praline side up; spread top with remaining whipped cream. Garnish with whole pecans and chocolate curls. Store in refrigerator.

HIGH ALTITUDE (3500-6500 FT): Add 1/3 cup flour to dry cake mix; increase water to 1-1/3 cups. Bake at 350°F for 30 to 35 minutes. Immediately remove from pans.

NUTRITIONAL INFORMATION PER SERVING: Calories 460 • Fat 30g • Sodium 340mg • Total Carbohydrate 43g • Protein 4g.

cook's notes

Cake can be prepared in a 13 x 9-inch pan. Bake at 325°F for 50 to 60 minutes or until cake springs back when touched lightly in center. Cool 5 minutes; invert onto serving platter. Cool completely. Frost cake or pipe with whipped cream. Garnish with pecan halves and chocolate curls. Serve with any remaining whipped cream. Store in refrigerator.

individual lemon-lime cream tarts

PREP TIME: 30 Minutes ✳ READY IN: 45 Minutes ✳ SERVINGS: 4

CRUST
1 refrigerated pie crust (from 15 oz. box), softened as directed on package

FILLING
1 (3 oz.) package cream cheese, softened

2 tablespoons powdered sugar

2 tablespoons whipping cream

1 teaspoon grated lime peel

1/4 cup lemon curd (from 10 oz. jar)

GARNISH
Whipped cream

Strips of lime peel

1 Heat oven to 450°F. Cut four 4-inch rounds from crust. Press each crust into 4-inch tart pan; prick bottom with fork. Bake for 5 to 9 minutes or until golden brown. Cool 15 minutes or until completely cooled.

2 Meanwhile, in small bowl, combine cream cheese, powdered sugar and whipping cream; beat until smooth. Divide evenly into cooled tart shells.

3 In small bowl, stir grated lime peel into lemon curd until smooth. Spoon evenly on top of cream cheese mixture in shells to within 1/4 inch of edges. Garnish with whipped cream and lime strips.

HIGH ALTITUDE (3500-6500 FT): Bake at 450°F for 7 to 11 minutes.

cook's notes

The tart crusts can be made ahead. Assemble and bake the crusts, then cool them. Wrap them tightly and freeze them for up to 1 week.

NUTRITIONAL INFORMATION PER SERVING: Calories 440 • Total Fat 28g • Saturated Fat 14g • Cholesterol 55mg • Sodium 290mg • Total Carbohydrate 45g • Dietary Fiber 1g • Sugars 19g • Protein 3g. DIETARY EXCHANGES: 1 Starch • 2 Fruit • 3 Other Carbohydrate • 5-1/2 Fat.

BOBBIE SONEFELD
Hopkins, South Carolina
Bake-Off® Contest 39, 2000
Grand Prize Winner

chocolate-almond mousse cake

PREP TIME: 50 Minutes ✳ READY IN: 1 Hour 10 Minutes ✳ SERVINGS: 16

CAKE

- 1 (1 lb. 2.25 oz.) package devil's food cake mix with pudding
- 1-1/3 cups water
- 1/2 cup vegetable oil
- 3 eggs

MOUSSE

- 12 oz. semisweet chocolate, cut into pieces
- 1/2 cup whipping cream
- 1/4 teaspoon almond extract
- 2-1/2 cups whipping cream, whipped

TOPPING

- 2 tablespoons sliced almonds, toasted

1 Heat oven to 350°F. Spray 15x10x1-inch baking pan with nonstick cooking spray. Line bottom with waxed paper; spray paper. Prepare cake mix as directed on package using water, oil and eggs. Pour batter into sprayed paper-lined pan.

2 Bake for 18 to 20 minutes or until cake springs back when touched lightly in center. Cool cake in pan on wire rack for 10 minutes. Invert cake onto wire rack; remove pan and paper. Cool 15 minutes or until completely cooled.

3 Meanwhile, melt chocolate and 1/2 cup whipping cream in medium saucepan over low heat, stirring constantly. Remove from heat. Stir in almond extract. Cool 10 minutes or until slightly cooled. Fold cooled chocolate mixture into whipped cream.

4 Trim edges of cake. Cut cake lengthwise into 2 long layers. Place 1 layer on serving platter. Spread with 1/3 of mousse. Repeat with remaining cake layer and 1/3 of mousse. Place remaining 1/3 of mousse in decorating bag fitted with star tip. Pipe border around bottom and top of cake. Decorate top of cake with mousse rosettes. Sprinkle almonds over top. Store in refrigerator.

NUTRITIONAL INFORMATION PER SERVING: Calories 460 • Total Fat 31g • Saturated Fat 14g • Cholesterol 90mg • Sodium 320mg • Total Carbohydrate 40g • Dietary Fiber 2g • Sugars 30g • Protein 5g. DIETARY EXCHANGES: 1-1/2 Starch • 6 Fat • 1 Other Carbohydrate • 2-1/2 Carbohydrate Choices.

cream cheese brownie pie

SERVINGS: 8

- 1 refrigerated pie crust (from 15 oz. pkg.)
- 1 (8 oz.) package cream cheese, softened
- 3 tablespoons sugar
- 1 teaspoon vanilla
- 3 eggs

- 1 (15.1 oz.) package fudge brownie mix with hot fudge swirl
- 1/4 cup oil
- 2 tablespoons water
- 1/2 cup chopped pecans

1 Heat oven to 350°F. Place pie crust in 9-inch pie pan according to package directions for one-crust filled pie.

2 In medium bowl, combine the cream cheese, sugar, vanilla and 1 of the eggs; beat until smooth. Set aside.

3 Reserve hot fudge packet from brownie mix for topping. In large bowl, combine brownie mix, oil, 1 tablespoon of the water and remaining 2 eggs; beat 50 strokes with spoon. Spread 1/2 cup brownie mixture in bottom of crust-lined pan. Spoon and carefully spread cream cheese mixture over brownie layer. Top with remaining brownie mixture; spread evenly. Sprinkle with pecans.

4 Bake for 40 to 50 minutes or until center is puffed and crust is golden brown. If necessary, cover edge of crust with strips of foil after 15 to 20 minutes of baking to prevent excessive browning. (Pie may have cracks on surface.)

5 Place hot fudge from packet in small microwavable bowl. Microwave on High for 30 seconds. Stir in remaining tablespoon water. Drizzle fudge over top of pie. Cool 3 hours or until completely cooled. Store in refrigerator.

HIGH ALTITUDE (3500-6500 FT): Add 3 tablespoons flour to dry brownie mix. Bake as directed above.

NUTRITIONAL INFORMATION PER SERVING: Calories 600 • Fat 36g • Sodium 370mg • Total Carbohydrate 60g • Protein 8g.

chocolate-map

PREP TIME: 15 Minutes ✳ READ

CHEESECAKE

- 1-1/2 cups graham cracker crumb
- 1 cup walnut pieces, toasted,
- 1/3 cup butter, melted
- 3 (8 oz.) packages cream ch
- 1 cup maple-flavored syrup
- 1/4 cup packed brown sugar

1 Heat oven to 350°F. In med
blended. Press in bottom a
8 to 10 minutes or until set.

2 Meanwhile, in large bowl,
and creamy. Gradually bea
speed, add eggs 1 at a time, be
beat until smooth.

3 Remove crust from oven.
into crust.

4 Return to oven. Bake 55 f
around edge of cheeseca
least 8 hours before serving.

5 Just before serving, in sm
Carefully remove side of
into wedges.

NUTRITIONAL INFORMATION PER SERVING
Carbohydrate 26g • Dietary Fiber 1g • Su

cranberry m

PREP TIME: 25 Minutes ✳

- 1-1/2 cups cranberry-raspbe
- 3/4 cup sugar
- 3 tablespoons cornstar
- 1/2 cup frozen cranberry-
(from 12 oz. containe

1 In small saucepan, mix
boiling over medium-l

2 Stir in crushed fruit.
Refrigerate 2 hours or

3 Stir chilled cranberry
mixture. Spoon into 6
each with raspberry and n

NUTRITIONAL INFORMATION PER SER
Total Carbohydrate 51g • Dietary Fibe

chocolate-almond mousse cake

kitchen tip

To melt white vanilla chips or candy coating, place 1 cup or 6 oz. at a time in medium microwavable bowl. Microwave on Medium for 3 to 4 minutes or until melted, stirring once halfway through cooking. Stir until smooth.

cook's notes

You can prepare the cake up 1 day in advance or just se in plastic wrap. Add the fil and frosting before serving

Cake layers can be fr for up to 2 months; place resealable plastic freezer Thaw cake at room temp ture; add the filling and fr and refrigerate as directe

new york white chocolate cheesecake

PREP TIME: 1 Hour ✳ READY IN: 7 Hours ✳ SERVINGS: 16

CRUST
- 1 (9 oz.) package chocolate wafer cookies, crushed (2-1/4 cups)
- 6 tablespoons butter or margarine, melted

FILLING
- 2 (8 oz.) packages cream cheese, softened
- 1/2 cup sugar
- 3 eggs
- 1 (12 oz.) package white vanilla chips or 12 oz. vanilla-flavored candy coating, chopped, melted (2 cups)
- 1 cup whipping cream
- 1 teaspoon vanilla

CHOCOLATE SAUCE
- 1/3 cup semisweet chocolate chips
- 1 tablespoon butter
- 1/4 cup boiling water
- 3/4 cup sugar
- 3 tablespoons corn syrup
- 1/2 teaspoon vanilla or mint extract

1 Place 12-inch square sheet of foil on rack below center oven rack in oven. Heat oven to 325°F. In medium bowl, combine crust ingredients; mix well. Press in bottom and about 1 inch up sides of ungreased 10-inch springform pan. Refrigerate while preparing filling.

2 Beat cream cheese in large bowl with electric mixer at Medium speed until smooth. Gradually add 1/2 cup sugar, beating until smooth. Add eggs, 1 at a time, beating well after each addition. Quickly add melted chips, whipping cream and vanilla; beat until smooth. Pour into crust-lined pan.

3 Bake for 55 to 65 minutes or until edges are set; center of cheesecake will be soft. Turn oven off; open oven door at least 4 inches. Let cheesecake sit in oven for 30 minutes or until center is set.

4 Remove cheesecake from oven. Cool in pan on wire rack for 1 hour or until completely cooled. Carefully remove sides of pan. Refrigerate at least 4 hours or overnight.

5 In small heavy saucepan, combine chocolate chips, 1 tablespoon butter and boiling water. Let stand 5 minutes. Whisk chocolate mixture until smooth. Add 3/4 cup sugar and corn syrup; mix well. Bring to a boil over medium-low heat, stirring constantly. Reduce heat to low; boil 8 minutes without stirring.

6 Remove saucepan from heat. Stir 1/2 teaspoon vanilla into chocolate sauce. Cool 15 minutes, stirring frequently. Sauce will thicken as it cools. Serve cheesecake with sauce. Store cheesecake and sauce in refrigerator.

HIGH ALTITUDE (3500-6500 FT): Wrap outside of springform pan with foil; prepare cheesecake as directed above. To help prevent cracking, place pan filled with 1 to 2 inches water on oven rack below cheesecake during baking. Bake at 325°F for 60 to 70 minutes.

NUTRITIONAL INFORMATION PER SERVING: Calories 485 • Total Fat 31g • Saturated Fat 17g • Cholesterol 105mg • Sodium 250mg • Total Carbohydrate 46g • Dietary Fiber 0g • Sugars 38g • Protein 6g. DIETARY EXCHANGES: 2 Starch • 1 Other Carbohydrate • 6 Fat.

new york white chocolate cheesecake

ROSE ANNE LEMON
Sierra Vista, Arizona
Bake-Off® Contest 32, 1986

almond macaroon cherry pie

SERVINGS: 8

1 refrigerated pie crust (from 15 oz. pkg.)	1/2 cup sliced almonds
FILLING	1/4 cup sugar
1 (21 oz.) can cherry fruit pie filling	1/8 teaspoon salt, if desired
1/4 to 1/2 teaspoon cinnamon	1/4 cup milk
1/8 teaspoon salt, if desired	1 tablespoon margarine or butter, melted
1 teaspoon lemon juice	1/4 teaspoon almond extract
TOPPING	1 egg, beaten
1 cup coconut	

1   Prepare pie crust according to package directions for one-crust filled pie using 9-inch pie pan. Reduce oven temperature to 400°F.

2   In large bowl, combine all filling ingredients; spoon into crust-lined pan. Bake for 20 minutes; remove from oven.

3   Meanwhile, in medium bowl, combine all topping ingredients; spread evenly over partially baked pie. Bake an additional 15 to 30 minutes or until crust and topping are golden brown. Cover pie with foil during last 5 to 10 minutes of baking if necessary to prevent excessive browning.

NUTRITIONAL INFORMATION PER SERVING: Calories 380 • Fat 16g • Sodium 200mg • Total Carbohydrate 58g • Protein 4g.

kitchen tip

Don't overbeat eggs for cheese-cake batter. Overbeating adds extra air and volume that can cause cracks.

pistachio-white chocolate cheesecake

PREP TIME: 40 Minutes ❋ READY IN: 6 Hours ❋ SERVINGS: 16

CRUST	1/2 cup sour cream
1 cup chocolate cookie crumbs	1/4 teaspoon almond extract
1/4 cup sugar	4 eggs
2 tablespoons butter, melted	1 (3.4 oz.) package instant pistachio pudding and pie filling mix
FILLING	1 (12 oz.) package white vanilla chips (2 cups)
20 oz. cream cheese, softened	1/2 cup chopped shelled pistachios
3/4 cup sugar	

1   Heat oven to 350°F. In medium bowl, combine cookie crumbs and 1/4 cup sugar; mix well. Stir in butter. Press crumb mixture in bottom of ungreased 9-inch springform pan.

2   Bake for 10 minutes. Cool 10 minutes. Wrap outside of pan, bottom and sides, with heavy-duty foil.

3   Reduce oven temperature to 325°F. Beat cream cheese in large bowl at Medium speed until creamy. Beat in 3/4 cup sugar until very soft and creamy. Add sour cream and almond extract; beat well. Reduce speed to Low; add eggs one at a time, beating just until combined and scraping down sides of bowl after each addition.

4   With wire whisk, beat in pudding mix until well mixed. Stir in vanilla chips. Pour into crust-lined pan. Sprinkle pistachios over top.

5   Bake at 325°F for 1 hour 15 minutes to 1 hour 20 minutes or until sides of cheesecake are set and slightly puffed but center still moves slightly when pan is tapped. Cool cheesecake in pan on wire rack for 1 hour. Cover; refrigerate at least 3 hours before serving. To serve, remove sides of pan. Cut cheesecake into wedges.

HIGH ALTITUDE (3500-6500 FT): Bake cheesecake at 325°F for 1 hour 25 minutes to 1 hour 35 minutes.

NUTRITIONAL INFORMATION PER SERVING: Calories 455 • Total Fat 29g • Saturated Fat 15g • Cholesterol 105mg • Sodium 300mg • Total Carbohydrate 43g • Dietary Fiber 1g • Sugars 35g • Protein 7g. DIETARY EXCHANGES: 2 Starch • 1 Fruit • 3 Other Carbohydrate • 5 Fat.

melba streusel pie

SERVINGS: 8

1   refrigerated pie crust (from 15 oz. pkg.)

TOPPING
3/4   cup all-purpose flour
1/2   cup firmly packed brown sugar
1/4   cup margarine or butter

FILLING
1/3   cup sugar

2   tablespoons cornstarch
1/4   teaspoon cinnamon
1   (16 oz.) package frozen peaches, thawed, drained
1   (10 oz.) package frozen raspberries in light syrup, thawed
1   tablespoon lemon juice

ELAINE STOECKEL
Minneapolis, Minnesota
Bake-Off® Contest 15, 1963

1 Prepare pie crust according to package directions for one-crust filled pie using 9-inch pie pan. Reduce oven temperature to 375°F.

2 In small bowl, combine flour and brown sugar; mix well. With fork or pastry blender, cut in margarine until mixture is crumbly; set aside.

3 In large bowl, combine sugar, cornstarch and cinnamon; mix well. Stir in fruits. Sprinkle with lemon juice; mix well. Pour into crust-lined pan. Bake for 35 to 40 minutes or until filling is partially set in center. Sprinkle evenly with topping mixture. Cover edge of crust with strips of foil to prevent excessive browning. Bake for an additional 12 to 15 minutes or until topping is light golden brown.

NUTRITIONAL INFORMATION PER SERVING: Calories 350 • Fat 13g • Sodium 210mg • Total Carbohydrate 55g • Protein 3g.

candy cane peppermint brownie

candy cane peppermint brownie

PREP TIME: 30 Minutes ✳ READY IN: 6 Hours ✳ SERVINGS: 10

1 (19.8 oz.) package fudge brownie mix	3 cups peppermint bon bon ice cream, softened
1/2 cup oil	
1/4 cup water	3 cups frozen extra-creamy whipped topping, thawed
3 eggs	
	1/2 cup crushed candy canes (about 7 large) or peppermint candies

1 Heat oven to 350°F. Line 13x9-inch pan with foil. Prepare brownie mix as directed on package, using oil, water and eggs. Pour into foil-lined pan. Bake for 28 to 30 minutes or until toothpick inserted 2 inches from side of pan comes out almost clean. Cool 1 hour or until completely cooled.

2 Lift brownie from pan with foil. Cut out 11-1/2x8-inch candy cane shape (see photo). Place on serving platter. Cut remaining brownie into bars; reserve for another use.

3 Mound ice cream onto candy cane-shaped brownie; spread evenly. Top with whipped topping, spreading evenly over top and sides. Sprinkle crushed candy diagonally on whipped topping to resemble candy cane. Cover loosely with foil; freeze at least 4 hours or overnight before serving.

HIGH ALTITUDE (3500-6500 FT): Prepare brownie mix using High Altitude package directions. Continue as directed above.

NUTRITIONAL INFORMATION PER SERVING: Calories 345 • Total Fat 17g • Saturated Fat 5g • Cholesterol 50mg • Sodium 150mg • Total Carbohydrate 44g • Dietary Fiber 0g • Sugars 33g • Protein 4g. DIETARY EXCHANGES: 1 Starch • 2 Other Carbohydrate • 3-1/2 Fat.

apple brown betty

PREP TIME: 10 Minutes ✳ READY IN: 1 Hour 20 Minutes ✳ SERVINGS: 8

5 cups sliced peeled apples (5 medium)	1 tablespoon lemon juice
1/2 cup firmly packed brown sugar	1 cup unseasoned dry bread crumbs
1 teaspoon grated lemon peel	1/2 cup margarine or butter; melted
1/4 teaspoon nutmeg	Half-and-half, if desired

1 Heat oven to 375°F. Grease 8-inch square (2-quart) baking dish. In large bowl, combine apples, brown sugar, lemon peel, nutmeg and lemon juice; mix well.

2 In medium bowl, combine bread crumbs and margarine; sprinkle 1/2 cup bread crumb mixture in greased baking dish. Spoon apple mixture over crumb mixture; top with remaining bread crumb mixture.

3 Bake for 45 to 50 minutes or until apples are almost tender. Uncover; bake an additional 15 to 20 minutes or until top is crisp and golden brown. Serve warm with half-and-half.

HIGH ALTITUDE (3500-6500 FT): Bake at 325°F for 45 to 50 minutes.

NUTRITIONAL INFORMATION PER SERVING: Calories 300 • Total Fat 16g • Saturated Fat 5g • Cholesterol 10mg • Sodium 270mg • Total Carbohydrate 35g • Dietary Fiber 2g • Sugars 23g • Protein 3g. DIETARY EXCHANGES: 2-1/2 Carbohydrate • 3 Fat.

cook's notes

Prepare ice cream parfaits with any remaining brownies. Cut them into tiny squares and layer them in tall glasses with additional ice cream, whipped topping and crushed candy canes. For particularly pretty parfaits, layer the ingredients twice.

frosted cranberry-cherry pie

PREP TIME: 15 Minutes ✳ READY IN: 2 Hours ✳ SERVINGS: 8

CRUST

- 1 (15 oz.) box refrigerated pie crusts, softened as directed on package

FILLING

- 1 (21 oz.) can cherry pie filling
- 1 (16 oz.) can whole berry cranberry sauce
- 3 tablespoons cornstarch
- 1/4 teaspoon cinnamon

GLAZE

- 1/2 cup powdered sugar
- 1 tablespoon light corn syrup
- 2 to 3 teaspoons water

GARNISH

- 1/4 cup sliced almonds, if desired

1   Heat oven to 425°F. Prepare pie crust as directed on package for two-crust pie using 9-inch glass pie plate.

2   In large bowl, combine all filling ingredients. Spoon into crust-lined pan. Top with second crust; seal edges and flute. Cut slits in several places in top crust.

3   Bake for 35 to 45 minutes or until crust is golden brown. Cover edge of crust with strips of foil after 10 to 15 minutes of baking to prevent excessive browning.

4   Remove pie from oven. Immediately, in small bowl, combine powdered sugar, corn syrup and enough water for desired drizzling consistency. Drizzle glaze over hot pie. Decorate or sprinkle with almonds. Cool at least 1 hour before serving.

NUTRITIONAL INFORMATION PER SERVING: Calories 460 • Total Fat 15g • Saturated Fat 6g • Cholesterol 10mg • Sodium 240mg • Total Carbohydrate 78g • Dietary Fiber 2g • Sugars 47g • Protein 3g. DIETARY EXCHANGES: 1 Starch • 4 Other Carbohydrate • 3 Fat.

amaretto crème brûlée

PREP TIME: 15 Minutes ✳ READY IN: 5 Hours 45 Minutes ✳ SERVINGS: 6

- 6 egg yolks
- 1/2 cup sugar
- 1 pint whipping cream (2 cups)
- 1/4 cup amaretto

- 1 teaspoon vanilla
- 1/8 teaspoon salt
- 2 tablespoons sugar
- 1/4 cup sliced almonds, toasted

1   Heat oven to 350°F. Place six 6-oz. oval or round ramekins or custard cups in 13x9-inch pan. In medium bowl, combine egg yolks and 1/2 cup sugar; beat with wire whisk until light and fluffy. Add whipping cream, amaretto, vanilla and salt; mix well.

2   Strain mixture into 4-cup measuring cup or another medium bowl. Pour about 1/2 cup mixture into each ramekin. Pour hot water into pan until halfway up sides of ramekins. Cover loosely with foil.

3   Bake for 40 to 50 minutes or until edges are set but center still jiggles slightly when gently shaken. Remove ramekins from water bath; place on wire racks to cool for 30 minutes. Pour out water from pan.

4   Transfer ramekins to same pan. Cover; refrigerate at least 3 hours or up to 24 hours before serving.

5   Sprinkle each ramekin with 1 teaspoon sugar. Watching constantly, broil custards 4 to 6 inches from heat for 1 to 4 minutes or until sugar bubbles and is caramelized. Refrigerate at least 1 hour or up to 3 hours to harden topping.

6   Just before serving, sprinkle toasted almonds over the chilled crème brûlée. Store in the refrigerator.

HIGH ALTITUDE (3500-6500 FT): Bake at 350°F for 55 to 60 minutes.

NUTRITIONAL INFORMATION PER SERVING: Calories 420 • Total Fat 32g • Saturated Fat 17g • Cholesterol 300mg • Sodium 85mg • Total Carbohydrate 28g • Dietary Fiber 0g • Sugars 26g • Protein 5g. DIETARY EXCHANGES: 2 Starch • 6 Fat.

country apple-pear tart

PREP TIME: 30 Minutes ❋ READY IN: 1 Hour 30 Minutes ❋ SERVINGS: 6

CRUST

1 refrigerated pie crust (from 15 oz. box), softened as directed on box

FILLING

2 cups thinly sliced peeled apples

2 cups thinly sliced peeled pears

3/4 cup fresh cranberries

1/3 cup granulated sugar

2 tablespoons all-purpose flour

1/4 teaspoon nutmeg

TOPPING

1/4 cup all-purpose flour

1/4 cup packed brown sugar

2 tablespoons butter

1 teaspoon milk

1 tablespoon granulated sugar

2 tablespoons sliced almonds

1 Heat oven to 425°F. Line cookie sheet with parchment paper. Remove crust from pouch; place on cookie sheet.

2 In large bowl, mix all filling ingredients until fruit is coated. Spoon filling evenly onto crust, spreading to within 2 inches of edges.

3 In small bowl, mix 1/4 cup flour, the brown sugar and butter until crumbly. Sprinkle mixture over filling. Fold edge of crust over filling, pleating crust to fit and leaving about 5 to 6 inches in center uncovered. Brush crust with milk; sprinkle with 1 tablespoon granulated sugar.

4 Bake 10 minutes. Reduce oven temperature to 350°F. Sprinkle almonds over filling. Bake 20 to 30 minutes longer or until edges are deep golden brown and fruit is tender.

5 Immediately loosen tart by running pancake turner under crust; place on cooling rack. Cool 30 minutes. Serve warm or cool.

NUTRITIONAL INFORMATION PER SERVING: Calories 390 • Total Fat 15g • Saturated Fat 7g • Cholesterol 15mg • Sodium 180mg • Total Carbohydrate 61g • Dietary Fiber 2g • Sugars 34g • Protein 3g. DIETARY EXCHANGES: 1 Starch • 3 Other Carbohydrate • 3 Fat.

cook's notes

Instead of combining apples and pears, try this recipe prepared with either all apples or all pears.

IMOGENE NOAR
Paramount, California
Bake-Off® Contest 19, 1968

special touch

Garnishing the cake with raspberries or other bits of fruit creates a lovely presentation. When all else fails, mint leaves make a great addition to individual slices.

cake 'n cheese cake

SERVINGS: 10

FILLING

1	(8 oz.) package cream cheese, softened
2/3	cup sugar
1/2	cup dairy sour cream
1	teaspoon vanilla
2	eggs

CAKE

1	cup all-purpose flour
1	teaspoon baking powder
	Dash salt

1/2	cup margarine or butter, softened
2/3	cup sugar
2	eggs
1	tablespoon milk
1	teaspoon vanilla

TOPPING

1	cup dairy sour cream
2	tablespoons sugar
1	teaspoon vanilla

1 Heat oven to 325°F. Grease and flour bottom only of 10-inch deep dish pie pan or 9-inch square pan. In small bowl, beat cream cheese and 2/3 cup sugar until light and fluffy. Add 1/2 cup sour cream and 1 teaspoon vanilla; blend well. Add eggs 1 at a time, beating at Low speed. Set aside.

2 In medium bowl, combine flour, baking powder and salt. In large bowl, beat margarine and 2/3 cup sugar until light and fluffy. Add eggs 1 at a time, beating well after each addition. Stir in milk and 1 teaspoon vanilla. Add dry ingredients at Low speed until moistened. Beat 1 minute at Medium speed. Spread batter in bottom and up sides of greased and floured pie pan, spreading thinner on sides. Pour cream cheese mixture over batter.

3 Bake for 40 to 45 minutes or until cheesecake is almost set in the center and the cake is golden brown.

4 Meanwhile, in small bowl, combine all topping ingredients. Remove cake from oven; spread evenly with topping. Bake an additional 5 minutes. Cool; refrigerate 3 to 4 hours before serving. Store in refrigerator.

HIGH ALTITUDE (3500-6500 FT): Decrease sugar in filling to 1/2 cup; decrease sugar in cake to 1/2 cup. Bake as directed above.

NUTRITIONAL INFORMATION PER SERVING: Calories 430 • Fat 27g • Sodium 260mg • Total Carbohydrate 41g • Protein 7g.

cranberry-caramel cake

PREP TIME: 35 Minutes ✳ READY IN: 2 Hours 30 Minutes ✳ SERVINGS: 16

CAKE

1   (18.25 oz.) package yellow cake mix with pudding

2   teaspoons pumpkin pie spice

1   cup eggnog

1/3   cup oil

4   eggs

1-1/2   cups fresh or frozen cranberries, coarsely chopped

1/2   cup chopped walnuts

CARAMEL SAUCE

1/2   cup butter

1-1/4   cups firmly packed brown sugar

2   tablespoons light corn syrup

1/2   cup whipping cream

1 Heat oven to 350°F. Grease and lightly flour 12-cup fluted tube pan. In large bowl, combine cake mix, pumpkin pie spice, eggnog, oil and eggs; beat with electric mixer at Low speed for 30 seconds. Beat 2 minutes at Medium speed. Stir in cranberries and walnuts. Pour batter into greased and floured pan.

2 Bake at 350°F for 45 to 55 minutes or until toothpick inserted near center comes out clean. Cool in pan 10 minutes. Invert cake onto wire rack; remove pan. Cool about 1 hour or until completely cooled.

3 To serve, melt butter in medium saucepan over medium-high heat. Stir in brown sugar and corn syrup. Bring to a boil. Cook about 1 minute or until sugar dissolves, stirring constantly. Stir in whipping cream. Return to a boil, stirring constantly. Remove from heat. Serve warm sauce over cake.

HIGH ALTITUDE (3500-6500 FT): For cake, add 1/4 cup flour to dry cake mix, decrease oil to 1/4 cup and add 2/3 cup water. Bake at 375°F for 45 to 50 minutes.

NUTRITIONAL INFORMATION PER SERVING: Calories 400 • Total Fat 21 g • Saturated Fat 8g • Cholesterol 85mg • Sodium 300mg • Total Carbohydrate 49g • Dietary Fiber 0g • Sugars 41 g • Protein 4g. DIETARY EXCHANGES: 1 Starch • 2 Other Carbohydrate • 4 Fat.

cook's notes

To prepare the sauce in the microwave, place butter in a 4-cup microwavable measuring cup. Microwave on High for 1 minute or until melted. Stir in brown sugar and corn syrup. Microwave on High for 2 to 3 minutes or until sugar dissolves, stirring once. Stir in whipping cream. Microwave on High for 45 to 60 seconds or until mixture boils, stirring once.

eggnog crème brûlée

PREP TIME: 20 Minutes ✳ READY IN: 4 Hours 25 Minutes ✳ SERVINGS: 8

3   cups whipping cream

5   egg yolks

2   eggs

1/2   cup sugar

2   tablespoons dark rum

1   tablespoon brandy

1   teaspoon vanilla

1/2   teaspoon nutmeg

1/2   cup firmly packed brown sugar

1 Heat oven to 325°F. Place eight 6-oz. ramekins or custard cups in 15x10x1-inch baking pan. Heat whipping cream in medium saucepan just to a simmer. Remove from heat.

2 In medium bowl, combine egg yolks and eggs; beat well. Stir in sugar until combined. With wire whisk, stir in hot whipping cream until well blended. Stir in rum, brandy, vanilla and nutmeg. Pour mixture into ramekins.

3 Place pan in oven; pour hot water into pan until 1/2 to 3/4 inch up sides of ramekins. Bake for 30 to 35 minutes or until centers are just set.

4 Carefully remove from oven. Place cups on wire rack to cool. Cool 30 minutes. Refrigerate at least 3 hours or overnight.

5 Before serving, place ramekins in 15x10x1-inch baking pan. Top each with 1 tablespoon brown sugar. Broil 4 to 6 inches from heat for 1 to 2 minutes or until sugar is melted. (Watch closely.) Store in refrigerator.

NUTRITIONAL INFORMATION PER SERVING: Calories 490 • Total Fat 38g • Saturated Fat 22g • Cholesterol 310mg • Sodium 60mg • Total Carbohydrate 29g • Dietary Fiber 0g • Sugars 29g • Protein 5g. DIETARY EXCHANGES: 2 Fruit • 2 Other Carbohydrate • 1 Medium-Fat Meat • 6-1/2 Fat.

cook's notes

To sugar-coat the cooled custards, hold a strainer over each ramekin and press the brown sugar through. The even layer of sugar on the custards will melt evenly under the broiler.

lemon ricotta cheesecake

PREP TIME: 40 Minutes ✳ READY IN: 6 Hours ✳ SERVINGS: 16

CRUST
- 1 cup unseasoned dry bread crumbs
- 1/2 cup slivered almonds
- 1/3 cup sugar
- 6 tablespoons butter, melted

FILLING
- 2 (8 oz.) packages cream cheese, softened
- 1-1/4 cups sugar
- 2 to 3 tablespoons grated lemon peel (1 large)
- 2 tablespoons fresh lemon juice
- 1 (15 oz.) container whole-milk ricotta cheese
- 3 eggs

GARNISH
- 1/2 cup whipping cream
- 16 candied lemon slices

1 Heat oven to 350°F. In food processor bowl with metal blade, combine bread crumbs, almonds and 1/3 cup sugar; pulse until almonds are finely ground. Add butter; pulse until well mixed. Press crumb mixture in bottom and 2 inches up sides of ungreased 9-inch springform pan.

2 Bake for 10 to 15 minutes or until crust is light golden brown around edges. Remove crust from oven; place on wire rack. Cool 10 minutes. Wrap outside of pan, bottom and sides with heavy-duty foil.

3 Reduce oven temperature to 325°F. Beat cream cheese in large bowl on Medium speed until fluffy. Add 1-1/4 cups sugar; beat until very soft and creamy. Add lemon peel and lemon juice; mix well. Beat in ricotta cheese. Add eggs one at a time, beating just until combined and scraping down sides of bowl after each addition. Pour into crust-lined pan.

4 Bake for 1 hour 10 minutes to 1 hour 20 minutes or until sides of cheesecake are set and puffed but center still moves slightly when pan is tapped. Cool cheesecake in pan on wire rack for 1 hour. Cover; refrigerate at least 3 hours or overnight before serving.

5 Just before serving, whip cream in medium bowl until soft peaks form. Spoon 16 mounds of whipped cream evenly around edge of cheesecake. Top each with candied lemon slice. To serve, remove sides of pan. Cut cheesecake into wedges.

HIGH ALTITUDE (3500-6500 FT): Bake the cheesecake at 325°F for 1 hour 20 minutes to 1 hour 30 minutes.

NUTRITIONAL INFORMATION PER SERVING: Calories 360 • Total Fat 23g • Saturated Fat 13g • Cholesterol 105mg • Sodium 220mg • Total Carbohydrate 31g • Dietary Fiber 1g • Sugars 24g • Protein 8g. DIETARY EXCHANGES: 1-1/2 Fruit • 2 Other Carbohydrate • 5 Fat.

gingered pear pie

PREP TIME: 25 Minutes ✳ READY IN: 1 Hour 10 Minutes ✳ SERVINGS: 8

CRUST
- 1 (15 oz.) box refrigerated pie crusts, softened as directed on box

FILLING
- 3/4 cup sugar
- 2 tablespoons cornstarch
- 3 tablespoons chopped crystallized ginger
- 6 cups thinly sliced pears (about 6 medium)

TOPPING
- 1 tablespoon water
- 4 teaspoons sugar

1 Prepare pie crust as directed on box for two-crust pie using 9-inch glass pie plate. Heat oven to 425°F.

2 In large bowl, mix 3/4 cup sugar and cornstarch. Add ginger; toss to coat. Add pears; mix well. Spoon into crust-lined pie plate. Top with second crust; seal edges and flute. Cut slits or shapes in several places in top crust. Brush crust with water; sprinkle with 4 teaspoons sugar.

3 Bake 40 to 45 minutes or until pears are tender and crust is golden brown. Cover edge of crust with strips of foil after first 15 to 20 minutes of baking to prevent excessive browning.

NUTRITIONAL INFORMATION PER SERVING: Calories 410 • Total Fat 14g • Saturated Fat 6g • Cholesterol 15mg • Sodium 210mg • Total Carbohydrate 70g • Dietary Fiber 3g • Sugars 38g • Protein 2g. DIETARY EXCHANGES: 1 Starch • 3-1/2 Fruit • 4-1/2 Other Carbohydrate • 2-1/2 Fat.

lemon ricotta cheesecake

general recipe index

alphabetical recipe index